Pelican Books
Pelican Library of Business and M̶a̶n̶a̶g̶e̶m̶e̶n̶t̶
Advisory Editor: T. Kempner

Understanding Company Fina̶n̶c̶e̶

R. H. Parker was born in North Walsham, Norfolk, in 1932. He read
Economics at University College, London, from 1951 to 1954. He then
served three years' articles in the City of London before becoming a
member of the Institute of Chartered Accountants in England and
Wales in 1958. Since then he has practised accounting and taught at
universities and business schools in Australia, Britain, France and
Nigeria. He is the author of *Management Accounting: An Historical
Perspective* (1969), joint author of *Topics in Business Finance and
Accounting* (1964), and co-editor of *Readings in the Concept and
Measurement of Income* (1969), and has published numerous articles in
accounting and financial journals.

Since 1970 R. H. Parker has been Professor of Accountancy at the
University of Dundee. He is a member of the council of the British
Accounting and Finance Association and the editorial board of *Abacus*,
published by Sydney University Press. His main professional interests
are in the international, comparative and historical aspects of
accounting.

R. H. Parker Understanding
Company
Financial
Statements

Penguin Books

For Theresa and Michael

Acknowledgements

For 'The Hardship of Accounting' from *The Poetry of Robert Frost*, edited by Edward Connery Lathem, quoted on p. 36: to the Estate of Robert Frost, Edward Connery Lathem and to Jonathan Cape Ltd. Copyright 1936 by Robert Frost. Copyright © 1964 by Lesley Frost Ballantine. Copyright © 1969 by Holt, Rinehart & Winston, Inc. Reprinted by permission of Holt, Rinehart & Winston, Inc.

Penguin Books Ltd, Harmondsworth, Middlesex, England
Penguin Books Inc., 7100 Ambassador Road, Baltimore, Maryland 21207, U.S.A.
Penguin Books Australia Ltd, Ringwood, Victoria, Australia

First published in Pelican Books 1972
Reprinted 1973
Copyright © R. H. Parker, 1972
Made and printed in Great Britain by
Richard Clay (The Chaucer Press) Ltd
Bungay, Suffolk
Set in Monotype Ehrhardt

Contents

Preface 8

1. **Companies and their Reports** 9

    The purpose and design of this book 9
    Contents of a company annual report 10
    What is a company? 12
    Memorandum and articles of association 15
    The chairman's statement 15
    Interim reports 16
    Annual financial statements 16

2. **The Financial Statements** 17

    Assets, liabilities and net worth 17
    The consolidated balance sheet 21
    Current assets, current liabilities and working capital 21
    Fixed assets 22
    Depreciation 23
    Goodwill and patents 26
    Loan capital 27
    Share capital and reserves 29
    Consolidated profit and loss account 32
    Source and disposition statement (Funds statement) 33
    Depreciation as a 'source' of funds 34
    Cash flow 35

3. **Taxation and Audit** 36

    Taxation 36
    Corporation tax 37
    Capital allowances and investment incentives 39

Personal tax   41
Profits tax   42
Capital gains tax   42
Close companies   43
Tax law   43
Audit   43

4. **Tools of Analysis**   46

Financial ratios   46
Yields   47
The need for comparisons   47
Industry ratios   48
Sources of information   49

5. **Profitability and Return on Investment**   51

Profitability   51
Return on investment   51
Exceptional items   56

6. **Liquidity and Cash Flows**   57

Liquidity   57
Current and quick ratios   60
Average collection period   62
Window-dressing   63

7. **Sources of Funds and Capital Structure**   65

Sources of funds   65
Capital structure   65
Cost of capital   67
Risk: gearing and times interest earned   71
Dividend policy   75
Bonus issues and rights issues   79
Convertible loan stock   81
Leasing   82

8. **Accounting Principles and Inflation**   84

Accounting principles   84
Inflation   89

9. **Summary and Reading Guide** 92

Companies 92
Financial statements 93
Taxation 94
Audit 95
Tools of analysis 95
Profitability and return on investment 95
Liquidity and cash flows 96
Sources of funds and capital structure 96
Accounting principles and inflation 97
Personal investment 98

Appendixes

A. Debits and credits (Double entry) 99
B. Glossary of accounting and financial terms 102

INSET

C. Annual report and accounts of Alenco Ltd for the year ended 30 September 1969
D. Extracts from the annual report and accounts of Guest, Keen and Nettlefolds, Ltd for the 52 weeks ended 2 January 1971

Index 129

Preface

An eminent company lawyer has written of the published financial statements of companies that: 'To the average investor or creditor – "the man on the Clapham omnibus" – they are cryptograms which he is incapable of solving.'* This small book is an attempt to make the task easier. It is written for the general reader and the beginning student, not for my fellow accountants, and does not pretend to be more than an elementary introduction to a difficult subject. No previous knowledge is assumed.

I am greatly indebted to Alenco Ltd and Guest, Keen and Nettlefolds, Ltd for allowing me to reprint their annual reports. The Alenco annual report was designed by Walter Truman-Cox FSIA and printed by Mears Caldwell & Hacker Ltd. Guest, Keen and Nettlefolds' report was designed by L. Douglas Horman and printed by St Clements Fosh and Cross Ltd. Members of Alenco's staff, Mr G. S. Lowden of Dundee, Professor E. Stamp of the University of Lancaster and others made valuable comments on previous drafts of the manuscript, but any errors and misinterpretations that may remain are of course my responsibility.

The burdens of typing and proof-reading were bravely borne by Mrs S. Summers and Miss P. Lindsay.

*L. C. B. Gower, *The Principles of Modern Company Law* (London: Stevens, 3rd editn 1969), p. 454.

1. Companies and their Reports

In sooth a goodly company

REV. RICHARD HARRIS BARHAM, *The Jackdaw of Rheims*

THE PURPOSE AND DESIGN OF THIS BOOK

The purpose of this book is to show the reader how to understand, analyse and interpret the reports sent by companies to their shareholders, and more especially the financial statements contained therein. In order to do this, we shall look in detail at the 1969 report of a company called Alenco Ltd. We shall also refer occasionally to Alenco's 1968 and earlier reports and to the reports of other companies, particularly that of Guest, Keen and Nettlefolds, Ltd.

In this first chapter we survey in general terms the contents of a company annual report and look briefly at the nature and constitution of the limited liability company. Chapter 2 describes the various financial statements and introduces many important financial and accounting concepts. This is a vital chapter, which provides the basis for the analysis contained in later chapters. Chapter 3 explains as briefly as possible the nature of company taxation and the function of the auditors. Chapter 4 describes certain tools of analysis. Chapter 5 is concerned with profitability and return on investment, chapter 6 with liquidity and cash flows, and chapter 7 with sources of funds and capital structure. Chapter 8 deals with accounting principles and the effects of inflation on accounting. Chapter 9 summarizes the whole book.

Finance and accounting are specialist subjects. This does not mean that they need remain incomprehensible to the layman. It does mean, however, that technical terms cannot be entirely avoided. One would not, after all, learn to drive a car without learning words such as 'clutch' and 'accelerator'. In order to make the learning process as painless as possible, all technical terms are explained as they are introduced and a glossary is provided for reference (Appendix B). It is hoped that some readers will want to know more about finance and accounting after reading this book. For such readers the references given in chapter 9 should be useful.

CONTENTS OF A COMPANY ANNUAL REPORT

The 1969 annual report of Alenco Ltd is reproduced as Appendix C by kind permission of the company.* The original has a page size about twice that of the reproduction and is in a number of different colours. Alenco's report has been chosen for two reasons. First, the company has, much more than most companies, made a real effort to make its financial statements intelligible to the non-specialist. Alenco was in fact the winner in 1967 of the award given annually by *The Accountant* (a widely read weekly professional journal) for the best annual report of a small company.† Secondly, because it is a relatively small company (group sales in 1968/9 of just under £10 million – now in excess of £12 million), its report is not so complicated as to be unsuitable for detailed study in an introductory book of this kind.

The content of Alenco's report, as distinct from its superior presentation, is typical of that of most companies. To get some idea of this content it is worth leafing quickly through it.

Who are Alenco Ltd and what do they do? On the last page but one of the report (App. C, p. 24) we learn that Alenco Ltd of Slough is the holding company of a number of subsidiaries, the whole of whose share capitals it owns, directly or indirectly. It owns completely five companies in the United Kingdom and three overseas. Apart from a Swiss company, Patex S.A., all the subsidiaries are engaged in manufacturing pipe fittings, valves, tubes, thread sealing tape and other industrial components.

Turning back to the beginning of the report we find first of all the notice calling the annual general meeting of the members (shareholders) of the company. Every company must by law hold such a meeting once a year, with an interval of not more than fifteen months between meetings.

---

*This was the most recent report available when this book was written. Subject to supplies, the company will be pleased to send a copy of its current report to interested enquirers.

† Guest, Keen & Nettlefolds won the award for large companies in the same year.

The business of the meeting is very formal:

To receive the directors' report and accounts for the year ended 30 September 1969.
To declare a final dividend on the ordinary shares. (Dividends are recommended by directors but approved and declared by the shareholders).
To elect a director.
To authorize the directors to fix the remuneration of the auditors.

The next page of the report gives the names of the directors, the secretary, the auditors (see chapter 3) and the bankers of the company. The registered office or official address of the company is also given.

The next item is the directors' report.* This briefly discusses the results of the past year and how they were affected by the sale of one subsidiary (S. S. Stott Ltd) and the acquisition of a new one (H. & L. Austin Engineering Ltd), by the devaluation of the French franc on 11 August 1969, and by the fluctuating price of copper-based metals.

Details are also given of such things as a new group headquarters; the principal activities of the group; dividends; changes in the composition of the board of directors; the interests of the directors in the company and its ultimate holding company; exports; the number of employees; charitable and political contributions; and the resignation of one of the joint auditors. The ultimate holding company is stated to be The Charterhouse Group Ltd.

There now follows the most important and, for many, the most difficult section of the report: the financial statements. These consist of a consolidated profit and loss account, a consolidated balance sheet, the balance sheet of Alenco Ltd itself, several pages of notes, the report of the auditors, a source and disposition statement and a few pages of statistics and graphs. All these will be looked at in more detail later. For the moment it is enough to note that the consolidated profit and loss account shows the results of the operations of the Alenco *group of companies* for the *year ended* 30 September 1969; the consolidated balance sheet the financial position of the *group as at* 30 September 1969; the balance sheet of Alenco Ltd the financial position of *the holding company only as at* 30 September 1969; and the source and dis-

*See also Glossary.

position statement the changes in the assets and liabilities of the group *during the year* 1968/9.

WHAT IS A COMPANY?

In Britain the most important form of business organization is the limited liability company. The chief characteristics of such a company are a corporate personality distinct from that of its owners or shareholders; the limiting of the liability of the shareholders to the amount invested (which is not the case for a sole trader or partnership where personal assets are available to pay business debts); and, in principle at least, a perpetual life: companies are born but they do not have to die of old age.

It was not until 1844 that incorporation became possible other than by the slow and difficult process of a special Act of Parliament or a Royal Charter. It took another 11 years for incorporation by registration to be linked with limited liability by the Limited Liability Act of 1855. The foundations of modern British company law (and also that of Australia, Canada, New Zealand, and South Africa and many other Commonwealth or former Commonwealth countries) were laid in the Companies Act of 1862. The law has been continually revised since, notably in 1908, 1929, 1948 and 1967. At the time of writing the legislation in force is contained in the Companies Acts, 1948 and 1967. The report of the Company Law Committee of 1962 (the Jenkins Report) contains many recommendations which have not yet been made law.

By the end of 1970 there were about 519,000 companies registered in Great Britain, of which about 15,500 or just under 3 per cent were 'public' companies and about 503,500 were 'private' companies. In 1970, 30,262 new companies were registered with a nominal capital of £121 million.*

To explain the differences between public and private ('proprietary' in Australia and South Africa) companies it is necessary to look at the ways in which companies can be classified. The distinction between public and private companies is based on three criteria: the right to

*Department of Trade and Industry, *Companies in 1970* (H.M.S.O., 1971).

transfer the shares of the company; the number of shareholders of the company; and the right to make a public issue of shares or debentures. A private company is one which, by its articles of association (i.e., its internal regulations, see p. 15) restricts the right to transfer its shares, limits the number of its members to 50 (with certain exceptions), and prohibits any invitation to the public to subscribe for any shares or debentures of the company.

Note that a public company does not *have* to make a public issue of shares or debentures; it simply has the right to do so if it wishes. Thus not all public companies' shares are quoted on a stock exchange and the division between private and public companies is not the same as that between companies with quoted shares and those with unquoted shares. It is a necessary but not a sufficient condition for quotation that the company be a public company.

All companies in the United Kingdom must have at least two shareholders; public companies must have at least seven shareholders. There is no maximum limit to the number of shareholders of a public company. At 2 January 1971, for example, G.K.N. had 83,788 ordinary stockholders* (App. D, p. 48).

'Exempt' private companies no longer exist in the U.K. They were essentially family companies possessing the privilege of not having to file their financial statements with the Registrar of Companies in London (for companies with a registered office in England or Wales) or Edinburgh (for companies with a registered office in Scotland). These files are a useful source of information which can be readily searched.

There are other ways of classifying companies. Companies can take the power, and nearly always do so, to hold shares in other companies. A 'holding company' and a 'subsidiary company' exist where the former is a shareholder of the latter *and* controls the composition of the latter's board of directors; *or* where the former holds more than half in nominal value of the latter's equity share capital. It is possible for the subsidiary itself to have subsidiaries. These are the sub-subsidiaries of the first holding company. In the example below, A. Ltd is a holding company, B. Ltd a subsidiary, and C. Ltd a sub-subsidiary.

*The distinction between shareholders and stockholders, and between shares and stock, is not of practical importance. The terms are increasingly used interchangeably.

A. Ltd

|

holds 80 per cent of equity share capital of

|

B. Ltd

|

which holds 60 per cent of equity share capital of

|

C. Ltd

Note that A. Ltd's interest in C. Ltd is only 48 per cent – i.e. 80 per cent of 60 per cent.

The holding–subsidiary relationship is very common and practically all the annual reports which the reader is likely to be interested in will be those of *groups* of companies. We have already noticed (p. 10) that Alenco Ltd is a holding company. A closer look at the directors' report (App. C, p. 5) reveals that it is not only also a fully owned subsidiary company of Charterhouse Industrial Holdings Ltd,* but that that company in turn is a subsidiary of The Charterhouse Group Ltd. It is possible for subsidiaries to hold shares in each other but the Companies Act 1948 makes it illegal, with minor exceptions, for a subsidiary to hold shares in its holding company, or for any company to purchase its own shares.

The annual reports with which we shall be concerned, then, will be those of groups or sub-groups of companies. The holding company will usually be a public company. Other members of the group will be British public or private companies or companies incorporated overseas.† All the companies concerned will have share capital. It is worth noting in passing that not all companies do have share capital. Some are 'limited by guarantee', i.e. the members of the company have undertaken to contribute a fixed amount to the assets of the company

*Since re-named Charterhouse Industries Ltd.

† The American equivalent of Ltd is Inc. (i.e. incorporated). The nearest French and German equivalents to our public companies are *sociétés anonymes* (S.A.) and *Aktiengesellschaften* (A.G.); of our private companies, *sociétés à responsabilité limitée* (S.A.R.L.) and *Gesellschaften mit beschränkter Haftung* (G.m.b.H.). The names of Australian and South African private companies include the abbreviation Pty for Proprietary. The well-known Broken Hill Proprietary Co. Ltd (B.H.P.) is, however, a public company.

in the event of its being wound up. Some companies are even un-limited: since these have the privilege of not publishing their accounts they are not relevant to this book. They are used by professionals who desire corporate form but are not permitted to limit their liability or by those who value the privilege of non-publication more than the limitation of liability. They have become more important since the Companies Act 1967 removed that privilege from exempt private companies.

It is expressly provided in the Companies Act 1948 that groups of companies such as the Alenco group which are wholly owned by other groups need not publish separate accounts and Alenco are greatly to be complimented for doing so. This also illustrates the point that while published financial statements are formally for shareholders only, they are also of great interest to employees, customers, financial analysts and academic accountants.

MEMORANDUM AND ARTICLES OF ASSOCIATION

It will be convenient occasionally in this book to refer to two documents known as the Memorandum of Association and the Articles of Association. Every company must have both. The main contents of the memorandum are the name of the company, a statement whether the registered office is in England or in Scotland, a list of the objects for which the company has been formed, and a statement that the liability of the members is limited. The list of objects is important since a company cannot do anything which is beyond its powers (*ultra vires*). In practice the problem is avoided by listing every conceivable (and often inconceivable) object that the company is ever likely to have.

The articles are the internal regulations of the company and usually deal with such matters as the rights of particular classes of shares, transfer of shares, powers and duties of directors, accounts, dividends and reserves, quorums for meetings of shareholders and directors. A model set of articles (Table A), which can be adopted in full or in a modified form, is appended to the Companies Act 1948.

THE CHAIRMAN'S STATEMENT

Alenco has not included a chairman's statement in its annual report since it became a wholly-owned part of the Charterhouse group in 1968.

Such a statement, though not required by law, is published by many companies. The content varies. Guest, Keen and Nettlefolds for 1970 for instance (App. D, pp. 4–7) includes references to:

> trading results
> presentation of report and accounts
> the year in retrospect
> United Kingdom operations
> overseas operations
> exports
> capital expenditure
> finance
> the prospect for 1971

It is usual to refer to future prospects and fairly common to include comments on wider issues such as strikes (see G.K.N.'s statement, p. 4) and inflation (see the passage quoted in chapter 8, pp. 89–90, from the 1970 statement of The Distillers Company Ltd).

INTERIM REPORTS

Twelve months is a long time to wait for information about the details of the financial progress of a company. It has therefore become increasingly common for major companies to issue interim reports at half-yearly and sometimes quarterly intervals. Public companies seeking a quotation on the stock exchange are in fact required to circularize a half-yearly interim report to shareholders not later than six months from the date of the notice calling an annual general meeting. Companies with exceptionally large numbers of shareholders are allowed to insert such interim reports instead in two leading London newspapers (e.g. the *Financial Times* and *The Times*) or one such newspaper and one provincial newspaper.

G.K.N. issued an interim report on 18 August 1970, giving details of its unaudited results for the 26 weeks ended 4 June 1970.

ANNUAL FINANCIAL STATEMENTS

It is, however, with the annual financial statements that this book is mainly concerned. Now that we have sufficient background information, we can look at them in more detail.

2. The Financial Statements

The statements was interesting but tough

MARK TWAIN, *The Adventures of Huckleberry Finn*, ch. 17

ASSETS, LIABILITIES AND NET WORTH

At the core of any company's annual report are the financial statements. Those for Alenco Ltd and its subsidiaries for the year ended
30 September 1969 are reproduced as Appendix C. We shall start by
discussing the consolidated balance sheet (pp. 8–9). This, as the explanation (p. 9) states, is a statement showing the combined financial position
of Alenco Ltd and its eight subsidiary companies at 30 September
1969 as if they were one company, i.e. it shows the financial position of
the whole Alenco group. The statement entitled simply 'Balance
Sheet' (pp. 10–11) shows the financial position of Alenco Ltd itself,
not of the group. We shall explore this difference in more detail later
(pp. 26–7 below). For the moment we shall concentrate on the consolidated balance sheet only.

Perhaps the most obvious point about the consolidated balance
sheet is that it balances:

Source of Funds (£5,661,000) = Employment of Funds (£5,661,000)

How is this achieved? The explanation is quite simple. It must be
true of any company that

> what the company owns
> *less* what it owes
> *equals* what it is worth

Expressing this in rather more technical language we can write:

$$\text{assets} - \text{liabilities} = \text{net worth}^*$$

or, alternatively:

$$\text{assets} = \text{liabilities} + \text{net worth}.$$

*Not all accountants approve of the term 'net worth'. See chapter 8, pp. 88–9.

Since the assets represent the way in which funds have been *employed*, and liabilities and net worth represent *sources* of funds (i.e. a company can either borrow to obtain funds or use those belonging to the shareholders), we can rewrite this in the language of Alenco's report as:

employment of funds = source of funds

Looking at Alenco's consolidated balance sheet we see that funds have been obtained from ordinary shareholders (£4,746,000), preference shareholders (£165,000) and an unsecured loan (£750,000), and have been used to acquire fixed assets (£2,550,000), patents (£42,000), current assets (£5,538,000) and goodwill (£959,000). Shown as deductions in the employment list are current liabilities (£2,792,000) and deferred taxation (£636,000). Since an employment of funds is always associated simultaneously with a source of funds a balance sheet will (mistakes of arithmetic apart) always balance. This is also the basis of that other accounting mystery – double entry (debits and credits: see Appendix A).

The second important financial statement is the consolidated profit and loss account* (App. C, pp. 6–7 for that of Alenco Ltd and its subsidiaries). It will be noted that whilst a balance sheet is for a particular moment in time, a profit and loss account (the American phrase is 'income statement') is for a period, in this case for the year ended 30 September 1969. It shows the results of the year's activities. The Alenco group, for example, made sales outside the group of £9,669,000 in 1968/9. After deducting all expenses except tax, a profit was left of £922,000. This was further reduced to £515,000 to give profit after taxation. Out of this amount dividends have been or will be paid amounting altogether to £498,000. This leaves £17,000 to be retained (ploughed back). This amount also forms part of the revenue reserves item in the consolidated balance sheet.

It is worth looking more closely at this link between the profit and loss account and the balance sheet. How can a company grow, i.e. how can it increase its assets? Look again at the identity

assets = liabilities + net worth.

It is clear that the only way to increase assets is to increase the lia-

*Sometimes divided into a profit and loss account proper and a profit and loss appropriation account.

bilities (i.e. to borrow) or to increase the net worth. How can a company increase the latter? There are two possibilities: it can issue more shares or it can plough back profits (assuming, of course, it is making some). Ploughing back profits is the simplest but not necessarily the cheapest source of long-term finance for a company. Also, the more a company ploughs back the less, in the short run at least, there will be available for paying dividends.

The sources and uses of funds of a company *for a period* are sometimes included in a third financial statement whose name has not yet been standardized. Some companies call it a funds statement or a flow of funds statement. The Alenco group calls it a Source and Disposition Statement (App. C, p. 21). In 1968/9 the group obtained funds from profit before taxation, from depreciation (the way in which depreciation may be said to provide funds is discussed later, pp. 34–5), from the amount realized on disposal of S. S. Stott Ltd and from an unsecured loan. These funds were used mainly to acquire H. & L. Austin Engineering Ltd, to purchase new fixed assets and patents, to pay taxation, management charges, loan interest and dividends, and to finance the group's increased working capital. Alenco has drawn up its statement in such a way as to emphasize the reduction in net cash and bank resources, but note that sources of funds (£2,242,000) equals use, employment or disposition of funds (£2,649,000–£407,000).

By using simple algebra it is possible to show quite clearly the links between the three financial statements discussed above. Let us use the following symbols:

a = assets
l = liabilities
nw = net worth
s = share capital and capital reserves
rp = retained or ploughed back
    profits (i.e. revenue reserves)

r = revenues (e.g. sales, fees)
e = expenses other than taxation
t = taxation
d = dividends
Δ = net increase in

The identity for any balance sheet will then be

$$a = l + nw$$

which can be expanded to

$$a = l + s + rp. \tag{i}$$

The source and disposition statement shows the net increase in each item and can therefore be written as

$$\Delta a = \Delta l + \Delta s + \Delta rp. \tag{ii}$$

The profit and loss account is merely an expansion of the last item on the right-hand side (Δrp or net increase in retained profits). The equation is

$$\Delta rp = r - e - t - d. \tag{iii}$$

Equation (ii) can therefore be expanded to read

$$\Delta a = \Delta l + \Delta s + r - e - t - d. \tag{iv}$$

For those who dislike algebra these four equations and their relationships are shown in the following diagrams. It should be noted that the relative proportions of liabilities and net worth have changed, although, of course, the sum of the two categories must always by definition be equal to the assets.

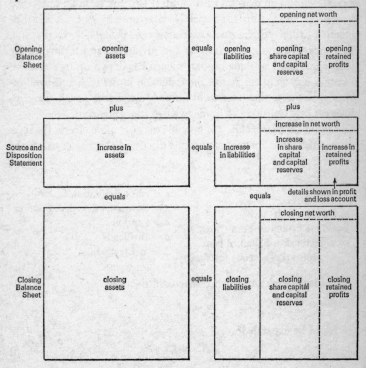

THE CONSOLIDATED BALANCE SHEET

It is not sufficient to record assets, liabilities and net worth as three totals. It is necessary to subdivide each category, and thus expand the accounting identity. In its consolidated balance sheet Alenco divides its sources of funds into:

> ordinary share capital and reserves
> preference share capital
> unsecured loan

and its employment of funds into:

> fixed assets
> patents
> net current assets (current assets *less* current liabilities)
> deferred taxation (a *negative* item)
> goodwill

Some consolidated balance sheets also include the item minority interests or outside shareholders' interests in subsidiaries. This will occur where some of the subsidiaries in the group are not wholly owned by the parent company. See, for example, the consolidated balance sheet of Guest, Keen and Nettlefolds (Appendix D, p. 34).

The next few sections of this chapter are devoted to brief discussions of each major balance sheet item.

CURRENT ASSETS, CURRENT LIABILITIES
AND WORKING CAPITAL

Alenco has four sorts of assets: current, fixed, goodwill, and patents. Current assets consist of those assets which are either in the form of cash or can reasonably be expected to be turned into cash within one year from the date of the balance sheet. The Alenco group at 30 September 1969 had current assets valued at £5,538,000, comprised of cash and bank balances and deposits of £67,000, debtors (accounts receivable in the United States) of £2,786,000 and stocks (inventories in the U.S.A.) of £2,685,000. The debtors figure is usually net of an allowance (or provision) for doubtful debts. The figure for stocks may vary according to the rules for valuation adopted. Alenco's policy is set out in their note 13 (App. C, p. 15) as follows:

Stocks were in the main valued on the following bases:
Raw materials at the lower of cost and net realisable value.

Finished parts and work in progress at the lower of cost and net realisable value. Cost in this context is confined to the cost of direct materials, variable wages and variable expenses; no addition has been made for fixed overhead expenses or depreciation.

The use of lower of cost or net realizable value is standard practice in Britain. The valuation of stock poses many problems and has been much discussed by accountants. One of the arguments revolves around the inclusion of fixed overhead expenses (those expenses which do not change over the usual level of manufacturing activity) and depreciation as part of the cost of manufactured goods. Some companies include them; others, like Alenco, prefer to exclude them.

Similarly, current liabilities are defined as those liabilities which are expected to have to be paid within one year from the date of the balance sheet. The Alenco group at 30 September had creditors (accounts payable in America) of £1,816,000, largely for materials supplied and expenses incurred in the normal course of business; a current taxation liability of £468,000; bank loans and overdraft of £169,000; and a proposed dividend of £339,000 (to be paid, subject to the formal approval of the shareholders, at the annual general meeting on 6 March 1970 – see consolidated profit and loss account, Appendix C, p. 6). The total of the current liabilities is thus £2,792,000, which, when deducted from the current assets of £5,538,000, gives net current assets of £2,746,000. Net current assets are also referred to as net working capital or (more usually) just working capital. The relationship between current assets and current liabilities is very important and is discussed in detail in chapter 6 on liquidity.

FIXED ASSETS

Fixed assets are usually defined as those which a company has acquired with the intention of using, not reselling. Stocks are not regarded as fixed assets since they are either acquired for immediate resale (e.g. a tobacconist selling cigarettes), as raw materials for use in manufacturing operations, or are the finished or partly finished ('work-in-progress') results of such operations. It will be seen from the consolidated balance sheet and note 15 that the fixed assets of the Alenco group at 30 September 1969 were land and buildings of £1,318,000 and plant, equipment and vehicles of £1,232,000. It is worth noting that these would be *current* assets of a company whose business it was to *sell* land, buildings, plant, equipment or vehicles.

Note 15 to the group accounts gives more detailed information of the group's fixed assets, starting with the figures for 30 September 1968 at cost or valuation. 'Cost' in accounting usually means the historical cost of acquisition or manufacture (if the asset was made by the company for its own use). Historical cost is favoured by accountants because it is thought to be objective and can be verified by an independent third party (i.e. by the auditor). It can, however, get seriously out of line with current market values, especially in times of inflation. Many influential accountants therefore consider that financial statements should be adjusted to take account of changes in specific and/or general prices, but no agreement has been reached on the methods to be used.* Meanwhile the historical cost approach predominates in practice and the reader must always look carefully at the practices of the particular company whose accounts he is analysing.

So far as the Alenco group is concerned, most of its land and buildings were valued at 30 September 1966 at £1,290,000 and now have a book value of £1,200,000, the difference being the effect of charging depreciation. Other land and buildings, including those held on short leases, cost £149,000, and now have a book value of £118,000. During the year additions to land and buildings were made amounting to £63,000. This item should be traced into the source and disposition statement (p. 17).

DEPRECIATION

The concept of depreciation means different things to different people, but in an accounting context it normally means spreading the cost (sometimes after revaluation) of a fixed asset over its estimated useful

*See further chapter 8.

economic life. Alenco's practice is explained in note 7 to the accounts:

Depreciation is calculated on a straight line basis by reference to the original cost (reduced by investment grants) or subsequent revaluation of the assets.

Alenco thus uses the straight line or linear method of depreciation. This is the simplest method and consists of dividing the cost less estimated scrap value of an asset by the estimated economic life. If, for example, a machine costs £1,200 and is expected to have a scrap value of £130 at the end of an estimated economic life of ten years, then the annual depreciation expense using this method will be £1,070/10 = £107.

Another common method in Britain and North America is the reducing balance method. As the name implies, the amount of depreciation charged each year decreases over the life of the asset. If for example a rate of 20 per cent were chosen for the asset which cost £1,200, the annual depreciation charges would be calculated as shown on p. 25.

The machine has been written down to its approximate scrap value. The correct percentage can be found by trial and error or by use of the formula:

$$ 1 - \sqrt[n]{\frac{s}{c}} $$

where n is the number of years, s the estimated scrap value and c the cost. In this case

$$ 1 - \sqrt[10]{\frac{130}{1200}} = 0 \cdot 2. $$

The charging of depreciation simultaneously: 1. reduces the recorded amount of the fixed asset, and 2. reduces net profit.

In the Alenco consolidated profit and loss account, for example, there is a depreciation item for 1969 of £324,000. This relates both to fixed assets and patents. Note 7 shows that £313,000 was charged on fixed assets, £15,000 was written off patents and that £4,000 was added back as adjustment on disposals. The source and disposition statement includes £11,000 as the proceeds of the sale of fixed assets; note 15 shows that they had a written down value of £7,000 (cost or

	£
Cost	1,200
Year 1 Depreciation 20% of £1,200	240
	960
Year 2 „ 20% of £960	192
	768
Year 3 „ 20% of £768	154
	614
Year 4 „ 20% of £614	123
	491
Year 5 „ 20% of £491	98
	393
Year 6 „ 20% of £393	79
	314
Year 7 „ 20% of £314	63
	251
Year 8 „ 20% of £251	50
	201
Year 9 „ 20% of £201	40
	161
Year 10 „ 20% of £161	32
	£129

valuation £78,000 *less* accumulated depreciation £71,000) in the company's books. This gives rise to the profit on disposal of £4,000.

The amounts given for the fixed assets and patents in the consolidated balance sheet are net of all accumulated depreciation, not only that of the current year but of all previous years since the purchase of the assets concerned.

Investment grants were available until recently from the government on the purchase of certain assets. Alenco's note 15 shows that it received investment grants of £67,000 during 1968/9 relating to expenditure of £369,000 on plant, equipment and vehicles. The grant is paid to the company in cash and thus, unlike the capital allowances described in the next chapter (pp. 39–41), does not depend upon whether or not a company has any taxable income. Alenco chose to calculate depreciation on the original cost as reduced by investment grants receivable. Some companies (e.g. I.C.I.) calculated depreciation on the gross amount.

GOODWILL AND PATENTS

A company is not just a collection of assets. It is, or should be, a going concern whose total value, by reason of its proven ability to earn profits, is greater than the sum of its parts. It is the difference between the total value and the sum of the parts which constitutes goodwill. It should not be regarded as in any way a fictitious asset: to be valuable an asset does not have to be tangible. Goodwill is, however, very difficult to value objectively and it is for this reason that it very seldom appears in a balance sheet unless it has been purchased, and even then it is often written off quite quickly.

This explains why the Alenco group balance sheet does not include any goodwill derived from the balance sheets of the individual companies of the group. As note 18 (App. C, p. 18) explains, the goodwill figure of £959,000 represents 'the excess of the cost of shares in subsidiary companies over the book value of their net tangible assets at the dates of acquisition'. This is sometimes known as 'goodwill on consolidation'.

Goodwill on consolidation can, by definition, appear only in a consolidated balance sheet. It is appropriate at this point to consider the differences between the balance sheet of the Alenco group (pp. 8–9) and of Alenco Ltd itself (pp. 10–11). Apart from the size of the figures, it will be seen that the main difference is that the items goodwill and patents appear only in the consolidated balance sheet, whilst the item subsidiary companies appears only in the holding company's balance sheet. The absence of patents* arises merely from the fact that these

---

*Patents are grants by the Crown to the authors of new inventions giving them the sole and exclusive right to use, exercise and sell their inventions and to secure the profits arising therefrom for a limited period.

are held only by the operating companies in the group (it will be noticed that Alenco Ltd has no stocks either). What is important is the absence from the consolidated balance sheet of the subsidiary companies item. This includes the cost (£2,520,000) to Alenco Ltd of buying the shares in the subsidiaries and also the amounts owed by the subsidiary companies to the holding company (£2,404,000) less the amounts owed *to* the subsidiaries (£38,000). When the accounts of Alenco Ltd and its subsidiaries are consolidated these intra-group debts cancel out, to leave only debtors and creditors outside the group. (Remember that the Alenco group is itself part of a larger group; its indebtedness to the larger group is not eliminated: see note 14, p. 15.)

The consolidated balance sheet does not include the shares in subsidiaries item, since this is replaced by the net tangible assets of the subsidiaries, plus, as we have just noted, goodwill on consolidation as a balancing figure. The Companies Act requires the publication of both balance sheets. Shareholders of the holding company should concentrate their attention mainly on the consolidated balance sheet.

LOAN CAPITAL

To the extent that a company cannot or does not wish to obtain long-term funds from its shareholders, it must borrow from outsiders. Such borrowings are called loan capital or medium and long-term debt. Alenco's loan capital consists of an unsecured loan of £750,000 from Charterhouse Industrial Holdings Ltd* (see consolidated balance sheet, p. 8).

Alenco's ultimate holding company, The Charterhouse Group Ltd, had loan capital at 30 September 1970 of £17,696,000. This consisted partly of 7 per cent debenture stock 1986/91 secured by a first floating charge on the assets of its major industrial subsidiaries and repayable at par on 30 September 1991 together with interest accrued to the date of repayment, the company, however, reserving the right, on giving three months' notice in writing, to repay on or after 30 September 1986, all or any part of the stock at par, together with interest accrued to the date of repayment.

There are a number of terms in the preceding paragraph which need

* Since re-named Charterhouse Industries Ltd.

further explanation. The word 'debenture' simply refers to a document evidencing a long-term borrowing or loan. Debentures are usually, but not necessarily, secured on the assets of the company, i.e. if the company fails in its obligation to pay interest or repay the loan, certain property of the company can be sold in order to provide the necessary funds. The phrase unsecured debenture is unusual, unsecured loan, as in the case of Alenco, being preferred in practice. Debenture stock means that instead of issuing individual debentures the company has created one loan fund to be divided among a class of lenders each of whom will receive a debenture stock certificate. Companies may, and often do, make more than one issue of debentures, the terms of issue and, in particular, the rate of interest varying according to the financial circumstances of the time. Such issues may be made at par (i.e. at face value), at a discount (less than face value) or at a premium (more than face value). Issue at a discount increases the effective interest rate payable; issue at a premium (rare) reduces it. Issues are often made at a discount in order to keep the interest rate on the par value (known as the coupon rate) a reasonably round figure, whilst allowing the effective rate to be adjusted more finely.

Debentures and loans may be secured by a fixed charge on a particular asset or, as in the Charterhouse case, by a general or floating charge on all the assets or particular classes of assets. A floating charge, unlike a fixed charge, allows a company to dispose of the assets charged in the usual course of business without obtaining special permission from the lender. Stock-in-trade is a particularly suitable asset to be charged in this manner. If assets are, or may be, used as security for more than one loan, it is necessary to state the order of priority of the lenders. The Charterhouse Group Ltd's debenture stock is stated to be secured by a *first* floating charge.

Some debentures are irredeemable, i.e. they will never have to be repaid (unless the company is wound up), but most are redeemable. It is common, as is the case here, to specify not only the latest date, but also to give the company the power to redeem earlier if it so wishes. This is especially useful if debentures are issued in times of high interest rates like the present, and if there is an expectation of lower rates later.

How much loan capital to issue and when and in what form to

issue it, are vital matters to any company. We shall look at this problem in chapter 7.

SHARE CAPITAL AND RESERVES

Apart from the unsecured loan, the sources of funds section of Alenco's consolidated balance sheet is made up of the following items:

ordinary share capital and reserves
      divided into: ordinary share capital of Alenco Ltd
                     share premium account
                     other capital reserves
                     revenue reserves
preference share capital.

Shareholders differ from debenture holders in that they are members (owners) of the company not lenders, in that they receive dividends (a share of the profits) not interest and in that, except in special circumstances, the cost of their shares will not be repaid to them by their company. Quoted shares can of course be sold on a stock exchange, but the company itself is in general forbidden by law from buying back or redeeming its own shares. An exception is the redeemable preference share (see Glossary).

There are two main types of shares: ordinary and preference. The difference between an ordinary shareholder and a preference shareholder is very important.* The latter is usually entitled only to a dividend at a fixed rate (6 per cent in the case of Alenco, see App. C, note 9, p.14) but has priority of repayment in the event of the company being wound up. This is not always so, however, and the exact rights must always be looked up in the company's articles of association (see chapter 1, p. 15 above). Preference shares may be cumulative or non-cumulative. Alenco's are cumulative, which means that if the company misses a dividend payment, it carries it forward to the next year. Any arrears of preference dividends must be shown in a note to the balance

---

* In the case of Alenco Ltd, the distinctions between ordinary share capital, preference share capital and loan capital are rather artificial since all are held by Charterhouse Industrial Holdings Ltd (since re-named Charterhouse Industries Ltd). Nevertheless the legal, accounting and financial differences remain and in most companies are of great practical importance.

sheet. Non-cumulative preference dividends, on the other hand, do not have to be carried forward.

The ordinary shareholder is not entitled to a fixed dividend, the size of his dividend varying according to the profits made by the company. It can be seen from the consolidated profit and loss account (pp. 6–7) than an interim ordinary dividend of $8\frac{1}{2}$ per cent was paid on 29 August 1969 and that (subject to the approval of the proprietors at the annual general meeting) a final ordinary dividend of $19\frac{1}{4}$ per cent is to be paid on 6 March 1970. The total ordinary dividend was thus $27\frac{3}{4}$ per cent. Since this percentage is applied to the *par* value of the shares the total amount paid and payable is $27\frac{3}{4}$ per cent of £1,760,000 (the ordinary share capital of Alenco Ltd given in the balance sheets) or approximately £488,000 (actually £488,400; the financial statements are rounded off to the nearest £'000).

Although dividends are always stated in relation to par value, their ratio to total ordinary shareholders' funds (= ordinary share capital and reserves) is more important, since the latter represent the shareholders' total stake in the company. In 1968/9 this ratio was $\frac{488,000 \times 100}{4,746,000} = 10\cdot3\%$. From the figures for 1967/8 also given in the consolidated profit and loss account and consolidated balance sheet it can be calculated that the percentage the previous year was $\frac{440,000 \times 100}{4,940,000} = 8\cdot9\%$. The percentages for each year from 1960/61 onwards are given in Table 14 on p. 78.

More important still to an investor is the relationship between the dividend and the current *market price* of the share. This is known as the dividend yield and is discussed in chapter 7 in the context of earnings yields and price–earnings ratios. For the moment, it should be noted that every share must have a par value* (Alenco's ordinary shares have a par value of 25p (5s) each, its preference shares a par value of £1 each), but that this is not necessarily the same as the issue price of the shares or their market price. Shares can be issued at more or (very rarely) less than the par value. Issue at a price greater than par gives rise to a *share premium*. Alenco has a share premium of £207,000 which, as the explanation in the consolidated balance sheet

*No par value shares are common in North America but illegal in the U.K.

states, cannot be distributed as dividends. A share premium can, however, be used to make a bonus issue (see below). Once a share has been issued its market price fluctuates from day to day in accordance with supply and demand. If the shares can be bought and sold on a stock exchange* then its current market price can easily be obtained from the financial pages of a newspaper or from the *Stock Exchange Daily Official List*. The most complete newspaper list is given in the *Financial Times*. The information given in that paper's daily share information service is further discussed in chapter 7.

A company does not have to issue all its shares at once, nor does it have to request full payment on the shares immediately. Alenco has authority to issue, i.e. it has authorized capital of 8,000,000 ordinary shares of 25p (5s) each, and 500,000 6 per cent cumulative preference shares of £1 each (Appendix C, note 9, p. 14). As at 30 September 1969 it had issued 7,040,000 ordinary shares (par value £1,760,000) and 165,000 preference shares (par value £165,000). All the shares are described as being fully paid, that is the company does not have the right to call up any further amounts from the shareholders. They could have been partly paid. For example, a 25p share could be payable 5p on application for the shares, a further 5p on allotment when the directors decide who the shares are going to be issued to, and the remaining 15p in calls. Thus, in summary, one can distinguish authorized, issued, called-up and paid-up share capital.

The 1968 consolidated balance sheet (not reproduced in this book) stated that the figure of £1,760,000 for ordinary share capital represented the par value of the ordinary shares originally issued and as subsequently increased by rights and bonus issues. A rights issue is one in which the existing shareholders have the right, if they so wish, to subscribe for new shares at a stated price. If they do not wish to do so they can sell the rights on a stock exchange. Most issues of shares are rights issues in Britain; in many European countries companies *must* offer new shares to the existing shareholders first.

A bonus issue (also called a scrip issue in Britain and a stock dividend in the United States) can be regarded as a rights issue whose stated price is zero. Alenco's preference shares were, according to a statement

---

*As one of the consequences of its becoming a wholly owned subsidiary of the Charterhouse group, Alenco's shares have not been quoted since September 1968.

in the 1968 consolidated balance sheet, all originally issued as bonus shares to the ordinary shareholders. The word 'bonus' is rather misleading as we shall see in chapter 7, where both rights and bonus issues are further discussed.

The ordinary share capital and reserves of the Alenco group as at 30 September 1969 amounted to £4,746,000. We have already encountered the ordinary share capital (£1,760,000) and the share premium (£207,000). The other two items are called 'other capital reserves' (£502,000) and 'revenue reserves' (£2,277,000). The essential difference between capital and revenue reserves is that the former are not regarded as being normally available for dividend. The distinction is not without its difficulties and has not been obligatory since the Companies Act 1967.

Alenco has two sorts of capital reserves: the share premium and those reserves arising from capital profits on, for example, the sale of a subsidiary (see note 10, p. 14). Revenue reserves represent the retained profits of the group after charging taxation and deducting dividends.

It is very important not to confuse reserves with cash. To say that a company has large reserves is not the same thing as saying that it has lots of cash. If a company has reserves it must have net assets of equal amount, but these net assets may be of any kind (e.g. machinery, stock-in-trade). Thus it is perfectly possible (and often sensible) for a company to have both large reserves and a large bank overdraft. The Alenco group's reserves at 30 September 1969 amounted to £2,986,000 (i.e. share premium of £207,000, other capital reserves of £502,000 and revenue reserves of £2,277,000); it had cash and bank balances and deposits of £67,000 and bank loans and overdrafts of £169,000, i.e. *negative* net cash resources of £102,000.

CONSOLIDATED PROFIT AND LOSS ACCOUNT

The ordinary shareholders' funds of the group were increased in 1968/9 by the adding to revenue reserves of £17,000 of retained profits. This is the last item in the consolidated profit and loss account (p. 6). To see how it arose we must start with the sales of the group which amounted to £9,669,000. Note that only sales to customers *outside the group* are included. The inclusion of sales within the group would not be justified; they would merely inflate both the sales and the purchases.

It is obligatory for companies to provide in the directors' report an analysis of sales according to principal activities* and to state the value of goods exported. Alenco's export sales in 1968/9 amounted to £1,059,000 (App. C, p. 5).

From the sales are deducted the cost of raw materials, the wages and salaries, depreciation (discussed earlier in this chapter) and other expenses. The wages and salaries include the directors' emoluments. An analysis of the latter, compulsory since the Companies Act 1967, is given in note 6 (p. 13).†

Deduction of all these costs from sales gives a trading profit, independent of the method of financing, of £979,000 or 10·1 per cent of sales. Deduction of the net interest payable by the group (£29,000) gives a profit attributable to proprietors before taxation of £950,000. The proprietors (i.e. Charterhouse) are entitled to £5,000 as a management charge and £23,000 of loan interest, so the profit before taxation is £922,000. Taxation is £407,000, leaving £515,000 to be paid out to the shareholders or retained in the business. The preference shareholders receive £10,000 (6 per cent of £165,000 rounded to the nearest £1,000). As we have already seen the ordinary dividends are of two kinds: an interim of 8½ per cent paid on 29 August 1969, and a proposed final dividend of 19¼ per cent payable on 6 March 1970.

The deduction of the dividends from the profit after taxation leaves the £17,000 carried forward as an increase in the revenue reserves.

Profit earned needs to be related to investment made and compared if possible with the performance of similar firms. Profitability and return on investment form the main subjects of chapter 5.

SOURCE AND DISPOSITION STATEMENT (FUNDS STATEMENT)

It will be remembered that a source and disposition statement shows *changes* during the year in assets, liabilities, share capital and retained profits and that the last item is made up of revenues less expenses (in-

---

*The Stock Exchange recommends that a geographical analysis be also shown. See G.K.N.'s Directors' Report, App. D, p. 11.

† See Glossary under 'Directors' Emoluments'.

cluding depreciation), less tax, less dividends. The statement shows what assets have been acquired and how they have been financed. Looking at the Alenco group's statement for the year ended September 1969 we can see that the most important uses of funds were:

	£
the acquisition of H. & L. Austin Engineering Ltd	845,000
proprietors' charges and appropriations (mainly dividends paid)	574,000
increase in working capital	439,000
taxation paid	391,000

These were financed as follows:

	£
profit before taxation	950,000
depreciation	324,000
unsecured loan	750,000
amount realised on disposal of S. S. Stott Ltd	218,000

DEPRECIATION AS A 'SOURCE' OF FUNDS

We have already stated (p. 24) that the charging of depreciation simultaneously reduces (1) the recorded amount of the fixed asset concerned and (2) the net profit. How then can it also be regarded as a 'source' of funds, as in Alenco's statement? The simple answer is that depreciation is neither a source nor a use of funds. The use of funds obviously took place when the fixed asset was originally bought. It would be double counting to regard each year's depreciation as a further use of funds and it therefore follows that the relevant figure for profit from operations in a source and disposition statement is *profit before charging depreciation*. But the same arithmetical result can be reached by adding back depreciation to profit *after* charging depreciation. This is very commonly done, and is the practice followed by Alenco, but it should not mislead us into thinking that funds can be obtained by increasing the depreciation charge in the books.* If, for example, Alenco's depreciation had been £334,000

---

*Depreciation allowable for tax is another matter. The more which can be deducted, the greater profit from operations will be.

instead of £324,000 then its profit before taxation would have been £940,000 instead of £950,000 and its total sources of funds as shown in the Source and Disposition Statement (p. 21) would remain unchanged at £2,242,000.

CASH FLOW

Since for funds-flow purposes it is profit before charging depreciation which is important, it has become common to add back depreciation to profit and to call the result by the rather misleading name 'cash flow': a more accurate name would be 'funds provided by operations'. Sometimes cash flow is defined as *retained* profits plus depreciation. This can be regarded as the *net* cash flow as compared with the *gross* cash flow defined above. Note that cash flow is *not* the same as the change in the net cash and bank resources of the group.

3. Taxation and Audit

This short chapter deals briefly with two important matters of which all readers of company reports should have some knowledge – taxation and audit. No attempt will be made to go into either in detail; company taxation in particular can become fearsomely complicated.

TAXATION

There are several references to taxation in the Alenco report. Taxation provided on the group profit for 1968/9 is stated in the consolidated profit and loss account to be £407,000 (£401,000 in 1967/8), i.e. just over 44 per cent of the profit chargeable to taxation of £922,000 (about 42 per cent of a profit of £958,000 in 1967/8). In the consolidated balance sheet of 30 September 1969 deferred taxation of £636,000 appears as a negative employment of funds (£681,000 in 1968) and current taxation of £468,000 as a current liability (£324,000 in 1968). Further details of the group's tax position are given by the company in notes 8 and 17 (App. C, pp. 14 and 18).

There are a number of special features in the 1968/9 figures which make them rather awkward to use for our purpose. We shall therefore look in detail at the 1967/8 figures instead.

CORPORATION TAX

Companies pay corporation tax, not income tax or personal tax. The corporation tax rate is imposed annually in arrears for the financial year 1 April to 31 March. For the financial year 1967 (i.e. from 1 April 1967 to 31 March 1968) it was 42½ per cent; for the financial year 1968 (1 April 1968 to 31 March 1969) 45 per cent; for the financial year 1969 (1 April 1969 to 31 March 1970) 42½ per cent; and for the financial year 1970 (1 April 1970 to 31 March 1971) 40 per cent. The tax is *assessed*, however, on the basis of a company's accounting period. In the case of Alenco this runs, as we know, from 1 October to 30 September. The tax is normally *payable* nine months after the end of the financial year in which the company's accounting period ends.

Applying the above to Alenco's taxable profit for its accounting period 1 October 1967 to 30 September 1968, we see that the first six months of this period (i.e. 1 October 1967 to 31 March 1968) fell within the financial year 1967, whilst the second six months (1 April 1968 to 30 September 1968) fell within the financial year 1968. Alenco estimated the total tax payable by the group for the whole twelve months (1 October 1967 to 30 September 1968) to be £382,000 (see note 8, p. 14) and charged this accordingly in its 1967/8 consolidated profit and loss account (there was also an extra £19,000 – explained below – making a total of £401,000). Payment was due nine months after 31 March 1969 (the last day of the financial year 1968), i.e., on 1 January 1970. The £382,000 was therefore *not* a current liability as at 31 September 1968 (since it was not payable within one year from the date of the balance sheet) but formed part of the deferred taxation item. It appears as such in note 17 to the 1969 report (p. 18).

By 30 September 1969 the estimated taxation on the 1967/8 profits had become a current liability and is included as part of current taxation in the current liabilities section of the 30 September 1969 balance sheet. It should be noted, however, that the amount finally paid may differ from the original estimate.

There remains to be explained £19,000 (the figure of £401,000 shown in the consolidated profit and loss account *less* the £382,000 of corporation tax just mentioned) and also £299,000 (£681,000 *less*

£382,000) of deferred taxation. As notes 8 and 17 in the 1969 Report explain, the £19,000 represents foreign taxation of £24,000 based on the profit of the year, less a transfer of £5,000 from the taxation equalization account; the £299,000 comes entirely from the taxation equalization account. This account arises from the fact that the depreciation written off fixed assets for taxation purposes (see below) may be greater or smaller than that provided in the accounts (see chapter 2). This has the effect of changing the time pattern of the tax liability; some companies therefore transfer appropriate amounts each year to or from a taxation equalization account and increase or decrease accordingly the charge for taxation in the consolidated profit and loss account. In 1967/8 Alenco reduced by £5,000 both the balance on the taxation equalization account and the tax on the profits for the year. The total deferred taxation of £681,000 is thus made up of £382,000 corporation tax payable on 1 January 1971 and £299,000 on taxation equalization account.

The current taxation liability of £324,000 at 30 September 1968 represents the U.K. corporation tax and foreign tax payable within one year from the balance sheet.

No provision has been made in the accounts for additional taxation which would only be payable if the retained profits of foreign subsidiaries were to be distributed to the parent company. An estimate is given, however, of the amount involved: £40,000 in 1968; £41,000 in 1969 (see note 12, p. 15).

In 1971 the government announced that it would reform the system whereby distributed profits (profits paid out as dividends) are treated more harshly than undistributed profits. Under this system distributed profits are taxed not only in the hands of the company but also in the hands of the shareholder. At the time of writing it is not known what reforms will be made. One possibility would be to have different tax rates for undistributed and distributed profits, the latter being lower than the former. Another possibility would be to follow the French method of giving the *shareholder* a credit for the tax paid by the company on its distributed profits (the so-called imputation method).

CAPITAL ALLOWANCES AND INVESTMENT INCENTIVES

As already noted in both this and the previous chapter, depreciation allowed for tax purposes usually differs from that shown in a company's accounts. The main reason for this is that whilst a company in reporting to its shareholders is interested in calculating profit as accurately as possible, the government is more interested in regulating investment.

The present system of capital allowances acts as an incentive to investment by allowing a very large write-off in the first year of ownership. For machinery and plant (which includes furniture, fixtures and fittings and some motor vehicles), new or second-hand, there is a first-year allowance of 60 per cent of the expenditure.* In the second and later years there is a writing-down allowance of 25 per cent on the reducing balance method. Chapter 2 included the example of a company which acquired an asset for £1,200 with an estimated economic life of ten years and an estimated scrap value of £130 at the end of that period. It was shown that the required annual writing-off percentage was 20 per cent. The capital allowances for tax purposes in this case are shown on p. 40.

The written-down value in the books at the end of the tenth year would be £129 (see p. 25) compared with a written-down value for tax purposes of £36. If the asset were in fact sold at this point for £129, there would be a balancing charge of £93 (£129–£36) increasing the company's taxable income. Where the sales price is less than the tax written-down value there is a balancing allowance instead.

In the above example, 60 per cent of the cost of the asset was allowed for tax in the first year, 70 per cent by the end of the second year, and 77·5 per cent by the end of the third year. Even more liberal treatment is available for ships, capital equipment for scientific research and immobile plant and machinery in development areas. In these cases a system of free depreciation applies, i.e. the company can write off the cost of these assets as quickly as it likes, for example a 100 per cent write-off in the year of purchase.

*80% for the period 20 July 1971 to 31 July 1973.

		£	Compared with book depreciation of
Cost		1,200	
Year 1	60% of £1,200	720	£240
		480	
2	25% of £480	120	192
		360	
3	25% of £360	90	154
		270	
4	25% of £270	67	123
		203	
5	25% of £203	51	98
		152	
6	25% of £152	38	79
		114	
7	25% of £114	28	63
		86	
8	25% of £86	22	50
		64	
9	25% of £64	16	40
		48	
10	25% of £48	12	32
		36	
		and so on	

The 60 per cent first-year allowance is not applicable to industrial buildings. For industrial buildings an initial allowance of 30 per cent or 40 per cent applies, together with a 4 per cent annual writing-down allowance which begins in the first year and is based on the straight-line method. The allowances for an industrial building costing £100,000 would be as follows assuming a 30 per cent initial allowance:

	£	£
Cost		100,000

		£	£
Year 1	Initial Allowance—		
	30% of £100,000	30,000	
	Writing-down Allowance		
	4% of £100,000	4,000	
			34,000
			66,000
2	Writing-down Allowance		4,000
			62,000
3	Writing-down Allowance		4,000
			58,000
			and so on

There are no capital allowances at all on non-industrial buildings such as retail shops, offices, dwelling-houses and hotels.

It is important to note that all the allowances described above are deductions from taxable income. If the latter is large enough to cover the allowances then their effect is to reduce the company's tax bill by the amount of the allowances multiplied by the corporation tax rate. A company which has no taxable income to offset against the allowances does not benefit at all.

This was not true of the recently discontinued system of investment grants which we have already encountered in chapter 2. These were not reductions in taxable income but payments of cash (equal during most of their period of existence to 20 per cent of the cost of the plant and machinery acquired in non-development areas and 40 per cent in development areas) to a company by the government. They were thus not dependent on the company making a taxable profit. Companies receiving investment grants did not receive first-year or initial allowances, but did receive writing-down allowances on the cost of the asset net of the grant.

PERSONAL TAX

From April 1973 onwards individuals will pay a graduated personal tax (replacing the income tax and surtax payable before that date).

At the time of writing a basic rate of 30 per cent is envisaged. This is a rounding down of the present standard rate of income tax (38·75 per cent) less earned income relief of 2/9, i.e., 30·14 per cent.

Although a company is not liable to income tax, surtax or personal tax, except in special circumstances, it must, when paying dividends or debenture interest, deduct income tax at the standard rate until April 1973 and personal tax at the basic rate thereafter, and account for the money to the Inland Revenue. This is one example – P.A.Y.E. (pay as you earn) is another – of the preference in our tax system for deduction of tax at source. Since the company is merely acting, in effect, as an unpaid collector of taxes the dividends and interest are shown gross of tax in the financial statements.

PROFITS TAX

Before the 1965 Finance Act companies were liable to income tax and also to a tax applicable only to companies known as 'profits tax'. Profits tax has been abolished.

CAPITAL GAINS TAX

Individuals are taxed not only on their income but also on certain capital gains, i.e. the excess of the price they receive on selling an asset over the price they paid for it (but see below). Capital gains are taxed at 30 per cent or (for gains up to £5,000) at half an individual's marginal tax rate (i.e. the highest rate of tax he pays), whichever is the lower. Gains on government securities are only subject to capital gains tax if realized within 12 months of the date of purchase.

Companies are not liable to capital gains tax on their capital gains, which are instead charged to corporation tax.

If a gain is made from selling an asset owned on 6 April 1965, only that part of the gain related to the period from 6 April 1965 to the date of sale is taxable. It is for this reason that many companies include a note in their annual reports giving the market value of their shares at that date. G.K.N.'s 1970 report, for example, contains the following (Appendix D, p. 3):

FINANCE ACT 1965

Capital Gains Tax

In certain circumstances the liability of a stockholder to long term capital gains tax is computed by reference to the market value of the shares on 6th April 1965.

The market value of £1 GKN ordinary stock on 6th April 1965 (adjusted for the 1 for 3 scrip issue in 1970) was 183p.

CLOSE COMPANIES

The owners of unincorporated businesses pay personal tax (income tax and, sometimes, surtax before 1973) on their profits. If there was no close company legislation, they could turn the business into a company, distribute no profits and pay only corporation tax, since shareholders are taxed only on profits paid out as dividends. In order to prevent this the Finance Act 1965 introduced the concept of the 'close company', defined as a company resident in the United Kingdom which is under the control of five or fewer participators or of participators who are directors. The detailed legislation is extremely complex.

TAX LAW

The most important statutes (Acts of Parliament) relating to the taxes described in this chapter are the Finance Act 1965, the Capital Allowances Act 1968, the Income and Corporation Taxes Act 1970 and the Taxes Management Act 1970. Every year there is at least one Finance Act amending the law. There is also a large body of case law relating to taxation. The law is thus always changing and some of the statements made in this chapter will need modification as the years go by.

AUDIT

The preparation of the financial statements of a company, and their presentation to the shareholders and to the tax authorities are the duties of the directors not of the auditors, although the latter, of course, often give valuable assistance.

Since there are often misconceptions about the functions of auditors, it is worth looking carefully at the report they give.

The Report of the Auditors to the members of Alenco Ltd (Appendix C, p. 20) reads as follows:

In our opinion, based on our examination and on the reports of other firms which have audited the accounts of certain subsidiaries, the accounts and notes set out on pages 6–19 comply with the Companies Acts 1948 and 1967 and, so far as concerns members of the company, give a true and fair view of the state of affairs at 30th September, 1969 of the company and of the group and of the profit of the group for the year ended on that date.

There are a number of interesting points to note about this report:

1. First of all, it is a *report*, not a certificate or a guarantee. The auditors report their opinion; they do not certify or guarantee anything. The discovery of mistakes or fraud is incidental.

2. Secondly, what they give their opinion on is the 'truth and fairness' of the accounts. This is not the same as saying that the accounts are 'correct' in every particular. It should be clear from the discussion of the financial statements in chapter 2 that the figures in balance sheets and profit and loss accounts are necessarily based to a certain extent on judgements. Depreciation is perhaps the most obvious example; should it be based on original cost or a revaluation? should the straight line or reducing balance method be used? how accurately has the accountant estimated the economic life and the scrap value? Clearly there are a number of reasonable depreciation figures; auditors would not seek to change a reasonable figure. (See also the discussion in chapter 8).

3. Thirdly, the auditors are reporting to the members (shareholders) of Alenco Ltd, not to the directors. Their function, as a late nineteenth century English judge put it, is to serve as a watchdog for the shareholders. They are appointed by the shareholders, usually on the recommendation of the directors.

The last item in the Directors' Report (Appendix C, p. 5) shows that during the year Messrs Thomson McLintock & Co. resigned as joint auditors and that Messrs Touche Ross & Co., (formerly Messrs Radford Edwards & Co.) are continuing in office. Retiring auditors are usually reappointed automatically (without the shareholders having to pass a resolution) unless they resign, lose their qualification or the shareholders pass a resolution appointing somebody else.

It is obviously important that auditors should not only be skilled in their profession but also be independent of the directors and managers of the company being audited. It is therefore provided by the Companies Acts that (1) auditors should either be members of a body of accountants established in the United Kingdom and recognized by the Board of Trade or be authorized by the Board to be appointed, and that (2) the auditor must not be an officer or servant of the company or of any company in the group, or a partner or employee of such officer or servant.

The amount of the auditors' remuneration must be stated in the annual report. For the Alenco group in the year 1968/9 it was £16,000 (note 3).

4. Tools of Analysis

... high Heaven rejects the lore
Of nicely-calculated less or more.

WILLIAM WORDSWORTH, *Inside of King's College Chapel, Cambridge*

The first three chapters of this book have been mainly descriptive. In the chapters which follow we turn to analysis and interpretation. We shall be concerned with three main questions:

1. Is the company under analysis making a satisfactory profit?
2. Is the company likely to run out of cash, or to keep cash idle?
3. How does the company decide the sources of its long-term funds?

These are the related problems of profitability, liquidity and capital structure.

Our tools of analysis will be the relationships which exist among the different items in the financial statements ('financial ratios') and the rates of return linking outflows with expected inflows ('yields').

FINANCIAL RATIOS

Financial ratios are normally expressed either as percentages or by the number of times one figure can be divided into another. For example, if a company has current assets of £10,000 and current liabilities of £5,000, we could say that current liabilities are 50 per cent of current assets, that current assets are 200 per cent of current liabilities, that the ratio: $\dfrac{\text{current assets}}{\text{current liabilities}}$ is 2.0, or that the ratio $\dfrac{\text{current liabilities}}{\text{current assets}}$ is 0.5. Which method is chosen is a matter of convenience and convention. In the example quoted it is customary to speak of a current ratio, $\dfrac{\text{current assets}}{\text{current liabilities}}$, of 2.0.

A percentage, as can be seen from the above, is merely a ratio multiplied by 100.

Not all ratios and percentages are significant or useful and one must beware of the temptation to calculate them for their own sake. It is unlikely, for example, that much can be gained from a scrutiny of the relationship between current liabilities and goodwill. The limitations of conventional accounting must always be kept in mind and accounting figures should not be treated as more precise than they really are. There is little sense in calculating a ratio to more than two decimal places.

YIELDS

A yield is a rate of return relating outflows to inflows. If, for example, I buy for £50 an irredeemable government bond with a par value of £100 on which interest of 4 per cent is payable annually, there is an immediate cash outflow of £50, followed by a series of cash inflows of £4 each year in perpetuity. The yield (gross of tax) is $\frac{4 \times 100}{50}\%$, i.e. 8%. If the bond were redeemable at a fixed price at some date in the future there would be a difference between the flat yield, which takes only the interest into account, and the redemption yield which takes the redemption price into account as well. For example, if the bond is redeemable twenty years hence at par, the flat yield is about 5·0 per cent and the redemption yield about 9·8 per cent. Yields such as these can be calculated using compound interest tables, specially compiled bond tables or a suitable computer program.

THE NEED FOR COMPARISONS

Any ratio, percentage, or yield is of little value in isolation. It is necessary to have some standard with which to compare it. The standard can be a budgeted one, set by the company for itself; an historical one, based on the past performance of the company; or an industry one, based on the observed ratios of companies in the same industry.

Budgeted standards are not usually available to shareholders or external financial analysts. Historical comparisons are often given in annual reports: see, for example, the Statistics and Ratios section (pp. 22–3) of Alenco's report. The inclusion of comparative figures for the past ten years is recommended by the Federation of Stock Exchanges.

INDUSTRY RATIOS

Industry ratios pose a much more difficult problem to the financial analyst. There are a number of reasons for this.

First, it is often difficult to decide which industry a company belongs to. Many industries are, in fact, composed of a surprisingly heterogeneous group of companies. In the official Standard Industrial Classification (S.I.C.) both Alenco and Guest, Keen and Nettlefolds are included in a group called 'metal goods not elsewhere classified'.

Secondly, the whole emphasis of the system of accounting at present in use is on *consistency* for a particular company over time rather than *comparability* among different companies at a single point in time, and the analyst must be constantly on his guard against differences in definition and in methods of valuation.

For these reasons not too much reliance can be placed on an industry comparison which is based on ratios obtained from published accounts. Companies can however obtain comparable ratios by taking part in a properly conducted interfirm comparison such as those conducted by the Centre for Interfirm Comparison.* Such ratios are however, by their very nature, confidential and unavailable to the external analyst.

In the next few chapters we shall make use of industry comparisons based on published accounts as well as historical comparisons, but shall try to avoid placing too much reliance on the former.

The final section of this chapter gives details of a number of useful sources of information relating to individual companies, to industries or to the company sector as a whole.

*Parker Street, Kingsway, London, WC2.

SOURCES OF INFORMATION

1. *Business Ratios* (Dun & Bradstreet Ltd)

This periodical, which was a very useful source of industry ratios (based on published accounts) relevant to profitability, liquidity and capital structure, regrettably ceased publication in 1970.

2. *The Times 1000* (published annually by *The Times*)

This lists each year, amongst other things, the thousand largest British industrial companies, with details of their turnover (both total and export); capital employed (defined as total tangible assets less current liabilities and sundry provisions, other than bank loans and overdrafts and future tax); net profit before interest and tax; net profit before interest and tax as a percentage of turnover; net profit before interest and tax as a percentage of capital employed; number of employees; and the market capitalization of the equity (i.e. the total market value of all the company's ordinary shares).

3. *Company Finance* (available annually by subscription from H.M.S.O.; it is M3 in the 'Business Monitor' series)

Contains tables showing for both quoted and non-quoted companies:

(i) a balance sheet summary;
(ii) sources of funds;
(iii) appropriation of trading and other income;
(iv) uses of funds;
(v) income and dividends and interest as percentage of assets;
(vi) financing of growth.

4. *Financial Statistics* (published monthly by the Central Statistical Office)

This includes, among many other things, tables summarizing:

(i) appropriation account of companies (i.e. company income and its allocation among dividends, interest, taxes and retentions);
(ii) sources and uses of capital funds of industrial and commercial companies;

(iii) selected liquid assets of industrial and commercial companies;

(iv) income and finance of quoted companies (three tables: balance sheet summary; sources of company funds; uses of company funds);

(v) capital issues and redemptions in the United Kingdom;

(vi) stock exchange transactions;

(vii) prices and yields of British government securities;

(viii) company security prices and yields.

5. *Economic Trends* (H.M.S.O., monthly)

6. *Monthly Digest of Statistics* (H.M.S.O.)

7. *National Income and Expenditure* (the 'Blue Book'; H.M.S.O., annually)

These three publications are not primarily concerned with company data, but do contain some information about companies.

8. *Moodies Investment Digest* (annual)

Summaries of the financial statements and share price movements of individual companies.

9. *Extel cards* (Extel Statistical Services Ltd, London)

The cards give information (kept continually up-to-date) of the same kind as (8) above.

5. Profitability and Return on Investment

For what is Worth in anything
But so much Money as 'twill bring.
SAMUEL BUTLER, *Hudibras*, I., i.

One of the first questions a shareholder is likely to ask of his company is: is it making a profit? If so, is it making a satisfactory profit? We have already seen in chapter 2 some of the difficulties which arise in trying to measure profit. Although accountants try to make their measurements as objective as possible, many financial figures, even those purporting to represent past events, are necessarily to some extent estimates. Profit is especially affected by the difficulties of measuring depreciation and valuing stock-in-trade, difficulties which are accentuated in times of changing price levels.*

In this chapter we shall look at the Alenco group's profit record for the three years ended 30 September 1969. Figures for 1967/8 and 1968/9 are given in the financial statements; most of those for 1966/7 can be found in the statistics and ratios section.

RETURN ON INVESTMENT

Sales and profits should not be looked at in isolation from the investment made to achieve them. We therefore make use of the following relationship which links profit before interest and tax, net tangible asssets and sales:

$$\frac{\text{profit}}{\text{net tangible assets}} = \frac{\text{profit}}{\text{sales}} \times \frac{\text{sales}}{\text{net tangible assets}}$$

The ratio on the left-hand side is the most usual (but not the only) measure of rate of return on investment. Profit is taken before interest and tax in order to separate managerial performance from the effects

*These problems are discussed further in chapter 8.

of different financial structures (see further chapter 7) and from changes in tax rates. The first term on the right-hand side is the net profit ratio, the second term measures the turnover of the net tangible assets. In interpreting these ratios the problems of valuation referred to above must be borne in mind. Before making comparisons between companies care must be taken to see that the definitions used are consistent.

Table 1 shows how the ratios can be calculated using Alenco's figures for the period 1966 to 1969. The slight differences between these figures and those given in the company's statistics and ratios section (App. C, pp. 22–3) arise from our deduction of the proprietors' management charge of £5,000 in 1967/8 and 1968/9 before arriving at profit before loan interest and tax.

	Sales	Profit before loan interest and tax	Net tangible assets	Net profit percentage	Sales as ratio of net tangible assets	Profit as percentage of net tangible assets
	(a)	(b)	(c)	(b)/(a) × 100	(a)/(c)	(b)/(c) × 100
	£000	£000	£000	%		%
1966/7	7,544	951	4,693	12·6	1·6	20·3
1967/8	8,085	958	4,817	11·8	1·7	19·9
1968/9	9,669	945	4,702	9·8	2·1	20·1

(*Source:* Alenco Ltd, Annual Report and Accounts for the year ended 30 September 1969.)

TABLE 1: *Calculation of Profitability Ratios, Alenco Group 1966–9*

It is apparent from these figures that Alenco's return on investment (profit as a percentage of net tangible assets) has been more or less constant over the period. The turnover of net tangible assets (sales as a ratio of net tangible assets) has improved but this has been offset by a decline in the net profit percentage.

Table 2 provides a comparison of Alenco's return on investment with that of quoted and non-quoted British manufacturing companies for the years 1966–9. It will be noted that Alenco is a relatively profitable group and that non-quoted manufacturing companies appear to be more profitable than quoted.

It is possible to carry further the analysis of Alenco's asset turnover

	Alenco group	Manufacturing companies (quoted)	Manufacturing companies (non-quoted)
	%	%	%
1967	20·3	11·9	14·2
1968	19·9	13·9	19·7
1969	20·1	13·3	16·9

(*Sources:* 1. Alenco Group: as for Table 1. 2. *Company Finance*, (H.M.S.O.), Third Issue, 1971, tables 1, 2, 4, 5.)

Note: Return on investment of manufacturing companies is gross trading profit, less depreciation provisions and amounts written off, as a percentage of net tangible fixed assets, stocks and work in progress, trade and other debtors, tax reserve certificates, treasury bills and cash, less current liabilities.

TABLE 2: *Return on Investment: Alenco Group and Quoted and Non-quoted Manufacturing Companies, 1967–9*

and net profit percentage. In Table 3 the rates of stock turnover and fixed asset turnover are calculated. The recent improvement in the latter is particularly noticeable.

Tables 4, 5 and 6 supplement the net profit percentage by providing details of expenses as well as sales and profits. The details are taken from Alenco's 1967, 1968 and 1969 annual reports. Table 4 gives the figures in thousands of pounds. To make the figures easier to follow, table 5 expresses each year's expenses and profit as a percentage of the sales of that year and table 6 shows sales, expenses and profit of each year as percentages of the base year 1967.

The three tables show that rising expenses have been eating into profits. For example, total expenses were 87·4% of sales in 1967 and 90·2% in 1969; and whereas sales rose by 28·2% over the three years, total expenses rose by 32·3%. Looking at individual expense items, it is apparent that:

(i) depreciation is a relatively unimportant item;

(ii) raw materials is the most important item – there was a big jump in 1969;

(iii) wages and salaries are second only to raw materials in importance, but have risen at a slower rate than sales over the three years;

(iv) the other expenses have increased as a percentage of sales from 13·2% to 14·3%.

	Sales	Stocks	Fixed assets and patents	Sales/stocks	Sales/fixed assets
	(a)	(b)	(c)	(a)/(b)	(a)/(c)
	£000	£000	£000		
1966/7	7,544	2,287	2,737	3·3	2·8
1967/8	8,085	2,432	2,671	3·3	3·0
1968/9	9,669	2,685	2,592	3·6	3·7

(*Source:* As for Table 1.)

TABLE 3: *The Alenco Group: Calculation of Rates of Turnover of Stocks and Fixed Assets, 1966–9*

Year ended 30 September ...	1969	1968	1967
	£000	£000	£000
Sales	9,669	8,085	7,544
Raw materials	3,835	2,873	2,801
Wages & salaries	3,183	2,847	2,522
Depreciation	324	305	276
Other expenses*	1,382	1,102	994
Total expenses	8,724	7,127	6,593
Profit before interest	945	958	951
Loan interest	23	—	
Profit before tax	922	958	951
Taxation	407	401	403
Profit after tax	515	557	548

*Includes non-loan interest and management charge.

(*Source:* Alenco Ltd, Annual Reports and Accounts for the years 1967 to 1969.)

TABLE 4: *The Alenco Group: Sales, Expenses and Profits, 1967–9, in Thousands of Pounds*

Year ended 30 September ...	1969	1968	1967
	%	%	%
Sales	100·0	100·0	100·0
Raw materials	39·7	35·5	37·1
Wages & salaries	32·9	35·2	33·4
Depreciation	3·3	3·8	3·7
Other expenses*	14·3	13·6	13·2
Total expenses	90·2	88·2†	87·4
Profit before interest	9·8	11·8	12·6
Loan interest	0·2	—	—
Profit before tax	9·5†	11·8	12·6
Taxation	4·2	4·9	5·3
Profit after tax	5·3	6·9	7·3

*Includes non-loan interest and management charge.
†Rounding error.

(*Source:* As for Table 4.)

TABLE 5: *The Alenco Group: Sales, Expenses and Profits, 1967–9, in Percentage Form; Sales of Each Year = 100.*

Year ended 30 September ...	1969	1968	1967
	%	%	%
Sales	128·2	107·2	100·0
Raw materials	136·9	102·6	100·0
Wages and salaries	126·2	112·9	100·0
Depreciation	117·4	110·5	100·0
Other expenses*	139·0	110·9	100·0
Total expenses	132·3	108·1	100·0
Profit before interest	99·4	100·7	100·0
Loan interest†	—	—	—
Profit before tax	97·0	100·7	100·0
Taxation	101·0	99·5	100·0
Profit after tax	94·0	101·6	100·0

*Includes non-loan interest and management charge.
†No percentages given because applicable only to 1969.

(*Source:* As for Table 4.)

TABLE 6: *The Alenco Group: Sales, Expenses and Profits, 1967–9, in Percentage Form; 1967 = 100*

EXCEPTIONAL ITEMS

In any analysis of profitability it is necessary to take into account exceptional or non-recurring items. For example, from the figures we have looked at so far it would appear that Alenco's profits in 1968 were only slightly higher than in 1967. In fact, information given in the 1968 directors' report (not reproduced in this book) reveals that:

1. the profits of the French subsidiary (Ermeto S. A.) were seriously affected by the disturbances in France during the months of May and June, 1968 and that in the directors' opinion the adverse impact was about £80,000;
2. the group benefited by about £50,000 (*nil* in 1967) by reason of the fluctuating price of copper-based metals.

If these two influences are removed the 1968 profit before interest becomes £988,000 instead of £958,000 which increases the return on investment from 19·9 per cent to 20·4 per cent. (In making this revised calculation it must be remembered that the £30,000 difference would have changed the net tangible assets as well as the profits.)

In 1968/9 the group again benefited by about £50,000 from the fluctuating cost of copper-based metals but the devaluation of the French franc on 11 August 1969 did not have a material effect on Alenco's sales and profits (see directors' report, App. C, pp. 3, 4).

6. Liquidity and Cash Flows

One may not doubt that, somehow, good
Shall come of water and of mud;
And, sure, the reverent eye must see
A purpose in liquidity.

RUPERT BROOKE, *Heaven*

LIQUIDITY

It is very important that a company should be profitable; it is just as important that it should be liquid. We have already seen (pp. 18–19) that an increase in profits must by definition lead to an increase in a company's net assets. There is no reason however why its *liquid* assets such as cash in the bank should automatically increase. A profitable and fast-expanding company may in fact find that it has tied up so much of its profits in fixed assets, stocks and debtors that it has difficulty in paying its debts as they fall due. To help prevent such a situation developing a company should prepare a cash budget, i.e. a plan of future cash receipts and payments based on specified assumptions about such things as sales growth, credit terms, issues of shares and expansion of plant. A simplified example demonstrating how a profitable company may run into liquidity problems is given below.

X.Y.Z. Ltd, is formed on 1 January 1972 to make boomerangs at a cost of £1·50 each and to sell them for £2 each. All bills are paid immediately and debts are collected within 30 days. The stock of boomerangs manufactured and paid for in January, for example, will be sold in February and the cash proceeds collected in March. The company's provisional plans are to sell 400 boomerangs in February 1972, 600 in March, 800 in April and so on. At 1 January the company has £600 in cash (raised by an issue of shares) – i.e. just sufficient to cover the manufacture of the first 400 boomerangs – but no other assets.

Before actually starting production the company draws up the following monthly budgets relating to profits and cash resources (Table 7).

The figures show that although the planned profit for the year is

Budgeted Profit and Loss Statement

	Jan. £	Feb. £	Mar. £	Apr. £	May £	June £	July £	Aug. £	Sep. £	Oct. £	Nov. £	Dec. £	Total £
Sales	—	800	1,200	1,600	2,000	2,400	2,800	3,200	3,600	4,000	4,400	4,800	30,800
Cost of sales	—	600	900	1,200	1,500	1,800	2,100	2,400	2,700	3,000	3,300	3,600	23,100
Profit	—	200	300	400	500	600	700	800	900	1,000	1,100	1,200	7,700

Note: The sales figures are equal to the quantity sold multiplied by £2; the cost of sales figures to the quantity sold multiplied by £1.50; the profit figures to the quantity sold multiplied by £0.50. Note that the cost of sales figures give the cost of the goods *sold* during the month *not* the cost of the goods *manufactured* during the month.

Cash Budget	Jan. £	Feb. £	Mar. £	Apr. £	May £	June £	July £	Aug. £	Sep. £	Oct. £	Nov. £	Dec. £
Balance at beginning of month	+600	—	-900	-1,300	-1,600	-1,800	-1,900	-1,900	-1,800	-1,600	-1,300	-900
Cash received from debtors	—	—	+800	+1,200	+1,600	+2,000	+2,400	+2,800	+3,200	+3,600	+4,000	+4,400
	+600	—	-100	-100	—	+200	+500	+900	+1,400	+2,000	+2,700	+3,500
Cash payments to creditors	-600	-900	-1,200	-1,500	-1,800	-2,100	-2,400	-2,700	-3,000	-3,300	-3,600	-3,900
Balance at end of month	—	-900	-1,300	-1,600	-1,800	-1,900	-1,900	-1,800	-1,600	-1,300	-900	-400

Note: Cash received from debtors is equal to the sales of the previous month; cash payments to creditors to the cost of sales of the next month.

TABLE 7: *X.Y.Z. Ltd: Cash Budget and Budgeted Profit and Loss Statement, 1972*

£7,700, cash will fall by £1,000 from a positive £600 to a negative £400. There is thus £8,700 to be accounted for. We can see what will happen by comparing the balance sheet at 1 January with that which will result at 31 December (Table 8).

Balance Sheets

	1 Jan. 1972	*31 Dec. 1972*	*Difference*
	£	£	£
Cash	+600	−400	−1,000
Debtors	—	+4,800	+4,800
Stocks	—	+3,900	+3,900
	+600	+8,300	+7,700
Share capital	+600	+600	—
Retained profits	—	+7,700	+7,700
	+600	+8,300	+7,700

Note: The cash figure at 31 December is taken from the cash budget; the debtors represent the December sales the cash for which will not be collected until January; the stocks represent the cost of goods manufactured and paid for in December for sale in January 1973.

TABLE 8: *X.Y.Z. Ltd: Balance Sheets, 1 January & 31 December 1972*

The difference column, which is in fact a simple source and disposition statement, shows the position quite clearly. All the profits, plus the original cash (£600), plus another £400 are tied up in debtors and stocks. It is interesting to note, however, that by the end of January 1973 the company's liquidity crisis will be over:

	Jan. 1973
Balance at beginning of month	−400
Cash received from debtors	+4,800
	+4,400
Cash payments to creditors	−4,200
	£+200

The catch is, of course, that in its present under-capitalized situation the company will never reach January 1973, in spite of its excellent profit-making potential, unless it can raise more cash by borrowing, by collecting its debts faster or by keeping down the size of its stocks.

If sales continue to rise similarly in 1973 and costs also remain the same, the company will run into the opposite problem: excess liquidity. The purpose of drawing up cash budgets is to ensure both that the company does not run out of cash and also that it does not keep cash idle when it can be profitably invested.

CURRENT AND QUICK RATIOS

Although cash budgets are thus an essential part of internal company financial management they are unavailable to the external financial analyst who must therefore perforce make use of rather less precise measures of liquidity. What he tries to do, in fact, is to approximate the possible future cash flows as closely as possible. It will be remembered that current assets and current liabilities were defined in chapter 2 as those assets and liabilities which can reasonably be expected to take the form of cash within one year from the date of the balance sheet. One crude measure of liquidity, therefore, is the relationship between the current assets and current liabilities. This is known as the 'current ratio', and is defined as follows: $\text{current ratio} = \dfrac{\text{current assets}}{\text{current liabilities}}$.

A more immediate measure of liquidity can be found by excluding stock-in-trade from the numerator. The resulting ratio is known as the quick, liquid or acid-test ratio:

$$\text{quick ratio} = \frac{\text{current assets} - \text{stock-in-trade}}{\text{current liabilities}}.$$

It has the incidental advantage of being more easily compared among companies, since it does not depend, as does the current ratio to some extent, on the method chosen to value the stock-in-trade.

The current assets, stock-in-trade and current liabilities of the Alenco group at 30 September each year from 1960 to 1969 are given in the statistics and ratios section of its annual report (App. C, pp.

22–3). In Table 9 below the figures for the last five years have been extracted and the current and quick ratios calculated.

	Current assets (a)	Stock-in -trade (b)	Current assets less Stock-in-trade (c) = (a) − (b)	Current liabilities (d)	Current ratio (a)/(d)	Quick ratio (c)/(d)
	£000	£000	£000	£000		
1965	4,058	2,317	1,741	2,125	1·91	0·82
1966	4,219	2,294	1,925	1,947	2·17	0·99
1967	4,447	2,287	2,160	1,840	2·42	1·17
1968	4,941	2,432	2,509	2,114	2·34	1·19
1969	5,538	2,685	2,853	2,792	1·98	1·02

(*Source:* Alenco Ltd, Annual Report and Accounts for the year ended 30 September 1969.)

TABLE 9: *Alenco Ltd: Calculation of Current and Quick Ratios, 1965–9*

Tables 10 and 11 compare the current and quick ratios of the Alenco group and of quoted and non-quoted British manufacturing companies in general for the years 1965 to 1969.

	Alenco group	Manufacturing companies (quoted)	Manufacturing companies (non-quoted)
1965	1·91	1·93	1·43
1966	2·17	1·87	1·40
1967	2·42	1·94	1·44
1968	2·34	1·84	1·39
1969	1·98	1·68	1·37

(*Sources:* 1. Alenco Ltd, Annual Report and Accounts for the year ended 30 September 1969. 2. *Company Finance*, (H.M.S.O.), Second Issue, 1970, tables 1, 7 and 13 and Third Issue, 1971, tables 1 and 4.)

TABLE 10: *Comparison of Current Ratios*

It can be seen that so far as Alenco is concerned the trend of both ratios has been the same, with the group becoming steadily more liquid up to 1967. Since 1968 the Alenco group has been completely

	Alenco group	Manufacturing companies (quoted)	Manufacturing companies (non-quoted)
1965	0·82	0·97	0·76
1966	0·99	0·96	0·75
1967	1·17	1·03	0·81
1968	1·19	1·06	0·81
1969	1·02	0·96	0·81

(*Sources:* as for Table 10.)

TABLE 11: *Comparison of Quick Ratios*

owned by the Charterhouse group and its liquidity position needs to be looked at in this wider context. At 30 September 1969 its current and quick ratios were very close to the traditional rule-of-thumb standards of 2·0 and 1·0 respectively.

Non-quoted manufacturing companies in general are clearly less liquid than quoted manufacturing companies but both follow the same trends.

AVERAGE COLLECTION PERIOD

What other indicators of liquidity are there? An important one is the speed at which debts are collected. The average collection period for debtors can be calculated as follows, if one assumes that all sales are for credit:

$$\frac{\text{debtors} \times 365}{\text{sales}} \text{ days.}$$

In applying this ratio to a company such as Alenco it must be remembered that: 1. as the explanation to the consolidated balance sheet states, the debtors figure given there results largely but not wholly from sales to customers in the normal course of business and that the average collection period will be overstated for this reason, and that 2. the ratio is a weighted average: it is possible, for example, that the credit terms granted by the French subsidiary may because of local customs differ quite substantially from those in Britain.

Bearing these points in mind we can now calculate Alenco's average collection period from 1964/5 to 1968/9:

1964/5	83 days
1965/6	89 ,,
1966/7	95 ,,
1967/8	92 ,,
1968/9	105 ,,

It seems fair to interpret these figures as evidence of increasing difficulty in debt-collection resulting from the various credit squeezes to which British industry has been subjected. Investigations carried out by the Engineering Industries Association show that this is a problem shared by the engineering industry as a whole.*

WINDOW-DRESSING

We will end this chapter with an illustration of a problem which arises from the nature of ratios. Suppose that a company has current assets of £800,000, current liabilities of £500,000 and quick assets of £550,000. Its *net* current assets and *net* quick assets will therefore be £300,000 and £50,000 respectively. If we keep these *net* amounts constant but vary the gross figures using current assets to pay off current liabilities, then the current and quick ratios will vary as shown in Table 12.

(a) Current assets	(b) Current liabilities	(c) Quick assets	(d) Current ratio a/b	(e) Quick ratio c/b
£800,000	£500,000	£550,000	1·60	1·10
700,000	400,000	450,000	1·75	1·12
600,000	300,000	350,000	2·00	1·17
500,000	200,000	250,000	2·50	1·25
400,000	100,000	150,000	4·00	1·50
350,000	50,000	100,000	7·00	2·00
301,000	1,000	51,000	301·00	51·00

TABLE 12: *Illustration of Window-Dressing*

*See the report in *The Accountant*, 4 June 1970, pp. 835-6.

Obviously we have exaggerated to make a point, but there is clearly some latitude for window-dressing. Within limits, a company may be able to arrange its current assets and liabilities so as to have the desired ratios at balance-sheet time.

7. Sources of Funds and Capital Structure

Les affaires, c'est bien simple: c'est l'argent des autres.
ALEXANDRE DUMAS, *fils*, *La question d'argent*

SOURCES OF FUNDS

The funds available to a company are obtained either from its share-holders or by borrowing. The former include not only issues of shares but also the retention of profits. The latter range from long-term debt to trade credit. The composition at any time of these sources and more especially the long-term sources, is referred to as the 'capital structure' of a company. Table 13 gives some idea of the relative importance of various sources for quoted companies in the United Kingdom for the years 1964/9. Three points stand out in particular:

1. by far the most important source of funds for British companies is the ordinary shareholders, especially through the medium of reserves (which consist mainly of retained profits).
2. long-term loans have steadily gained in relative importance in recent years. We shall see later that the provisions of the Finance Act 1965 have something to do with this.
3. preference shares are becoming less important, the amount of preference share capital falling both absolutely and relatively during the period.

CAPITAL STRUCTURE

Is there such a thing as an optimal capital structure for a particular company? This is a question which has aroused much academic debate. In principle there probably is such a structure, but it is not easy in practice for a company either to discover what it is or to achieve it.

The main problem is to choose the best mix of debt (loans, debentures) and equity (ordinary shares, reserves, retained profits). There is

	1964 £m.	%	1965 £m.	%	1966 £m.	%	1967 £m.	%	1968 £m.	%	1969 £m.	%
Ordinary shares	5,866	33	6,106	32	6,179	31	5,950	29	6,020	29	6,199	28
Reserves	7,813	45	8,641	46	9,006	45	9,197	45	9,331	44	9,686	45
Ordinary shareholders' funds	13,679	78	14,747	78	15,185	76	15,147	75*	15,351	73	15,885	73
Preference shares	1,042	6	1,028	5	925	5	837	4	734	3	606	3
	14,721	84	15,775	83	16,110	81	15,984	79	16,085	76	16,491	76
Minority interests	519	3	588	3	604	3	705	3	813	4	900	4
Long-term loans	2,277	13	2,622	14	3,158	16	3,634	18	4,151	20	4,355	20
	17,517	100	18,985	100	19,872	100	20,323	100	21,049	100	21,746	100
Bank overdrafts and loans	1,302		1,645		1,875		1,871		2,114		2,601	

* Rounding error.

(*Source:* Calculated from figures given in *Company Finance* (1970), Second Issue, Tables 4 & 13 and Third Issue (1971), Table 1.)

TABLE 13: *Sources of Funds, U.K. Quoted Companies, 1964–9.*

no easy way of doing this. It is possible to list the factors which ought to be considered, but assessing the weight to be given to each remains very largely a matter of judgement and experience. The factors are:

1. *Cost:* The current and future costs of each potential source of capital should be estimated and compared. It should be borne in mind that the costs of each source are not necessarily independent of each other. An increase in debt now, for example, may push up the cost of equity later. Other things being equal it is desirable to minimize the average overall cost of capital to the company.

2. *Risk:* It is unwise (and often disastrous) to place a company in a position where it may be unable, if profits fall even temporarily, to pay interest as it falls due or to meet redemptions. It is equally undesirable to be forced to cut or omit the ordinary dividend (see the section below on dividend policy).

3. *Control:* Except where there is no other alternative, a company should not make any issue of shares which will have the effect of removing or diluting control by the existing shareholders.

4. *Acceptability:* A company can only borrow if others are willing to lend to it. Few companies can afford the luxury of a capital structure which is unacceptable to financial institutions.

5. *Transferability:* Shares may be quoted or unquoted. Many private companies have made issues of shares to the public in order to obtain a stock exchange quotation and improve the transferability of their shares. Such a procedure may also have advantages in relation to estate duty.

COST OF CAPITAL

Although a company cannot always choose what appears to be the cheapest source of capital, because of the need to pay attention to risk, control, acceptability and transferability, it should always estimate the cost of each potential source and the effect on the overall average cost.

The usual practice is to work out first of all the cost of each potential source of capital. This is most easily done in the case of debentures. Suppose that a company can issue £100,000 10 per cent debentures at par, repayable at par in twenty years time. The before-tax cost is obviously 10 per cent, the after-tax cost, assuming a corporation tax rate of 40 per cent, is 6 per cent. If preference shares were issued instead, the before and after tax rates would be equal, since preference dividends, unlike debenture interest, are not deductible for tax purposes. This explains why since the introduction of corporation tax in 1965 many companies have replaced their preference share capital by loan stock.

The arithmetic becomes rather more difficult if the loan stock is not issued at par. In December 1970, for example, Imperial Chemical Industries Ltd made an issue of £40 million 10¾ per cent Unsecured Loan Stock 1991/6 at £98 per cent, payable £20 per £100 stock on application, £40 on 1 March 1971 and £38 on 29 April 1971. That is, for every £98 received over the period December 1970 to April, 1971 the company promised to pay interest of £10·75 each year and to repay the stock at par (£100) between 1991 and 1996. Using tables (or a computer program) it can be calculated that the yield to the last redemption date (1996) is a fraction under 11 per cent.

The real cost of issuing debentures is reduced during a period of inflation by the fact that the cash paid out by the company will be of lower purchasing power than the cash it receives at the date of issue.

Calculation of the cost of an issue of ordinary shares is more diffi-cult. An analogous calculation to the one above would suggest that it is equal to the gross dividend yield, calculated as follows:

$$\frac{\text{current dividend per ordinary share} \times 100}{\text{market price per share}}.$$

Dividend yields may be most easily found from the stock exchange pages of the *Financial Times* and other newspapers. The *F.T.* Share Information Service gives quite a lot of information about shares every day. The following typical entry has been extracted from the *Financial Times* of 16 December 1971 (referring to the day before):

1971		Stock	Closing price	+ or −	Div. % or amount	Times covered	Gross yield p.c.	P/E ratio
High	Low							
179	125⅝	Distillers 50p	159	−1	12¾	1·5	4·0	17·1

This tells us that the current market price of the 50p ordinary shares of The Distillers Company Ltd is 159 compared with a high of 179 and a low of 125⅝ so far during 1971 and a price the day before of 160p. The most recent annual dividend was 12¾ per cent, i.e. 6·375p per share (12¾ per cent of 50p). Dividing 6·375p by the closing market price of 159p and multiplying by 100 produces the gross dividend yield of 4·0 per cent.

The dividend yield of any company can be compared with dividend yields in general and those of other companies in the same equity group or sub-section by looking at the table in the *Financial Times* headed F.T. – Actuaries Share Indices. On 15 December 1971 the 500 Share dividend yield was 3·48 per cent. Distillers is included in the 'Wines and Spirits' sub-section, whose average dividend yield was 3·96 per cent.

These yields can be contrasted with the 8·69 per cent yield on 2½ per cent Consols (an irredeemable government stock), the average redemption yield of 7·48 per cent on six 20-year government stocks and the average yield of 9·23 per cent on fifteen 20-year redeemable debentures and loans. All yields are quoted gross of tax but even after allowing for corporation tax at 40 per cent, the redeemable debentures and loans yield of 5·54 per cent after tax is still significantly higher than the dividend yields.

Given the relative riskiness of fixed-interest and variable dividend securities this is at first sight a surprising situation. Before August 1959, in fact, the average dividend yield was higher than the yield on government bonds. Since then a reverse yield gap, as it is called, has existed. The main reason for the reverse yield gap is the realization by investors that only equities offer protection against the effects of inflation. This has raised share prices relatively and lowered yields.

The dividend yield cannot, however, be regarded as an adequate measure of the cost of equity capital. It fails to take account of 1. the fact that future dividends may be different from the current dividend, and 2. that the price of the shares may change. Neither of these considerations is relevant to long-term debt with its fixed interest payments and fixed redemption prices.

Because of these defects in the dividend yield it is usual to regard the cost of issuing ordinary shares as equal either to the *earnings yield* or to the *dividend yield plus a growth rate*. The earnings yield is calculated as follows:

$$\frac{\text{earnings per ordinary share after tax} \times 100}{\text{market price per ordinary share}}.$$

In recent years it has become very common to express the same relationship in the form of a *price-earnings ratio* (P/E ratio) which is simply the reciprocal of the earnings yield multiplied by 100, i.e.

$$\frac{\text{market price per ordinary share}}{\text{earnings per ordinary share after tax}}.$$

In other words, the P/E ratio expresses the multiple of the last reported earnings that the market is willing to pay for the ordinary shares. The higher the P/E ratio (the lower the earnings yield) the more the market thinks of the company and the cheaper the cost of equity capital to the company.

From the extract from the *Financial Times* it can be seen that Distillers' price-earnings ratio on 15 December 1971 was 17.1. Its earnings yield must therefore have been $\frac{100}{17.1}\% = 5.85\%$ after tax. The 500 share figures were 18.59 and 5.38 per cent; those of the wines and spirits sub-section 17.44 and 5.73 per cent.

The P/E ratio of Distillers is calculated as follows. The profit attributable to the ordinary shareholders of the company for the year ended 31 March 1971 was £33,747,000. There were 363,169,544 ordinary shares of 50p each at that date. The earnings per share (EPS) is therefore $\frac{33,747,000 \times 100}{363,169,544}$ p = 9.3p. Dividing the market price of 159p by 9.3p gives a P/E ratio of 17.1.

An alternative approach to the cost of equity capital which has received strong support in the literature on financial theory is to add a growth rate to the dividend yield. If one considers, for example, that Distillers' dividends are likely to grow in future at an average annual rate of 3 per cent, then the cost of its equity capital would be estimated to be 4 per cent + 3 per cent = 7 per cent.

Use of the earnings yield or the dividend yield plus a growth rate will almost always produce a cost of equity capital for a company greater than its after-tax cost of long-term debt. The next stage is to consider the effect of risk.

RISK: GEARING AND TIMES INTEREST EARNED

Risk can be measured to some extent by the use of ratios measuring

1. gearing
2. times interest earned.

The use of these ratios does not, however, remove the need for judgement.

Gearing (or leverage as the Americans call it) is the relationship between the funds provided to a company by its ordinary shareholders and the long-term sources of funds carrying a fixed interest charge or dividend (e.g. unsecured loans, debentures and preference shares). The degree of gearing can be measured in terms of either capital or income. A company's capital structure is said to be highly geared when the fixed charges claim an above average proportion of the company's resources of either capital or income.

There is more than one way of defining and calculating 'gearing ratio'. If we define it as $\dfrac{\text{long-term loans} + \text{preference shares}}{\text{ordinary shareholders' funds}}$ we can calculate the following ratios from Table 13 (which, it will be remembered, referred to quoted companies):

	%
1964	24
1965	25
1966	27
1967	30
1968	32
1969	31

Or we could add bank overdrafts and loans to the numerator on the grounds that to a large extent they may be renewed each year and therefore should be treated as long-term sources of funds even though included under the heading of current liabilities in *Company Finance*.

The relevant figures are also given in Table 13. The gearing ratios now become:

	%
1964	34
1965	36
1966	39
1967	42
1968	46
1969	48

Both the above definitions are based on book values. Market values could (some would say should) be used instead if they are available. The definition would now become:

$$\frac{\text{market value of fixed interest securities}}{\text{market value of ordinary share capital}}.$$

Whichever definition we choose, we find a trend towards higher gearing ratios. Given the relative cheapness of long-term loans, especially since the Finance Act 1965, this is not at all surprising.

Some companies are more highly geared than others, especially those which have relatively stable profits, and assets such as land and buildings which can be specifically identified and are unlikely to fall in value over time, therefore providing good security. An example of such a company is Arthur Bell & Sons Ltd, the scotch whisky distillers of Perth. The consolidated figures below have been abstracted from their 1970 annual report.

	£m.
Ordinary share capital	4·000
Capital reserves	0·614
Revenue reserves	2·467
Ordinary shareholders' funds	7·081
5½% Preference share capital	0·400
7¼% Debenture stock, 1986/91	2·500
Bank overdraft	3·509
Profit before interest and tax	1·457
Debenture interest (gross)	0·181
Bank overdraft interest (gross)	0·212
Other loan interest (gross)	0·002

Depending whether we include the bank overdraft* in the numerator or not the gearing ratios can be calculated to be:

		%
(i)	(without overdraft)	41
(ii)	(with overdraft)	91

Times interest earned is really just a different way of looking at gearing. It is defined as:

$$\frac{\text{profit before interest and tax}}{\text{interest (gross)}}.$$

The figures for Arthur Bell & Sons Ltd (calculated from the data given above) are:

(i)	(excluding overdraft interest)	8·0
(ii)	(including overdraft interest)	3·7

The major disadvantage of the times interest earned method is that it ignores the existence of reserves, i.e. the retained profits of previous years, upon which the company could call if necessary (if they are in liquid form). The same drawback applies to the 'priority percentages' approach in which the analyst calculates the percentage of earnings that is required to service each category of loan and share capital.

The effect of gearing on profits available to ordinary shareholders can be seen from the following example.

X Ltd is a very highly geared company and Y Ltd a relatively low-geared one. Their long-term sources of funds are as follows:

	X	Y
Ordinary share capital	100,000	200,000
Retained profits	100,000	200,000
Ordinary shareholders' funds	200,000	400,000
10% Debenture	300,000	100,000
	£500,000	£500,000
Gearing ratio (debentures as % of ordinary shareholders' funds)	150%	25%

*In 1971 the company reduced its bank borrowings by the issue for cash of 2,500,000 50p Ordinary shares at 130p per share.

If profit before interest and tax is £80,000 for both companies, the distributions will be as follows, assuming a 40 per cent tax rate and no retention of profit:

	X	Y
(a) Profit before interest and tax	80,000	80,000
(b) Debenture interest (gross)	30,000	10,000
	50,000	70,000
Tax at 40%	20,000	28,000
Ordinary dividend	£30,000	£42,000
Times interest earned (*a/b*)	2·67	8·00

The ordinary dividend rate will be 30 per cent on par for company X and 21 per cent on par for company Y.

If, however, the profit before interest and tax is £160,000, the position will be as follows:

	X	Y
(a) Profit before interest and tax	160,000	160,000
(b) Debenture interest (gross)	30,000	10,000
	130,000	150,000
Tax at 40%	52,000	60,000
Ordinary dividend	£78,000	£90,000
Times interest earned (*a/b*)	5·33	16·00

The ordinary dividend rate on par becomes 78 per cent for company X and 45 per cent for company Y. Note that whilst profits before interest and tax have doubled, X's ordinary dividend rate has gone up 2·60 times and Y's 2·14 times. It is clear that gearing enables a company to trade on the equity, as the Americans say, and increase the ordinary share holders' return at a faster rate than the increase in profits. The higher the gearing the greater the relative rate.

Unfortunately the converse also applies. Suppose that the profit before interest and tax falls to £30,000. The position will then be as follows:

	X	Y
(a) Profit before interest and tax	30,000	30,000
(b) Debenture interest (gross)	30,000	10,000
	—	20,000
Tax at 40%	—	8,000
Ordinary dividend	£ —	£12,000
Times interest earned (a/b)	1·00	3·00

The dividend rate of company X falls to zero and of company Y to 6 per cent. If profits fell even further company X would not be able to pay the debenture interest out of its current profits and would have to call upon past retained profits (reserves). Once these were exhausted it would be in serious trouble. Company Y is in a much better position to meet such an emergency. It must also be remembered, of course, that a company which has tied up its assets too much in fixed assets and stocks may run into similar problems even though its profits have not fallen. Profits are not the same thing as ready cash.

The moral is that companies whose profits are low or likely to fluctuate violently should not be too highly geared. Investors in such companies are running risks and will in any case prefer ordinary shares to fixed-interest debentures. From a company point of view the attraction of a relatively cheap source of funds must be balanced against the risks involved.

DIVIDEND POLICY

How does a company determine the size of the dividend it pays each year, or, putting the same question round the other way, how does a company decide how much of its profits to retain each year? A number of factors are important:

1. the effect of dividend policy on the present and future cost of capital to the company;
2. taxation;
3. government policy.

The most convenient source of funds to a company is retained profits. A company which pays very high dividends loses this source and may have to raise money in the capital market. Issues of debentures and other loans usually have a lower cost of capital than either new issues of shares or retained profits but, as we have just seen, there are dangers in a too highly-geared capital structure. New issues of shares are more expensive than retained profits because of the issue costs involved.*

On the other hand, most expanding companies will have to go to the market sooner or later and one of the points potential investors will look at is the dividend record. A company whose dividend has declined or fluctuated violently is not likely to be favourably regarded. For this reason companies prefer to maintain their dividends even if earnings fall.

Since the market is interested in future dividends it prefers to see current dividends reasonably well covered by current earnings. This is some sort of guarantee that the dividend will be at least maintained in the future since if profits fall there will be past retained profits to draw upon. The measure of dividend cover is

$$\frac{\text{earnings per share}}{\text{ordinary dividend per share}} = \frac{100}{\text{dividend yield} \times \text{P/E ratio}}.$$

Referring back to the extract from the *Financial Times* we can see that Distillers' dividend was covered by earnings 1·5 times (9·3/6·375).

On the whole, then, cost-of-capital considerations push companies towards constant or steadily increasing dividend payouts. Two factors which tend to limit the size of the dividend are taxation and government policy. In spite of the fairly recent introduction of capital gains tax in Britain, our tax system still favours capital increases rather than income increases. There are many shareholders who are more interested in capital gains than dividends. Again, a number of governments since the war, in their efforts to contain rises in wages and prices, have placed statutory limitations on the size of company dividends.

We are now in a position to look at Alenco's dividend policy. Table 14 gives information about Alenco's dividend policy for the last nine years. It has been adapted from the statistics and ratios section of the

---

*Retained profits are not a costless source of funds. They can be regarded as a notional distribution of profits which are immediately re-invested in the company.

1968 Report and brought up to date with information from the 1969 Report.

To interpret properly the information given in the table it is necessary to take account of:

1. the change in the tax treatment of dividends which resulted from the Finance Act 1965;
2. the effect of bonus issues.

Before the 1965 Finance Act companies deducted and retained income tax at the standard rate from dividends. This meant that the cost to the company was not the gross dividend but the dividend net of tax. All pre-1966 figures in the table are therefore net of tax. For example in 1961 Alenco paid a 30 per cent dividend on a par value of £880,000. 30 per cent of £880,000 is £264,000. The net cost to Alenco, however, at the then standard rate of 8s. 9d. (£0·4375) was £148,000. For 1966, the transition year, the figures are given both net and gross. From 1967 onwards the figures are gross. The row showing the dividend as a percentage of ordinary shareholders' funds is based entirely on the *gross* cost.

Whilst the percentages just mentioned can be considered a series, this is not so of the rates declared. The important row is that showing the index after allowing for bonus issues. In 1963 the dividend rate fell from $32\frac{1}{2}$ to $17\frac{1}{2}$ per cent, whereas the index rose from 108 to 117. At the same time the ordinary share capital doubled from £880,000 to £1,760,000. It can be deduced from these figures that the fall in the rate declared was due to a one for one bonus issue. Without the issue the rate declared would have risen to 35 per cent (i.e. to twice $17\frac{1}{2}$ per cent). A rise of $2\frac{1}{2}$ on $32\frac{1}{2}$ to 35 (the rate) is equal to a rise of 9 on 108 to 117 (the index). Bonus issues are discussed further in the next section of this chapter.

In discussing Alenco's dividend policy it is necessary to distinguish between the period before 1968, the year in which Alenco became a fully-owned subsidiary within the Charterhouse group, and the period since 1968. Before 1968 the policy appears to have been one of maintaining or increasing the dividend payout each year. The index, after allowing for bonus issues, rose steadily from 100 in the base year 1961 to 117 in 1963, jumped to 150 in 1964, and stayed constant at 157 for

	1961 £000	1962 £000	1963 £000	1964 £000	1965 £000	1966 £000	1967 £000	1968 £000	1969 £000
Ordinary shareholders' funds									
Ordinary share capital	880	880	1,760	1,760	1,760	1,760	1,760	1,760	1,760
Reserves	1,537	1,771	1,082	1,409	1,905	2,074	3,056	3,180	2,986
	2,417	2,651	2,842	3,169	3,665	4,434	4,816	4,940	4,746
Profit after tax attributable to ordinary shareholders	331	387	392	549	720	671	538	547	505
As a % of ordinary shareholders' funds	13.7%	14.6%	13.8%	17.3%	19.6%	15.1%	11.2%	11.1%	10.6%
Dividends									
Cost of ordinary dividends – net	148	175	189	243	243	125	414	440	488
gross						202			
Rate declared	30%	32½%	17½%	22½%	23½%	23½%	23½%	25%	27¾%
As a % of ordinary shareholders' funds	10.0%	10.8%	10.8%	12.5%	11.3%	9.3%	9.1%	8.9%	10.3%
Index allowing for bonus issues	100	108	117	150	157	157	157	167	185
Times covered – net	2.4	2.3	2.1	2.3	3.0	2.8	1.3	1.2	1.0
gross						1.6			

(*Source*: Alenco Ltd, Annual Report and Accounts, 1968 and 1969.)

TABLE 14: *Alenco Ltd: Statistics and Ratios Concerning Dividends, 1961–9.*

the three years 1965 to 1967. In other words the dividend payout increased by 57 per cent in seven years. During the same period the profit after tax attributable to ordinary shareholders rose by 62 per cent (from £331,000 to £538,000), with a number of ups and downs. This is a fairly typical policy: dividends are increased in accordance with the general trend of profits but fluctuations are ironed out.

Since 1968 Alenco has not had an independent dividend policy. Charterhouse has followed the normal practice of sweeping up the profits of the U.K. subsidiaries of the Alenco group and then making finance available where necessary by means of loans. This explains both the rise in the index to 167 in 1968 and 185 in 1969 and the fall in the dividend cover to 1·0 in 1969.

BONUS ISSUES AND RIGHTS ISSUES

It is now time to look more closely at bonus issues (also known as 'scrip issues', 'capitalization issues' and, in the United States, 'stock dividends'). To clear up the misunderstandings which often arise we shall use a simple example.* Consider a company whose summarized balance sheet is as follows:

Ordinary share capital	40,000	Assets	150,000
(40,000 shares of £1 each)			
Revenue reserves	60,000	*Less* Liabilities	50,000
	£100,000		£100,000

The company decides to write up (revalue) its assets to their current market value of £160,000 and at the same time to make a bonus issue of one new share for two old shares. This is what the balance sheet will look like after these operations have been carried out:

Ordinary share capital	60,000	Assets (as revalued)	160,000
(60,000 shares of £1 each)			
Revenue reserves	50,000	*Less* Liabilities	50,000
	£110,000		£110,000

*For a real example, see G.K.N.'s 1970 annual report, App. D, p. 39.

All that has happened is a book-keeping entry. In order to increase the ordinary share capital from £40,000 to £60,000, the accountant has *decreased* the revenue reserves from £60,000 to £50,000 and *increased* the assets from £150,000 to £160,000. It is important to realize that the recognition of the increase in market value of the assets has in no way increased the physical assets of the company. The shareholders have not received any cash, only more paper. Are they any better off? In principle, no. There is no reason why the market value of 6 shares now should differ from that of the 4 shares held previously, i.e. the market price *per share* ought to fall proportionately. It may not do so, partly because unrelated factors may be affecting share prices at the same time, partly because the revaluation and the issue may have drawn favourable attention to the future prospects of the company. Of course, if the company announces at the same time that the total *amount* to be paid out in dividends to shareholders will be increased then the shareholders really are better off and the market price will tend to rise.

One point often forgotten is that a bonus issue which involves capitalizing reserves (i.e., in effect, turning them into share capital) actually *decreases* the profits available for distribution. Such an issue does, of course, imply that the management is confident of earning more profits in the future.

A bonus issue can be regarded as a *rights issue* in which the subscription price for the new shares is zero. For a rights issue the price is usually fixed a little below the current market price. Let us suppose that our imaginary company decides to make a rights issue instead of a bonus issue, that the current market price of the shares is £2 each and that a 1 for 4 rights issue is announced at a subscription price of £1·50 per new share. This means that the directors wish to raise another £15,000 (10,000 × £1·50) of ordinary share capital. After the issue the balance sheet will look like this:

Ordinary share capital	50,000	Assets (original figure plus	
(50,000 shares of £1 each)		£15,000 cash)	165,000
Share premium	5,000	*Less* Liabilities	50,000
(10,000 × £0·50)			
Revenue reserves	60,000		
	£115,000		£115,000

Notice that the ordinary share capital is shown at its par value and the excess of the issue price above par is shown separately as a share premium.

The market value of the 50,000 shares should be (40,000 × £2) + (10,000 × £1·50) = £95,000. The theoretical market price per new share will therefore be $\frac{£95,000}{£50,000} = £1·90$. If this is in fact the price the existing shareholder will be no better or worse off than before the issue, *provided that he has either subscribed for the new shares or sold his rights.* The theoretical value of one right can be worked out as follows:

If the shareholder were to take no action he would end up with, say, 4 shares valued at £1·90 each plus £1·50 in cash, instead of 5 shares valued at £1·90 each. He would have £9·10 instead of £9·50, a loss of £0·40 per 4 old shares or £0·10 per new share. This could have been calculated from the formula:

$$r = \frac{m - s}{n + 1}$$

where r is the theoretical value of one right, m is the market price per share, s the subscription price per share and n the number of rights required to purchase one new share. Thus:

$$r = \frac{£2·00 - 1·50}{4 + 1} = £0·10$$

CONVERTIBLE LOAN STOCK

So far in this book we have drawn a rather rigid dividing line between debenture-holders who are merely long-term creditors of a company and shareholders who are its owners. It will have been apparent however, that preference share capital has some of the characteristics of long-term debt. Another hybrid security of importance is the convertible loan.

The 1970 annual report of Guest, Keen and Nettlefolds Ltd, for example, includes the following item among the long-term loan capital (see Appendix D, p. 41):

6% convertible unsecured loan stock 1988/93 — £2·96 million

with the note:

The stock may be converted at 31st May in any of the years 1971 to 1975 inclusive into ordinary stock at the rate of £1 ordinary stock for every £3⅜ nominal of loan stock.

The attraction of such stock to an investor is that it enables him to buy a fixed-interest stock which he can later change into ordinary shares if he so wishes. Whether he will make the conversion or not depends, of course, on the relationship between the market price of the ordinary shares and the conversion price at the conversion date. The investor's hope is that he has found a cheaper way of buying the ordinary shares than direct purchase. The disadvantage to him is that the rate of interest offered on a convertible loan is less than that on a 'straight' loan.

Why should a company issue convertible stock? There are at least two possibilities:

1. the company wants to issue debt and adds the convertibility as an added attraction;

2. the company would prefer to issue equity but feels that the price of its ordinary shares is temporarily depressed. By setting the conversion price higher than the current price, the management can, if its expectations are fulfilled, effectively make a share issue at the desired price.

The possible disadvantages to the company are that either the market price fails to rise and it is saddled with unwanted debt or that the market price rises so quickly that it finds itself in effect selling equity more cheaply than it need have done.

LEASING

Instead of borrowing money to buy fixed assets, a company may decide to lease them, i.e. to enter into a long-term contract which allows it the use of the asset (but does not give it the ownership) in return for a periodic rental. Early termination of the lease is penalized. Sometimes the company already owns the assets and raises cash by selling them and then leasing them back. This is known as sale-and-leaseback.

The effect in either case is similar to an issue of long-term debt and it should be regarded and analysed as such. One important difference is that neither the asset leased nor the long-term liability to pay the rentals are shown in the balance sheet as such, although they may be disclosed in footnotes.

These omissions can lead to misleading ratios and some accountants, including myself, believe that the capitalized value of the lease rentals should be shown in the balance sheet as both an asset and a liability.

As in all financing decisions the effect on the tax payable by the company is an important factor in deciding whether or not to use leasing. If equipment is bought out of borrowed money, the company will be entitled to the capital allowances described in chapter 3 and the interest on the loan will be tax-deductible. If the equipment is leased the *lessor* will receive the benefit of the capital allowances but the lessee's annual taxable income will be reduced by the amount of the lease rental. It is not possible to state in general terms whether the tax effect will be favourable or unfavourable to the prospective lessee. Each case has to be analysed separately.

8. Accounting Principles and Inflation

Manners with Fortunes, Humours turn with Climes,
Tenets with Books, and Principles with Times.

ALEXANDER POPE, *Moral Essays*, 'Epistle to Cobham'

We have referred a number of times in this book to differences in accounting practice. We have noted, for example, that fixed assets may be depreciated by the straight-line method or by the reducing-balance method and that there was more than one way of accounting for investment grants. This leads to the questions of how accounting principles are established and whether they should be more uniform than they are at present. As readers of the financial pages of daily newspapers are aware, the problems of diversity of accounting practice and the desirability or non-desirability of more uniformity are controversial matters of great topical importance.

Linked with these problems is that of recognizing the effect of inflation on financial statements. This will undoubtedly be one of the matters most discussed by accountants and financial analysts during the 1970s.

We cannot hope in the space of one short chapter to consider these matters in detail, nor is it necessary for the average shareholder to become an expert in them. He should, however, have some understanding of the arguments since they revolve essentially around the main theme of this book: the annual financial statements as a guide to shareholder investment.

ACCOUNTING PRINCIPLES

Who lays down the principles on which financial statements are drawn up? The answer differs from country to country. In Britain the most important influences are company and tax legislation and the accounting profession.

The accounting provisions of the British Companies Acts are concerned mainly with disclosure and do not contain, as can be found in some European legislation, either a compulsory standard form for financial statements or detailed rules as to how assets should be valued and net profit calculated. The Acts do however impose two obligations on company directors: 1. to prepare balance sheets and profit and loss accounts which give a 'true and fair view', and 2. to give the detailed information specified in the Second Schedule to the 1967 Act.* No definition is given of the phrase 'true and fair view'.

This approach was commented on favourably in the report of the most recent committee on company law amendment:

In our view the general scheme of the Act in this respect is the right one, namely to indicate in general terms the objectives and the standard of disclosure required and also to prescribe certain specific information that must be given. The formula 'true and fair' seems to us satisfactory as an indication of the required standard, while it makes for certainty to prescribe certain specific information which the law regards as the minimum necessary for the purpose of attaining that standard.†

The Committee went on to state that 'it is primarily to the initiative of the professional associations that we must look if the general principles of the Act are to be effectively applied in practice' (para. 334). They referred in particular to the *Recommendations on Accounting Principles* issued periodically by the Institute of Chartered Accountants in England and Wales (the 'English Institute'). The first of these recommendations was issued in 1942. More recently, in December 1969, the Council of the English Institute issued a *Statement of Intent on Accounting Standards in the 1970s*. This announced the Council's intention to advance accounting standards along the following lines:

1. narrowing the areas of difference and variety in accounting practice;
2. disclosure of accounting bases;
3. disclosure of departures from established definitive accounting standards;

* See Glossary.
† *Report of the Company Law Committee* (Cmnd. 1749, 1962), para. 332.

4. wider exposure for major new proposals on accounting standards; and,

5. a continuing programme for encouraging improved accounting standards in legal and regulatory measures.

An Accounting Standards Steering Committee has been established, composed of twenty-one accountants in private practice, industry or academic life. This issues 'exposure drafts' for comment by interested parties. Later, a definitive statement is issued and disclosure must be made (by the auditor if the company itself does not do so) of any departures therefrom in published financial statements.

The first *Statement of Standard Accounting Practice* was issued in January 1971 and dealt with the urgent problem of accounting for the results of associated companies. These are companies, other than subsidiary companies, in which the interest of the investing group is effectively that of a partner in a joint venture or consortium *or* in which the investing group's interest is long term and is substantial (defined, inevitably somewhat arbitrarily, as not less than 20 per cent of the equity voting rights) and the investing group, having regard to the disposition of the other shareholders, is in a position to exercise a significant influence over the associated company.

There are a number of references to accounting for associated companies in Guest, Keen and Nettlefolds' 1970 annual report: in particular the item 'Share of Profits *less* Losses of Associated Companies' (equal to over 18 per cent of the profit for the year before taxation) in the consolidated profit and loss account, and the item 'Associated Company and Trade Investments' in the consolidated balance sheet. The important points to remember are that:

1. just as with subsidiaries, a share of the profit (or loss) of an associated company is brought into the consolidated results, not just dividends received;

2. unlike subsidiaries (see p. 26), the underlying assets and liabilities of an associated company are *not* brought into the consolidated balance sheet, which shows instead the cost of the original investment augmented by a share of the associated company's retained profits since acquisition.

The second *Statement of Standard Accounting Practice* was issued in November 1971. It requires the disclosure in the annual report of accounting policies followed for dealing with items which are judged material or critical in determining profit or loss and in stating the financial position.

The Institute's programme assumes that the Jenkins Committee was right and that the main responsibility for the development of accounting principles should be left with the accounting profession. It is in fact a response to suggestions that it would be preferable to deal with the problem by legislation or by the setting up of a government body such as the Securities and Exchange Commission in the United States.

It is sometimes suggested, for example, that companies should be forced to value assets and measure profit for annual report purposes in the same way as they do for tax purposes. This is not a very helpful suggestion for at least two reasons. In the first place, the rules relating to the calculation of profit for corporation tax purposes are only in part based on the kind of accounting which is relevant to shareholders. They have been greatly, and quite properly, influenced by considerations of fiscal policy. In particular, depreciation allowable for tax purposes (capital allowances) does not and is not meant to measure the extent to which fixed assets have actually been used up in operations. Its purpose, in part at least, is to encourage companies to invest more in certain assets. In general, fixed assets can be written off more quickly for tax purposes than their actual usage warrants. On the other hand, certain fixed assets such as non-industrial buildings cannot be depreciated at all for tax purposes.

Secondly, and this objection applies to company legislation as well as to tax legislation, it would bring into accounting a quite unnecessary rigidity and inflexibility. It would hand over accounting principles to parliamentary draftsmen and legislators who are unlikely to have much knowledge of accounting, and it would make changes very difficult. Accountants are continually being faced with new problems. Waiting for new legislation is not the best or quickest way to deal with them.

A more persuasive suggestion is the setting up of a government agency such as the Securities and Exchange Commission (S.E.C.) in the United States. This was established in the early 1930s following the great Wall Street crash and was given the power to determine accounting principles for all U.S. corporations whose securities are listed on stock exchanges. From the beginning, however, it has left this mainly in the hands of the American Institute of Certified Public Accountants, while retaining the right to overrule the Institute if it so wished. The existence of the S.E.C. has certainly encouraged the American Institute to be more active than it would otherwise have been. Perhaps in Britain the *threat* of the establishment of such a commission will be sufficient to keep the accounting profession on its toes.

Unless we believe that accounting principles are essentially arbitrary and that it does not matter what is done so long as everybody does it, the only way that they can be discovered is by research. Not a great deal of research into accounting has so far been carried out in Britain. Most of the recommendations of the English Institute have been in the nature of statements of 'best practice' and have tended, to use an American phrase, to rely on 'general acceptability' rather than theoretical soundness and to permit a diversity of sometimes conflicting accounting practices.

The reasons can be found in the two doctrines (principles is too strong a word) which have dominated the evolution of accounting in Britain – and, indeed, in most of the world except the Netherlands: objectivity and conservatism. Objectivity arises from the need to establish rules for recording financial transactions and events which as far as possible do not depend on the personal judgement of the recorder. This has led to a bias in favour of using cost of acquisition or historical cost as it is usually called. Suppose, however, that a company buys goods for resale for £1,000 but because it has misjudged market demand it later finds that it cannot sell them for more than £600. The doctrine of conservatism now suggests that their value should be written down accordingly. Similarly, the writing up of the value of unsold fixed assets, though fairly common in British practice, is often frowned upon by accountants because it is neither conservative nor based upon the objective evidence of a completed transaction.

Such considerations have led many accountants, including the English Institute, to deny that it is the function of a balance sheet to show how much a company is worth. Other accountants have argued, however, that a balance sheet which does not attempt to do this, in spite of all the difficulties involved, is of little use to the shareholders.

INFLATION

The problem becomes much worse in times of inflation, when balance sheet values based on historical cost rapidly become divorced from current market values and when the doctrines of objectivity and conservatism can lead paradoxically to an *overstatement* of profits. This is most easily understood in relation to fixed assets and depreciation. If fixed assets are valued at historical cost, then depreciation will usually be based on historical cost as well. This will result in a lower depreciation charge and hence a *higher* profit than if both the asset and the depreciation were written up to, say, current replacement cost. It can be strongly argued that the use of historical costs can lead to the publication of profit figures which are in part fictitious. The distribution of such profits would mean a running down of the *real* (as opposed to the money) capital of the company.

Company directors and accountants are of course aware of this problem but there are some who regard it as a problem of financial policy rather than of accounting measurement. They argue that the answer is the transfer of such fictitious profits to special capital reserves, so as to make them unavailable for distribution as dividends. One practical difficulty of this solution is that the fictitious profits are taxed as if they were real. The following quotation, taken from the chairman's statement in the 1970 annual report of The Distillers Company Ltd, sets out the problem very clearly:

Having regard to the wage explosion we have experienced in this country during the first half of 1970, of which the full effect will not be apparent for some time, it may be questionable by the end of the current fiscal year whether British industry can look upon the orthodox methods of accounting hitherto adopted in this country as providing a reasonable means of ascertaining profit. This is a matter which will have to be studied seriously by industry and the professional accounting bodies but it will, I believe, also require close examination by Her Majesty's Government. If the real capital of British industry is to be maintained, greater retentions of so-called profit will be necessary and the collection of taxes upon profits, including Corporation Tax, under a system which takes no account of the realities of the situation must be reviewed.

The Distillers Company Ltd makes no adjustment for inflation in its published financial statements as such. The chairman's statement in the 1971 report, however, contains the estimate that the conventional profit for 1970/1 of £55 million overstates the 'real' profit by £8 million (nearly 15%).

The authors of a booklet published by the Research Foundation of the English Institute in 1968 observed that:

... the majority of companies in the United Kingdom have made no attempt in their published annual statements to measure the extent to which their reported profits have been attributable to the progressive decline in the value of the currency in which they are measured, and those few which have done so have generally confined their calculations to one aspect only of this change, namely its bearing on the charges against profits for the amortisation of long-term expenditure on fixed assets.*

One exception is Guest, Keen and Nettlefolds Ltd., who state in their 1970 report (App. D, p. 36):

The total depreciation charged against profits takes into account the reduced purchasing power of money. The amount provided in excess of that required to write off the original cost of fixed assets over their estimated life is transferred to the depreciation reserve.

It should be noted that the company does not, however, revalue its fixed assets.

Such partial solutions appear to be insufficient. The logical answer is either a thoroughgoing recasting of the accounts to allow for price changes, as practised by the Philips company in the Netherlands, or the publication alongside the conventional historical cost accounts of a set of supplementary accounts adjusted for inflation, as recently suggested by a discussion paper on *Inflation and Accounts* issued by the Accounting Standards Steering Committee.

*Research Foundation of the Institute of Chartered Accountants in England and Wales, *Accounting for Stewardship in a Period of Inflation* (1968), p. 5.

It is difficult for any company, however large and important, to pioneer such changes alone. The initiative must come from the organized accountancy institutes. Meanwhile shareholders should realize that conventional financial statements lose some of their usefulness during periods of inflation.

The accounting principles upon which financial statements are drawn up are not uniform and much diversity of accounting practice still exists. Apart from company and tax legislation, the most important influence is the accounting profession. This is justified as long as accountants are continually researching into and trying to improve the usefulness of the statements submitted to shareholders. In times of inflation, financial statements become less useful if they remain based on historical cost modified by conservatism.

9. Summary and Reading Guide

The reader who has come this far has already learned a great deal about the annual reports of companies, about financial statements and about accounting and finance. The purpose of this chapter is to summarize what has been learned and to make suggestions about further reading.

COMPANIES

Chapter 1 was mainly about companies, the most important form of business organization in modern Britain. It was noted that although most (97 per cent) companies are private companies, the important ones and those which investors are mainly concerned with are public companies. Published annual reports are typically those of groups of companies, consisting of a holding company, subsidiaries and sub-subsidiaries. Two important documents which every company must have are the Memorandum of Association and the Articles of Association. The former sets out, *inter alia*, the objects of a company; the latter deals with its internal regulations.

Companies are governed by the Companies Acts 1948 to 1967 and the relevant case law, and it is desirable to have some knowledge of company law. Unfortunately most books on the subject are very long, very dull and not intended for the layman. An exception on all three counts is G. Naylor, *Guide to Shareholders' Rights* (Allen & Unwin, 1969).* An excellent book but one which is in places difficult reading for non-specialists, is L.C.B. Gower, *The Principles of Modern Company Law* (Stevens, 3rd editn 1969).

*All books referred to in this chapter are published in London unless otherwise stated.

FINANCIAL STATEMENTS

Chapter 2 dealt with financial statements. The three most important statements are:

1. *the balance sheet*, which shows the assets, the liabilities and the shareholders' funds at a particular point in time;
2. *the profit and loss account* (or income statement), which shows for an accounting period the revenues, expenses, net profit (before and after taxation) and often also the distribution of the profit; and
3. *the source and disposition statement* (funds statement), which shows the sources and uses of funds of a company over the same accounting period.

Assets are classified into *fixed* and *current* and liabilities into *current* and *long-term*. The difference between current assets and current liabilities is the working capital of a company. The fixed assets are depreciated over their estimated economic lives, depreciation in its accounting sense normally referring to the allocation over time of the acquisition cost less scrap value.

Long-term sources of funds of companies can be divided into *loan capital* (e.g. debentures) on the one hand and *shareholders' funds* (share capital and reserves) on the other. There is an important distinction between preference shares, usually carrying a fixed dividend rate and having priority in a winding up, and ordinary shares, which form the *equity* of the company. The par or face value of a share is not necessarily the same as its issue price (issues are often made at a premium) or its market price.

Depreciation cannot properly be regarded as either a source or a use of funds. Cash flow is usually defined as net profit after adding back depreciation, but 'funds provided by operations' would be a more accurate name.

The best introductory book on accounting and financial statements is probably R. J. Bull, *Accounting for Business* (Butterworth, 1969). More specialized and dealing specifically with the financial statements of companies is F. H. Jones, *Guide to Company Balance Sheets and Profit and Loss Accounts* (Cambridge, Heffer, 7th editn 1970). The legal requirements of the Companies Acts 1948 to 1967 in so far as they relate to accounting are conveniently summarized in the Institute of Chartered Accountants in England and Wales, *Guide to the Accounting Requirements of the Companies Acts 1948–1967* (Gee, 1967), the Institute of Chartered Accountants of Scotland, *The Companies Act 1967. Some Requirements and Implications* (Edinburgh, Accountants' Publishing Co., 2nd editn 1970) and A. G. Touche, *What to Include in Company Accounts Now* (Butterworth, 1967).

TAXATION

Chapter 3 dealt briefly with taxation and audit. Companies pay corporation tax not personal tax. The corporation tax rate is at present 40 per cent. The rate refers to a financial year but companies are assessed on the basis of their own accounting periods. The tax charge in the profit and loss account refers to the current profits but will not necessarily become payable within one year from the date of the balance sheet. If it is not, it is regarded as deferred taxation not as a current liability.

The depreciation provided in the books is not deductible for tax purposes but capital allowances are available instead. The present system combines a first-year allowance of 60 per cent and a reducing-balance writing-down allowance for plant and machinery with an initial allowance and a straight-line writing-down allowance for industrial buildings. In general, fixed assets are written down much faster for tax purposes than they are in the financial statements. This gives rise to tax equalization accounts.

Although companies do not pay personal tax they must deduct it at the basic rate from dividends and interest and account for it to the Inland Revenue. They are not liable to capital gains tax on their capital gains which are instead charged to corporation tax.

There are many large books on taxation. Readers with more modest ambitions will gain much from the current edition of *The British System of Taxation* (H.M.S.O.) and from Margot Naylor, *How to Reduce Your Tax Bill* (Allen & Unwin, revised editn 1970). Reference can also be made to the chapters on taxation in the books by Bull, Gower and Jones mentioned above and to T. D. Lynch (ed.),

Direct Taxation in the United Kingdom (Edinburgh, The Institute of Chartered Accountants of Scotland, 1968, with later supplements).

AUDIT

The main function of the auditors of a company is to report to the shareholders whether in their opinion the financial statements show a true and fair view.

TOOLS OF ANALYSIS

Chapter 4 was concerned with defining and explaining the uses and limitations of ratios, percentages and yields as tools for the analysis of financial statements. The need for comparisons and the difficulty of obtaining satisfactory industry ratios were stressed. A useful booklet on the latter problem is *Published Accounts – your yardsticks of performance*? obtainable from the Centre for Interfirm Comparison. There are chapters on the use of ratios in the books by Bull and Jones and in John Sizer, *An Insight into Management Accounting* (Penguin, 1969). On statistics in general see M. J. Moroney, *Facts from Figures* (Penguin, revised editn 1965).

PROFITABILITY AND RETURN ON INVESTMENT

Profitability and return on investment were discussed in chapter 5, in which the relationship between sales, expenses and profit was considered and stress laid on the relationship

$$\frac{\text{profit}}{\text{net tangible assets}} = \frac{\text{profit}}{\text{sales}} \times \frac{\text{sales}}{\text{net tangible assets}}$$

where the left-hand side represents return on investment and the right-hand the net profit ratio and the turnover of net tangible assets. The latter was broken down into turnover of stock and turnover of fixed assets.

LIQUIDITY AND CASH FLOWS

In chapter 6 it was pointed out that a company must be liquid as well as profitable and that making profits is not the same as accumulating cash. It was shown that the best way to control liquidity from inside the company was by means of a cash budget. The external analyst uses the current ratio and the quick ratio as rather cruder measures. Another indicator of liquidity is the average collection-period for debtors.

SOURCES OF FUNDS AND CAPITAL STRUCTURE

Chapter 7 discussed sources of funds and capital structure. It was pointed out that shareholders are still the most important source of long-term funds, especially through the medium of retained profits, but that loan capital has steadily gained in importance in recent years. This has led to higher gearing ratios.

The problem of capital structure is to obtain the best mix of debt and equity. Factors to be considered are cost, risk, control, acceptability and transferability. It was argued that either the earnings yield (reciprocal of the price-earnings ratio) or the dividend yield plus a growth rate is a better measure of the cost of equity than the dividend yield itself. Risk can to some extent be judged by looking at gearing ratios and times interest earned.

In deciding on its dividend policy a company will concern itself with the effect on the present and future cost of capital and the influences of taxation and government policy. Most companies try to maintain or slightly increase their dividends over a period of time.

Bonus issues of shares do not in any way change the physical assets of a company, although they are sometimes combined with a recognition in the financial statements of an already existing increase in market values. In principle, they leave shareholders no better off than before. Rights issues give existing shareholders the first chance to subscribe to new issues. A shareholder who does not either exercise or sell his right will be worse off.

The chapter ended with brief references to two other sources of funds: convertible loans and leasing.

Two useful introductory books on the matters discussed in chapters 5, 6 and 7 are G. D. Newbould, *Business Finance* (Harrap, 1970) and G. P. E. Clarkson and B. J. Elliott, *Managing Money and Finance* (Gower Press, 1969). At a more advanced level, R. J. Briston, *The Stock Exchange and Investment Analysis* (Allen & Unwin, 1970) is invaluable. There are a number of good American texts, e.g. J. C. Van Horne, *Financial Management and Policy* (Prentice-Hall, Englewood Cliffs, N.J., 2nd editn 1971). Some of the articles in B. V. Carsberg and H. C. Edey (ed.), *Modern Financial Management* (Penguin, 1969) are also of interest.

ACCOUNTING PRINCIPLES AND INFLATION

Accounting principles and inflation were discussed in chapter 8.

The most important influences on accounting principles in Britain are company and tax legislation and the accounting profession. The recent establishment by the profession of an Accounting Standards Steering Committee is a response to suggestions that accounting principles should be determined by legislation or by a government body akin to the United States Securities and Exchange Commission.

Accounting practice is dominated by objectivity and conservatism which have led to the use of a system of accounting based mainly on historical costs. Falls in asset values are nearly always recognized, rises much less frequently. This, paradoxically, can lead to an over-statement of profits during a period of inflation.

A lively and controversial book on accounting principles is E. Stamp and C. Marley, *Accounting Principles and the City Code: The Case for Reform* (Butterworth, 1970). The most important theoretical work on the problems of profit measurement is E. O. Edwards and P. W. Bell, *The Theory and Measurement of Business Income* (Berkeley and Los Angeles: University of California Press, 1961). There are several collections of articles dealing with the problem, e.g. R. H. Parker and G. C. Harcourt, *Readings in the Concept and Measurement of Income* (Cambridge University Press, 1969). R. S. Gynther, *Accounting for Price-Level Changes: Theory and Procedures* (Pergamon, 1966) deals expertly with both the practical and the theoretical problems of accounting for inflation.

PERSONAL INVESTMENT

This book has not dealt, except incidentally, with problems of personal investment. Its primary purpose has been to explain and interpret company annual reports and financial statements, not to advise the reader on how to invest his money. It is not perhaps out of place, however, to conclude by recommending two books which do this: G. Cummings, *The Complete Guide to Investment* (Penguin, 5th editn 1970) and Margot Naylor, *Your Money* (Hodder, revised editn 1967).

Appendix A.   Debits and Credits (Double Entry)

Welche Vorteile gewährt die doppelte Buchhaltung dem Kaufmanne!

JOHANN WOLFGANG VON GOETHE, Wilhelm Meisters Lehrjahre, I, x.

Most people know that accountants are concerned with debits and credits. Since it is possible to learn quite a lot about accounting and finance without using these terms, it has not been thought necessary to explain their meaning within the body of this book. Very little extra effort is required, however, to master double entry, so a brief explanation is given in this appendix.

It will be remembered that the following symbols were used in chapter 2:

a = assets
l = liabilities
nw = net worth
s = share capital and capital reserves
rp = retained or ploughed back profits (i.e. revenue reserves)
r = revenues (e.g. sales, fees)
e = expenses other than taxation
t = taxation
d = dividends
Δ = net increase in

The identity for any balance sheet is

$$a = l + nw$$

which can be expanded to

$$a = l + s + rp.$$

An increase on the left-hand side of the identity is called a debit (abbreviated to Dr.) an increase on the right-hand side a credit (abbreviated to Cr.). Similarly, decreases on the left-hand side are credits and decreases on the right-hand side are debits. Debit and credit are used here as technical terms and should not be confused with any other meanings of these words.

In chapter 2 we showed that an increase in retained profits (Δ rp) is equal to revenue less expenses, tax and dividends:

$$\Delta rp = r - e - t - d.$$

Now, since increases in retained profits are credits it follows that increases in revenues are also credits, whereas increases in expenses, taxes and dividends must be debits. Conversely, decreases in revenues are debits and decreases in expenses, taxes and dividends are credits.

We can sum up the rules as follows:

DEBITS ARE:

Increases in: assets
expenses
taxes
dividends

Decreases in: liabilities
net worth
share capital
capital reserves
retained profits
revenues

CREDITS ARE:

Increases in: liabilities
net worth
share capital
capital reserves
retained profits
revenues

Decreases in: assets
expenses
taxes
dividends

It seems curious at first sight that both increases in assets and expenses are debits. In fact, assets and expenses are much more closely linked than is usually realized. If a company buys for cash a machine which is expected to last ten years it is rightly regarded as having acquired the asset machine (therefore, debit 'machines') in exchange for the asset cash (decrease in cash, therefore credit 'cash'). Suppose, however, that technological change is so rapid that these machines have an economic life of only one year or less. Then, if the accounting period is one year the machine can be regarded as an expense of the period (therefore, debit 'machine expense', credit 'cash'). Thus, in one sense, an asset is merely an expense paid for in advance which needs to be spread over several accounting periods in the form of depreciation.

The system of debits and credits is referred to as double entry, since maintenance of the accounting identity ($a = l + nw$ in its simplest form) requires that any increase or decrease in one item be balanced by a corresponding increase or decrease in another item or items. There are always two sides to any transaction. Suppose, for example, that a company decreases its cash by £100. The other side of the transaction might be:

1. an *increase* in another asset such as a machine (so, debit 'machine', credit 'cash');
2. a *decrease* in a liability, such as a trade creditor (so, debit 'creditor', credit 'cash');
3. an *increase* in a negative net worth item such as expenses, taxes or dividends (so, debit 'expenses', 'taxes' or 'dividends', credit 'cash').

Note that cash is always credited (since the asset cash has been decreased) and that a negative credit is the same as a debit (and a negative debit the same as a credit).

Appendix B. Glossary of Accounting and Financial Terms

This glossary serves two purposes:

1. to collect in alphabetical order various definitions, descriptions and explanations scattered throughout the text;
2. to provide certain *additional* information especially concerning those matters which must by law be disclosed in the published financial statements of companies.

ACCELERATED DEPRECIATION: The writing off of depreciation, e.g. for tax purposes, at a faster rate than is justified by the rate of use of the asset concerned.

ACCOUNTING IDENTITY (or EQUATION): Another name for the Balance Sheet Identity (q.v.).

ACCOUNTING PERIOD: The period between two balance sheets, usually a year from the point of view of shareholders and taxation authorities. Corporation tax is assessed on the basis of a company's accounting period.

ACCOUNTING PRINCIPLES: The principles governing the preparation of financial statements.

ACCOUNTING STANDARDS STEERING COMMITTEE: Committee composed of members of the leading professional accounting bodies, and responsible for the drawing up of definitive statements on accounting principles.

ACCOUNTS PAYABLE: Amounts owing by a company; usually called creditors in Britain.

ACCOUNTS RECEIVABLE: Amounts owing to a company; usually called debtors in Britain.

ACCUMULATED DEPRECIATION: The cumulative amount of depreciation written off a fixed asset at a balance sheet date.

ACID TEST: Another name for the Quick Ratio (q.v.).

AKTIENGESELLSCHAFT (AG): The approximate German equivalent of the British public company.

ALLOTMENT: The allocation of shares by the directors of a company following applications for them by intending shareholders.

AMORTIZATION: The writing off over a period of an asset or a liability. Sometimes used synonymously with Depreciation (q.v.).

ANNUAL GENERAL MEETING (AGM): Meeting of the members (shareholders) of a company held annually at intervals of not more than fifteen months (but first AGM may be held within eighteen months of formation). Usual business transacted: reception of directors' report and accounts; declaration of dividend; election of directors; appointment of auditors.

ANNUAL REPORT: Report made annually by the directors of a company to its shareholders. Contains financial statements (accounts), directors' report and sometimes chairman's statement.

ANNUAL RETURN: Document which must be completed within 42 days of the Annual General Meeting (q.v.) and forthwith forwarded to the Registrar of Companies (q.v.). Main contents are:

1. address of registered office;
2. addresses where registers of members and debenture-holders are kept;
3. summary of share capital and debentures, giving number of issued shares of each class, the consideration for them, details of shares not fully paid-up, etc;
4. particulars of mortgages and charges;
5. list of names and addresses of past and present shareholders giving number of shares held and particulars of transfers;
6. names, addresses and occupations of directors and secretaries (and nationality of directors).

Copies of the financial statements, directors' report and auditors' report must be annexed to the return.

All the above can be inspected at the Companies Registry in London or Edinburgh on payment of a small fee.

APPLICATION MONEY: The amount per share or unit of stock payable on application for a new issue of shares or debentures.

ARITHMETIC MEAN: The 'average' of everyday speech, i.e. the sum of a list of numbers, divided by the number of numbers.

ARTICLES OF ASSOCIATION: The internal regulations of a company. Usually deal with: rights of various classes of shares; calls on shares; transfer, transmission and forfeiture of shares; alteration of share capital; general meetings (notice, proceedings); votes and proxies; directors (powers, duties, disqualification, rotation, proceedings); dividends and reserves; accounts; capitalization of profits; audit; winding up; and similar matters.

ASSET: Any property, tangible or intangible, which has a monetary value and which brings benefits to a company. Examples: machines, stock-in-trade, debtors, cash, goodwill.

ASSET REVALUATION RESERVE: Results from recognition in the shareholders' funds section of a balance sheet of the effect of writing up the value of an asset.

ASSET TURNOVER: Ratio of sales to net tangible assets.

ASSOCIATED COMPANY: A company in which an investing group or company's interest is either essentially that of a partner in a joint venture *or* is not less than 20% of the equity voting rights and gives a significant influence over policy. An appropriate share of the profits (or losses) of associated companies is included in the con-solidated profit and loss account.

AUDITORS: Independent experts who report to the shareholders of a company their opinion on the truth and fairness of published financial statements. Their remuneration (including expenses) must be disclosed in the published profit and loss account.

Auditors must either be members of a body of accountants established in the U.K. and recognized by the Board of Trade, or be authorized by the Board of Trade to be appointed. The auditor must not be an officer or servant of the company or of a company in the group; a body corporate; a partner or employee of an officer or servant of the company or a company in the group.

AUTHORIZED SHARE CAPITAL: The maximum share capital which

a company can issue at any given time. The amount, which can be altered by the shareholders in general meeting, is stated in the memorandum of association and must be disclosed in the balance sheet. Also called nominal share capital or registered share capital.

AVERAGE: A measure of central tendency such as the Arithmetic Mean or the Median (qq.v.).

AVERAGE COLLECTION PERIOD: The speed at which a company collects its debts: $\dfrac{\text{debtors} \times 365}{\text{credit sales}}$ days.

BALANCE SHEET: Statement of the assets, liabilities and shareholders' funds of a company at a particular date. The Companies Acts provide that share capital, reserves, provisions, liabilities, fixed assets, current assets and other assets must be separately identified and that every balance sheet should give a true and fair view of the state of affairs of the company.

BALANCE SHEET IDENTITY (or EQUATION): The identity: assets *equals* liabilities *plus* net worth.

BALANCING ALLOWANCE/CHARGE: The difference between the price at which a second-hand fixed asset is sold and its written-down value for tax purposes. If negative, there is an allowance decreasing taxable income; if positive, a charge increasing taxable income.

BEARER SECURITIES: Debentures or shares transferable by simple delivery.

BONDS: Fixed interest securities such as government loans or (in the U.S.A.) company debentures.

BONUS SHARES: Shares issued to existing shareholders without further payment on their part. Also referred to as a scrip issue, a capitalization issue and (in the U.S.A.) a stock dividend.

BOOK VALUE: The monetary amount of an asset as stated in its balance sheet. In Britain and the U.S.A. it usually represents acquisition cost less accumulated depreciation.

CALLED-UP SHARE CAPITAL: The amount of the Issued Share Capital (q.v.) which has been called-up, i.e. the amounts shareholders have been asked to pay to date. Equal to the paid-up share capital unless there are calls in arrear or calls have been paid in advance.

CALLS: Demands by a company for part or all of the balance owed on partly paid shares.

CAPITAL ALLOWANCES: In effect, the depreciation allowable for tax purposes. May differ quite substantially from that charged in the published financial statements.

CAPITAL EXPENDITURE: Expenditure on fixed assets. The amount of contracts for capital expenditure not provided for and the amount of capital expenditure authorized by the directors but not contracted for must be disclosed.

CAPITAL GAINS TAX: A tax on individuals. Companies pay corporation tax on their capital gains, not capital gains tax.

CAPITAL REDEMPTION RESERVE FUND: When Preference Shares (q.v.) are redeemed otherwise than out of a new issue of shares a sum equal to their nominal value must be transferred to an account with this name. For most purposes the Fund is treated as if it were Share Capital.

CAPITALIZATION ISSUE: *see* Bonus Issue.

CAPITAL RESERVES: Reserves (q.v.) not regarded by the directors as being normally available for dividends. Examples: share premium, capital redemption reserve fund, asset revaluation reserve. The distinction between capital reserves and Revenue Reserves (q.v.) is not obligatory in published balance sheets since the Companies Act 1967.

CAPITAL STRUCTURE: The composition of a company's sources of funds, especially long-term.

CASH BUDGET: A plan of future cash receipts and payments based on specified assumptions concerning sales growth, credit terms etc.

CASH FLOW: Net profit (sometimes, retained profits) before charging depreciation. Not the same as the change in the cash balance during the year. Funds provided by operations would be a better description.

CHAIRMAN'S STATEMENT: Statement made by the chairman of a company at its annual general meeting and often included in the annual report. There are no legal regulations relating to its contents but it often contains interesting and useful information.

CLOSE COMPANY: A company resident in the U.K. which is under the control of five or fewer participators, or of participators who are directors. Introduced by the Finance Act 1965.

COMMON STOCK: American term for Ordinary Shares (q.v.).

COMPANY: Rather imprecise term implying corporate activity. This book deals with companies registered under the Companies Act. The liability of such companies is limited except in the case of unlimited companies.

CONSERVATISM: An accounting doctrine which leads to pessimistic rather than optimistic valuations of assets.

CONSISTENCY: An accounting doctrine which emphasizes consistency of accounting principles over time for a particular company rather than comparability of the financial statements of different companies at any one point in time.

CONSOLIDATED ACCOUNTS: Another name for Group Accounts (q.v.).

CONSOLIDATED BALANCE SHEET: Balance sheet of a group of companies as distinct from the holding company only.

CONSOLIDATED PROFIT AND LOSS ACCOUNT: Profit and loss account of a group of companies as distinct from the holding company only. A holding company need not publish its own profit and loss account as well if the consolidated profit and loss account discloses the requisite details (*see* Profit and Loss Account) and also discloses what portion of the consolidated profit (or loss) has been dealt with in its accounts.

CONSOLIDATION OF SHARE CAPITAL: Combination of shares into larger units (e.g. combining two £0·50 shares into one of £1).

CONTINGENT LIABILITY: A liability which is contingent on some event which may or may not happen, e. g. losing a lawsuit and having to pay the costs. Disclosed as a footnote to the balance sheet.

CONVERTIBLE LOAN STOCK: Loan stock which may be converted at the option of the holder at a future date or dates into ordinary stock at given price ratios.

CORPORATION TAX: A tax on companies; not payable by individuals. The rate varies: for 1970/71 it was 40%.

COST OF CAPITAL: The cost to a company's ordinary shareholders of issuing shares or debentures, of retaining profits, or of other sources of funds.

COUPON RATE OF INTEREST: The rate of interest on the par value of a debenture or bond. Not necessarily equal to the effective rate.

CREDITORS: Amounts owing by a company resulting from (for example) the purchase of goods. The American term is 'accounts payable'.

CREDIT: *see* Double Entry.

CUM: Latin for 'with'. A price so quoted includes any dividend (div.), bonus issue, rights or other distribution.

CUMULATIVE PREFERENCE SHARES: Preference shares entitled to be paid the arrears of their dividend before any dividend is paid on the ordinary shares. Any arrears must be disclosed as a note to the balance sheet.

CURRENT ASSETS: Those assets which are either already cash or can reasonably be expected to become cash within one year from the date of the balance sheet. Examples: debtors, stock-in-trade. If the directors believe that any of the current assets will not realize their balance sheet values in the ordinary course of business this fact must be disclosed. The alternative terms 'circulating assets' and 'floating assets' are now obsolete.

CURRENT LIABILITIES: Liabilities (q.v.) which are expected to have been paid within one year from the date of the balance sheet (e.g. trade creditors, proposed final dividend, current taxation).

CURRENT RATIO: Ratio of current assets to current liabilities. A measure of liquidity.

CURRENT TAXATION: Tax payable within one year from the date of the balance sheet.

DEBENTURE DISCOUNT: Arises from issuing debentures at less than their par value. Disclosed in balance sheet to extent that not written off.

DEBENTURES: Loans, usually but not necessarily secured on the assets of the company. Usually redeemable but may be irredeemable.

DEBIT: *see* Double Entry.

DEBTORS: Amounts owing to the company, e.g. from the sale of goods. The American term is 'accounts receivable'. Usually shown in balance sheets net of an allowance ('provision') for doubtful debts.

DEFERRED TAXATION: Tax which is not payable within one year from the date of the balance sheet.

DEPRECIATION: Expense recording the using up of fixed assets through operations. Accountants usually measure it by allocating the historical (acquisition) cost less scrap value of the asset on a straight-line or reducing-balance basis. Amount of depreciation must be disclosed in the profit and loss account. The accumulated (provision for) depreciation is deducted from the cost in the balance sheet to give the net book value. Depreciation is neither a source nor a use of funds.

DILUTION: The decrease in control and/or earnings per share suffered by existing shareholders when a new issue of shares is wholly or partly subscribed to by new shareholders.

DIRECTORS' EMOLUMENTS: The following information must be disclosed:

1. amounts received by directors and past directors as emoluments, pensions and compensation in respect of services as directors and as executives;
2. emoluments of chairman and of highest paid director (if greater than chairman's);
3. number of directors whose emoluments amounted to not more than £2,500, number whose emoluments amounted to between £2,501 and £5,000 and so on in bands of £2,500;
4. number of directors who waived their emoluments and the aggregate amount waived;
5. number of *employees* in U.K. whose emoluments exceeded £10,000 but were not more than £12,500, exceeded £12,500 but were not more than £15,000 and so on in bands of £2,500.

(*Note*: (2) and (3) do not apply to anyone whose duties were discharged wholly or mainly outside the U.K.)

DIRECTORS' REPORT: Annual report by the directors of a company to the shareholders which must contain, *inter alia*, details of:

1. the principal activities of the company and any significant change in them during the financial year;

2. any significant change in the fixed assets of the group during the financial year and any substantial and significant difference between the market value and the balance sheet value of interests in land;

3. shares, stock or debentures issued during the financial year;

4. interest of any director in any significant contract entered into by the company;

5. group turnover and profit (or loss) before tax divided among classes of business that differ substantially (excepting banking and discounting business and any company which is not part of a group and whose turnover does not exceed £50,000);

6. amount (if more than £50) given by group for political or charitable purposes;

7. amounts recommended to be paid as dividends, and transfers to reserves;

8. exports (unless group turnover less than £50,000 or directors satisfy Board of Trade that not in national interest to disclose);

9. names of directors;

10. any arrangement to which company is party to enable directors to acquire benefits through acquisition of shares or debentures of the company or any other company;

11. each director's interest in shares or debentures of the company or other companies in the group;

12. average number of employees in U.K. under contracts of service of the group in each week together with their annual aggregate remuneration. (Not required where less than 100 employees or if company wholly owned subsidiary of company incorporated in Great Britain.)

DISCOUNTED CASH FLOW: The present value of future cash receipts and payments; i.e. their value after taking into account the delay in receiving or paying them.

DIVIDEND: That part of the profits of a company which is distributed to the shareholders. May be interim (paid during the financial year) or final (recommended by the directors for approval by the shareholders at the annual general meeting). Both must be disclosed gross of tax in the profit and loss account. The proposed final dividend is shown gross in balance sheet as a current liability. The company must deduct income tax at the standard rate (from 1973, personal tax at the basic rate).

DIVIDEND COVER: The ratio between earnings per share and the ordinary dividend per share.

DIVIDEND POLICY: A company's policy on how to divide its profits between distributions to shareholders (dividends) and re-investment (retained profits).

DIVIDEND YIELD: The relationship between the ordinary dividend and the market price per ordinary share.

DOUBLE ENTRY: A system of recording transactions based on the Balance Sheet Identity (q.v.). Broadly, increases in assets and decreases in liabilities and net worth items (including expenses) are *debits*, and increases in liabilities and net worth items (including revenues) and decreases in assets are *credits*.

EARNINGS PER SHARE: Net profit after tax attributable to the ordinary shareholders divided by the number of ordinary shares.

EARNINGS YIELD: The relationship between the earnings per ordinary share and the market price per ordinary share. The reciprocal of the Price-Earnings Ratio (q.v.) multiplied by 100.

EQUITY SHARE CAPITAL: Defined by the Companies Acts as any issued share capital which has unlimited rights to participate in either the distribution of dividends or capital. Often more narrowly defined to mean Ordinary Shares (q.v.) only.

EX: Latin for 'without'. A price so quoted excludes any dividend (div.), bonus issue, rights or other distribution.

EXEMPT PRIVATE COMPANY: No longer exists. Before the Companies Act 1967 was essentially a family company with the privilege of not having to publish its financial statements.

FINANCIAL RATIO: Relationship among items in financial statements.

FINANCIAL STATEMENTS: Statements showing the financial position (balance sheet), profit for a period (profit and loss account) and sources and uses of funds for a period (funds statement) of a company.

FINANCIAL YEAR: Runs for corporation tax purposes from 1 April to the following 31 March.

FIRST-YEAR ALLOWANCE: The amount deductible for tax purposes during the first year of life of plant and machinery.

FIXED ASSETS: Assets held for use in the business rather than for re-sale. In general there must be shown:

1. method or methods used to arrive at the amount of fixed assets under each heading;
2. for each class of asset the aggregate cost or valuation and the accumulated depreciation since the date of acquisition or valuation;
3. years of valuation and the amounts (also, if valued during financial year, name of valuers or their qualifications, and the bases of valuations);
4. aggregate of additions and aggregate of disposals during the year;
5. which land is freehold and which is leasehold; latter to be subdivided into long leases (not less than 50 years unexpired) and short leases.

FIXED OVERHEADS: Those overheads whose amount remains constant over the usual range of activity.

FLAT YIELD: A Yield (q.v.) which does not take account of the redemption value of a security.

FLOATING CHARGE: A charge which is not attached to any specific asset but to all assets or to a class of assets.

FIXED CHARGE: A charge which is attached to some specific asset or assets.

FLOW OF FUNDS STATEMENT: Another name for a Funds Statement (q.v.).

FOREIGN COMPANY: A company incorporated outside Great Britain.

FREE DEPRECIATION: The system where a company can write off the cost of a fixed asset for tax purposes in any manner it chooses. Currently applicable to ships, capital equipment for scientific research and to immobile industrial equipment in development areas.

FUNDS STATEMENT: A statement showing the sources of funds (e.g.

new issue of shares or debentures, retained profits) and the uses of funds (e.g. purchase of new fixed assets, increase in stocks) of a company over a period. Sometimes referred to as a 'flow of funds statement' or a 'source and disposition statement'.

FOREIGN CURRENCIES: The financial statements of foreign subsidiaries must be converted into sterling before they can be included in the consolidated statements. The basis of conversion must be disclosed.

GEARING: The relationship between the funds provided to a company by its ordinary shareholders and the long-term sources of funds carrying a fixed interest charge or dividend.

GESELLSCHAFT MIT BESCHRÄNKTER HAFTUNG (GmbH): The approximate German equivalent of the British private company.

GOODWILL: The difference between the value of a company as a whole and the algebraic sum of the values of the assets and liabilities taken separately. Usually recorded only when purchased. The balance-sheet figure therefore represents a past purchase price less amounts written off, not a current valuation.

GOODWILL ON CONSOLIDATION: The excess of the cost of shares in subsidiary companies over the book value of their net tangible assets at the dates of acquisition. Can only appear in a *consolidated* balance sheet.

GOODWILL, PATENTS AND TRADE MARKS: Must be shown as separate item (but not necessarily as separate items) in published balance sheets together with method used to arrive at the amounts shown. See also under separate headings.

GROUP ACCOUNTS: Also called consolidated accounts. The Companies Acts provide that they are to be submitted if a company has subsidiary companies and is not a wholly-owned subsidiary of another company incorporated in Great Britain.

A subsidiary may be omitted from the group accounts, if, in the opinion of its directors, its inclusion:

1. is impracticable;
2. would be of no real value to shareholders in view of the insignificant amounts involved;

3. would involve expense or delay out of proportion to the value to the members of the company;
4. would be misleading;

or, subject to the permission of the Board of Trade;

5. would be harmful to the company or any of its subsidiaries;
6. is unreasonable because the business of the holding company and subsidiary are so different that they cannot reasonably be treated as a single undertaking.

GUARANTEE, COMPANY LIMITED BY: Company the liability of whose members is limited to contributing a pre-determined amount in the event of the company being wound up. Companies may be limited by guarantee or by shares, or be unlimited.

HISTORICAL COST: The usual basis of valuation in published financial statements. Favoured because it is more objective and more easily verifiable by an auditor. Its use can be attacked on conceptual grounds especially in times of inflation. In practice historical cost is modified by conservatism.

HOLDING COMPANY: Company which controls another company, called its subsidiary. Balance sheet of holding company must show separately shares (including basis of valuation) and amounts owing to and owed by subsidiaries.

INCOME STATEMENT: American term for Profit and Loss Account (q.v.).

INCOME TAX: A tax on individuals, not payable by companies. The standard rate varies; in 1970/71 it was £0·3875. *See also* Personal Tax.

INDUSTRY RATIO: An average ratio for an industry.

INFLATION: A rise in the price-level. Not fully adjusted for in conventional financial statements.

INITIAL ALLOWANCE: Allowance for tax purposes (currently 30% or 40%) given in the first year of life of industrial buildings. Unlike an Investment Allowance (q.v.) it restricts the amount of the Writing-Down Allowances (q.v.) also given.

INTANGIBLE ASSETS: Goodwill, Patents and Trademarks (qq.v.).

INTERIM DIVIDEND: *see* Dividend.

INTERIM REPORT: Report issued by a company to its shareholders during a financial year, e.g. quarterly, half-yearly.

INVENTORIES: American term for Stock-in-Trade (q.v.).

INVESTMENT ALLOWANCE: Allowance for tax purposes formerly given in first year of life of some fixed assets. Unlike an Initial Allowance (q.v.) it did not restrict the amount of the Writing-Down Allowances (q.v.) also given. The total allowances granted were thus greater than the acquisition cost (less scrap value) of the asset.

INVESTMENT GRANT: A grant of cash formerly receivable from the government on the purchase of certain fixed assets.

INVESTMENTS: *see* Quoted Investments *and* Unquoted Investments.

INVESTMENT TRUST: Not really a trust but a company whose object is investment in the securities of other companies. Compare Unit Trust.

IRREDEEMABLE DEBENTURE: A Debenture (q.v.) which will never have to be repaid.

ISSUED SHARE CAPITAL: The amount of the Authorized Share Capital (q.v.) which has been issued; the remainder is the unissued share capital. The amount of the issued capital must be disclosed in the published balance sheet. Not necessarily equal to called-up or paid-up share capital.

ISSUE EXPENSES: Expenses of making an issue of shares or debentures. Disclosed in balance sheet to extent that not written off.

ISSUE PRICE: The price at which a share or debenture is issued. Since the issue may be at a premium or a discount, the issue price is not necessarily equal to the Par Value (q.v.).

LEASING: Entering into a long-term contract which allows the use of an asset in return for a periodic rental, but does not give ownership. Its effect is similar to financing the purchase of the asset by loan capital, but in leasing the asset and the liability are not usually shown in the balance sheet.

LEVERAGE: The American term for Gearing (q.v.).

LIABILITIES: Amounts owing by a company. The following must be disclosed in the published balance sheet:

    1. aggregate amount of bank loans and overdrafts;

2. aggregate amount of other loans made to the company which are:
(i) not repayable by instalments and repayable after 5 years from balance sheet date, or
(ii) repayable by instalments any of which fall due for payment after 5 years from balance sheet date, together with details of repayment and rates of interest (if number of loans is large a general indication will suffice);
3. amounts due to subsidiary companies;
4. amounts due to other group members distinguishing between debentures and other indebtedness;
5. recommended dividend (gross);
6. redeemed debentures which the company has the power to re-issue;
7. any liability secured (otherwise than by operation of law) on the assets of the company (the assets need not be specified).

LIMITED LIABILITY COMPANY: A company the liability of whose members is limited by shares or by guarantee. If by shares, liability is limited to the amount taken up or agreed to be taken up; if by guarantee, to the amount undertaken to be contributed in the event of winding-up.

LIQUID ASSETS: *see* Quick Assets.

LOAN CAPITAL: Funds acquired by non-short-term borrowing from sources other than the shareholders of the company.

LOANS RECEIVABLE: Must be shown in balance sheet under the following headings:

1. Loans to employees (or trustees for employees) or salaried directors to enable them to purchase fully paid shares in the company or its holding company;
2. Loans made during the year (whether repaid or not) by the company, a subsidiary, or by a third party secured or guaranteed by the company or subsidiary, to directors or officials of the company (except loans made in the ordinary course of business or loans not exceeding £2,000 made to employees).

LONG-TERM DEBT: Long-term sources of funds other than equity (share capital and reserves).

MARKET PRICE: The price at which a company's securities can be bought or sold on a stock exchange. Not necessarily equal to the Par Value or the Issue Price (qq.v.).

MEDIAN: One measure of the 'average'. The number in the middle when a list of numbers is arranged in order of magnitude.

MEMORANDUM OF ASSOCIATION: Document which gives:

1. the name of the company;
2. the situation of its registered office (England or Scotland);
3. the objects;
4. statement that the liability of the members is limited (unless the company is an unlimited one);
5. the authorized share capital and how it is divided (or, in the case of a company limited by guarantee, the maximum amount to be contributed by members on winding-up);
6. details of the subscribers (the persons 'desirous of being formed into a company').

MINORITY INTEREST: That part of a subsidiary company's shareholders' funds that is not held by the holding company. Usually shown as a separate item on the net worth and liabilities side of a consolidated balance sheet.

NET CURRENT ASSETS: Another name for Working Capital (q.v.).

NET PROFIT RATIO: Ratio of net profit to sales.

NET TANGIBLE ASSETS: Assets except for intangible assets (goodwill, patents and trademarks) *less* liabilities.

NET WORKING CAPITAL: Another name for Working Capital (q.v.).

NET WORTH: Assets *less* liabilities. The proprietorship section of a balance sheet, usually referred to in the case of a company as shareholders' funds or share capital and reserves.

NOMINAL SHARE CAPITAL: *see* Authorized Share Capital.

NON-VOTING SHARES: Shares with no voting rights. Non-voting ordinary shares are usually cheaper to buy than those carrying votes.

NO PAR VALUE SHARES: Shares with no nominal or par value. They are illegal in Britain.

OBJECTIVITY: Accounting doctrine which stresses the need to establish rules for recording financial transactions and events which so far as possible do not depend upon the personal judgement of the recorder.

ORDINARY SHARES: Shares entitled to share in the profits after payment of debenture interest and preference dividends. Often referred to as the equity capital.

PAID-UP SHARE CAPITAL: The amount of the Called-Up Share Capital (q.v.) which has been paid up by the shareholders.

PARENT COMPANY: *see* Holding Company.

PAR VALUE: The face or nominal value of a share or debenture. Not necessarily equal to the Issue Price or the current Market Price (qq.v.). Dividend and interest percentages refer to the par value, yields to the current market price.

PATENTS: Grants by the Crown to the authors of new inventions giving them the sole and exclusive right to use, exercise and sell their inventions and to secure the profits arising therefrom for a limited period.

PERSONAL TAX: A graduated tax payable by individuals and not, except in special circumstances, by companies. Replaces income tax and surtax from April 1973. Companies will deduct personal tax at the basic rate from dividends and interest and account for it to the Inland Revenue.

PLOUGHED BACK PROFITS: Profits which are retained and not paid out as dividends. Referred to in the balance sheet as retained profits, balance of profit and loss appropriation account, or as some kind of Reserve (q.v.).

PRE-ACQUISITION PROFITS: The accumulated profits of a subsidiary company up to the date of its acquisition (take-over) by the holding company.

PREFERENCE SHARES: Shares which usually are entitled to a fixed rate of dividend before a dividend is paid on the ordinary shares and to priority of repayment if the company is wound up. Participating preference shares are also entitled to a further dividend if profits are available. If a preference dividend is not paid the arrears must be disclosed as a footnote to the balance sheet. Arrears can only arise if the shares are *cumulative* as distinct from *non-cumulative*.

PRELIMINARY EXPENSES: Expenses of forming a company. Disclosed as an asset in the balance sheet to extent that not written off.

PRICE-EARNINGS RATIO: The multiple of the last reported earnings that the market is willing to pay for a company's ordinary shares. The reciprocal of the Earnings Yield (q.v.) multiplied by 100.

PRIOR CHARGES: Claims on a company's assets and profits that rank ahead of ordinary share capital.

PRIORITY PERCENTAGES: Method of calculating Gearing (q.v.) by computing the percentage of earnings that is required to service each category of loan and share capital.

PRIVATE COMPANY: A company which by its Articles of Association (q.v.):

1. restricts the right to transfer its shares;
2. limits the number of its members to fifty (with certain exceptions);
3. prohibits any invitation to the public to subscribe for any of its shares or debentures.

In 1970 there were about 503,500 private companies in Great Britain.

PROFIT: Revenues *less* expenses. May be reported before or after interest and/or tax.

PROFIT AND LOSS ACCOUNT: Gives details of a company's revenues, expenses and profit. Must by law give a 'true and fair view' of the profit or loss of the company for the financial year and disclose, *inter alia*:

1. provision for depreciation, renewals or diminution in value of fixed assets;
2. interest on the following loans (whether secured by debentures or not):
    (i) bank loans and overdrafts,
    (ii) loans repayable within 5 years by instalments,
    (iii) loans not repayable by instalments but due for repayment within 5 years,
    (iv) other loans;
3. taxation:
    (i) amount and basis of the charge for U.K. income tax and corporation tax,

(ii) income tax and corporation tax relieved by double taxation agreements,

(iii) overseas taxation,

(iv) any special circumstances affecting taxation liability for the financial year or succeeding financial years;

4. amounts provided for redemption of share capital and redemption of loans;

5. transfers to and from reserves;

6. income from:

(i) quoted investments,

(ii) unquoted investments;

7. rents (less outgoings) from land (if substantial);

8. charges for the hire of plant and machinery;

9. gross dividends paid and proposed;

10. charges or credits relating to prior years;

11. remuneration (including expenses) of the auditors;

12. amount and basis of turnover, except from banking and discounting (not required if company not part of a group and turnover does not exceed £250,000);

13. unusual, exceptional or non-recurring items and details of any change in the basis of accounting.

(*Note :* Above requirements include appropriations of profit. Thus published profit and loss account is really a profit and loss account proper plus a profit and loss appropriation account.)

PROFIT AND LOSS APPROPRIATION ACCOUNT: Continuation of profit and loss account proper giving details of profit appropriations, i.e. distribution as dividends and retention as reserves.

PROFITS TAX: A tax on companies; abolished by the Finance Act 1965.

PROPRIETARY COMPANY: Name given to a private company in Australia and South Africa.

PROSPECTUS: Any notice, circular, advertisement or other invitation offering shares or debentures to the public.

PROVISION: Defined by the Companies Acts as any amount written off or retained by way of providing for depreciation, renewals or diminution in the value of assets or providing for a known liability of which the amount cannot be determined with substantial accuracy. Examples: provision for depreciation, provision for doubtful debts. A charge against profit, not an appropriation of profit. Should not be confused with a Reserve (q.v.).

PROXY:

1. A person appointed to attend and vote at a company meeting on behalf of a shareholder;
2. The form, signed by the shareholder, which grants the above authority.

PUBLIC COMPANY: Any company which is not a Private Company (q.v.). Only 3% of British Companies are public. Not all public companies have their shares quoted on a stock exchange.

QUARTILE: When a list of numbers is arranged in order of magnitude the lower quartile is the number a quarter of the way up from the bottom, the upper quartile the number a quarter of the way down from the top.

QUICK ASSETS: Current assets *less* stock-in-trade.

QUICK RATIO: The relationship between quick assets and current liabilities. Also known as liquid ratio, or the acid test. A measure of liquidity.

QUOTED INVESTMENTS: Investments for which there is a quotation or permission to deal on a recognized stock exchange or on any reputable stock exchange outside Great Britain. Must be shown separately in the balance sheet.

REAL CAPITAL: The capital (net assets) of a company after allowing for changes in price levels (contrasted with 'money' capital).

RECOMMENDATIONS ON ACCOUNTING PRINCIPLES: Statements made by the Institute of Chartered Accountants in England and Wales relating to best accounting practice. They have persuasive authority only.

REDEEMABLE PREFERENCE SHARES: Preference shares which must or may be redeemed at the option of the company or (very rarely) the shareholder. The balance sheet must disclose the earliest and latest dates on which the company has power to redeem, whether at the option of the company or in any event, and also the amount of any premium on redemption.

REDEMPTION YIELD: A yield (q.v.) which takes into account not only the annual interest receivable but also the redemption value of a security.

REDUCING BALANCE DEPRECIATION: Method of depreciation in which the periodic amount written off decreases over the life of the asset. A fixed percentage is applied to a declining written-down value.

REGISTERED OFFICE: The official address of a company. The Memorandum of Association (q.v.) must state whether it is in England or Scotland.

REGISTERED SHARE CAPITAL: *see* Authorized Share Capital.

REGISTRAR OF COMPANIES: Government officer with whom annual reports (including financial statements) and other documents of companies must be filed: in London for companies registered in England and Wales, in Edinburgh for companies registered in Scotland.

RESERVE: Reserves arise either from the retention of profits or from specific capital transactions such as the issue of shares at a premium (*see* Share Premium) or the revaluation of assets (*see* Asset Revaluation Reserve). Must not include Provisions (q.v.) – unless the directors consider they are excessive – or the taxation equalization account. Not a charge against profits; not necessarily represented by cash on the other side of the balance sheet. Movements in reserves during the financial year must be disclosed.

RESERVE FUND: A Reserve (q.v.) which is represented by specially earmarked cash or investments on the other side of the balance sheet.

RETAINED PROFITS: Profits not distributed to shareholders but re-invested in the company. Their cost is less than a new issue of shares, because of the issue costs of the latter.

RETURN ON INVESTMENT: Ratio of profit (usually before interest and tax) to net tangible assets. A measure of profitability.

REVALUATION: The writing-up of an asset to its current market value.

REVENUE RESERVES: Reserves (q.v.) regarded by the directors as being normally available for dividend. The distinction between revenue reserves and Capital Reserves (q.v.) has not been obligatory in published balance sheets since the Companies Act 1967.

REVERSE YIELD GAP: A description of the fact that since August 1959 the average yield on government bonds has been greater than the average dividend yield on the ordinary shares of companies, despite the greater (monetary) security of the former.

RIGHTS ISSUE: An issue of shares in which the existing shareholders have a right to subscribe for the new shares at a stated price. The right can be sold if the shareholder does not wish to subscribe.

SALE-AND-LEASEBACK: Raising cash by selling an asset and then leasing it back in a long-term contract. *See also* Leasing.

SCRAP VALUE: The amount at which a fixed asset is expected to be sold at the end of its estimated economic life.

SCRIP ISSUE: *see* Bonus Issue.

SECOND SCHEDULE, COMPANIES ACT 1967: Sets out in detail what must, subject to the overriding obligation to show a true and fair view, be disclosed in the published financial statements of companies.

SECURITIES AND EXCHANGE COMMISSION (SEC): American federal body concerned with the operations of corporations (i.e. companies) and issues of and dealings in their securities. It has the right, which it has largely delegated to the American Institute of Certified Public Accountants, to establish accounting principles.

SECURITY: Two meanings:

1. A generic name for stocks, share, debentures etc;
2. The backing for a loan.

SHARE CAPITAL: Unless limited by guarantee, a company registered under the Companies Acts must have a share capital divided into shares of a fixed amount. The ownership of a share gives the shareholder a proportionate ownership of the company. The share capital is stated in the balance sheet at its par (nominal) value.

SHARE DISCOUNT: Results from issuing shares at less than their par value. Very rare. Disclosed in balance sheet to extent that not written off.

SHAREHOLDER: Member of a company whose part ownership (share in) of the company is evidenced by a share certificate.

SHAREHOLDERS' FUNDS: The proprietorship section of a company balance sheet. Includes the share capital and the reserves.

SHARE PREMIUM: Results from issuing shares at a price higher than their par value. Must be disclosed in the balance sheet as a Reserve (q.v.). Cannot be used to pay dividends but can be used to make an issue of Bonus Shares (q.v.).

SOCIÉTÉ ANONYME (SA): The approximate French equivalent of a British public company.

SOCIÉTÉ À RESPONSABILITÉ LIMITÉE (SARL): The approximate French equivalent of a British private company.

SOURCE AND DISPOSITION STATEMENT: Another name for a Funds Statement (q.v.).

STOCKBROKER: A member of a stock exchange who deals with the public.

STOCK DIVIDEND: *see* Bonus Issue.

STOCK EXCHANGE: A market where shares, debentures, government securities etc. are bought and sold. The London Stock Exchange is by far the largest in Britian but there are also provincial exchanges.

STOCK-IN-TRADE: Consists for a manufacturing company of raw materials, work-in-progress and finished goods. Usually valued at the lower of cost or market value.

STOCK TURNOVER: Ratio of sales (sometimes, cost of sales) to stock-in-trade.

STRAIGHT LINE DEPRECIATION: Obtained by dividing the cost less estimated scrap value of an asset by its estimated economic life. In Britain, the basis on which Capital Allowances (q.v.) for industrial buildings are calculated.

SUBDIVISION OF SHARE CAPITAL: Splitting of shares into smaller units (e.g. splitting one £1 share into two of £0·50).

SUBSIDIARY: Company controlled by another company called its holding company. A company is a subsidiary of another company if that other company:

> 1. is a member of it and controls the composition of its board of directors; or

2. holds more than half the nominal value of its Equity Share Capital (q.v.).

The following information *inter alia* about subsidiaries must be disclosed:

1. name of each subsidiary and country of incorporation if other than Great Britain (if incorporated in G.B. country of registration – England or Scotland – unless holding company registered in same country);
2. proportion of nominal value of each class of the issued share capital of each subsidiary which is held by the holding company (or its nominees) or by a subsidiary company (or its nominees);
3. name and (if known) country of incorporation of the ultimate holding company of a subsidiary company.

Note : (i) 1. and 2. apply also to share investments when a company holds more than 10% of nominal amount of any class of shares comprised in the equity share capital of a body corporate or where the share interest represents more than 10% of the assets of the company holding the shares.

(ii) Companies incorporated in or carrying on business abroad may be excluded from requirements 1., 2. and 3. with the agreement of the Board of Trade.

SURTAX: A tax on individuals over and above income tax. *See also* Personal Tax.

TABLE A: A model set of Articles of Association (q.v.) which can be adopted by a company in full or in a modified form.

TAKE-OVER BID: An offer to purchase the share capital of a company.

TAXABLE INCOME: Income liable to tax. Not usually equal to the profit reported in a company's financial statements.

TAXATION EQUALIZATION ACCOUNT: Arises mainly from the fact that the capital allowances permitted for tax purposes differ from the depreciation charged in the company's books.

TIMES INTEREST EARNED: The number of times that a company's interest is covered or earned by its profit before interest and tax.

TRADE CREDIT: Short-term source of funds resulting from credit granted by suppliers of goods bought.

TRADE MARK: A distinctive identification, protected by law, of a manufactured product or of a service.

TRADING ON THE EQUITY: American expression describing the process of using fixed-interest sources of capital to boost the return on the equity (ordinary shares).

TRUE AND FAIR VIEW: By law the balance sheet and profit and loss account must give a 'true and fair view'. This phrase is undefined but depends upon both the application of generally accepted accounting principles and the exercise of judgement.

TURNOVER: Sales. The profit and loss account must disclose the amount and basis of turnover for the financial year. The directors' report must disclose group turnover and profit (or loss) before tax divided among classes of business that differ substantially. (*Exceptions*: banking and discounting business and any company which is not part of a group and whose turnover does not exceed £250,000.)

ULTRA VIRES: Latin for 'beyond the powers'. Especially applied to acts of a company not authorized by the objects clause of its memorandum of association.

UNIT TRUST: Undertaking formed to invest in securities (mainly ordinary shares) under the terms of a trust deed. Compare Investment Trust.

UNLIMITED COMPANY: A Company (q.v.) the liability of whose members is limited neither by shares nor by guarantee.

UNQUOTED INVESTMENTS: Investments for which there is not a quotation or permission to deal on a recognized stock exchange or on any reputable stock exchange outside Great Britain. If they consist of equity of other companies directors must either give an estimate of their value or information about income received, profits etc.

UNSECURED LOAN: Money borrowed by a company without the giving of security.

VARIABLE OVERHEADS: Overheads which vary proportionately with manufacturing activity.

WINDOW-DRESSING: The manipulation of financial ratios so as to produce a desired result on the balance sheet date.

WORKING CAPITAL: Current assets *less* current liabilities.

WORK-IN-PROGRESS: Partly completed manufactured goods.

WRITING-DOWN ALLOWANCE: The annual amount deductible for tax purposes on plant and machinery (currently 25% on a reducing-balance basis) and on industrial buildings (currently 4% on a straight-line basis).

WRITTEN-DOWN VALUE: The value of an asset in the books of a company or for tax purposes after depreciation has been written off.

YIELD: The rate of return relating cash invested to cash received (or expected to be received).

Appendixes C and D

Both the Alenco report (Appendix C) and the Guest, Keen and Nettlefolds report (Appendix D) as printed here are photographic reproductions of the originals, reduced to book size. The Alenco report has been given in full, but certain information in the GKN report (general reviews of subsidiary firms, colour photographs of products, factories, etc.) has been omitted since it is irrelevant to the purposes of this book. Both reports were printed in colour, which for technical reasons it has not been practicable to reproduce, but which is in no way essential to the presentation of the facts concerning the two companies.

Appendix C

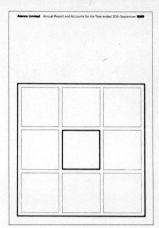

Contents

	Page
Notice of Meeting	1
Directors	2
Directors' Report	3
Consolidated Profit and Loss Account and Explanations	6
Consolidated Balance Sheet and Explanations	8
Balance Sheet and Explanations	10
Notes on the Accounts	12
Report of the Auditors	20
Source and Disposition Statement	21
Statistics and Ratios	22
The Alenco Group	24
Graphs	25

Alenco Limited

Annual Report and Accounts 1969

Notice of Meeting

Notice is hereby given that the nineteenth Annual General Meeting of the members of Alenco Limited will be held at the registered office of the company, Alenco House, 3/5 The Grove, Slough, Buckinghamshire on Thursday 22nd January, 1970 at 12.00 noon for the following purposes:

1 To receive the directors' report and accounts for the year ended 30th September, 1969

2 To declare a final dividend on the ordinary shares

3 To elect a director

4 To authorise the directors to fix the remuneration of the auditors

By order of the Board   S. A. Gardner, Secretary
Alenco House, 3/5 The Grove, Slough, Buckinghamshire   31st December, 1969

A member entitled to attend and vote at the above meeting may appoint one or more proxies to attend and on a poll to vote instead of him. A proxy need not be a member of the company.

A member of The Charterhouse Group

Alenco Limited

Directors	P. N. M. Rudder (Chairman)
	J. M. Blake C Eng MIEE (Managing Director)
	R. E. Burrows MA, FCA, ACWA
	R. Couraud (French)
	S. A. Gardner
	R. B. Halford
	K. M. S. Maconick MA
Secretary	S. A. Gardner
Registered office	Alenco House, 3/5 The Grove, Slough, Buckinghamshire
Auditors	Touche Ross & Co
Bankers	National Westminster Bank Ltd
	Barclays Bank Ltd

Alenco Limited   **Directors' Report**

The Directors have pleasure in submitting their Annual Report and the Accounts of the company for the year ended 30th September, 1969.

	1969	1968
Results		
The accounts of the company show that:		
Group profit attributable to proprietors before tax was	950,000	963,000
Proprietors' charges (including loan interest in 1969) amounted to	28,000	5,000
Leaving a profit chargeable to taxation of	922,000	958,000
Taxation provided on this profit totalled	407,000	401,000
Leaving a balance available for appropriation of	515,000	557,000
The cost of dividends paid and proposed is	498,000	450,000
Leaving a balance of unappropriated profit for the year of	£17,000	£107,000

In considering these results due regard must be had to the following factors:

Changes in the group

S. S. Stott Limited

For a number of years S. S. Stott Limited had been manufacturing mechanical handling equipment at Haslingden, Lancashire with only modest success. In the Spring of 1969 the directors decided that satisfactory long-term growth for this company was more likely to be achieved by association with a company specialising in the same field. Such a company was found and negotiations were successfully concluded on 12th August, 1969 when all the issued share capital of S. S. Stott Limited was sold to Thomas Robinson & Son Limited of Rochdale. The results of the Alenco group accordingly exclude those of this company for the whole of the year ended 30th September, 1969.

H. & L. Austin Engineering Ltd

In furtherance of the group's policy to expand its activities in the field of engineering components and in order to introduce a competence in technical plastics, the whole of the issued share capital of H. & L. Austin Engineering Limited and its subsidiary companies was acquired on 30th May, 1969, with effect from 1st October, 1968. This group of companies specialises in the manufacture of industrial products in polytetrafluorethylene (PTFE) – chiefly thread sealing tape and braided hoses – which it sells in both the United Kingdom and overseas; its export successes in the previous year earned the Queen's Award to Industry for 1969.

The acquisition of H. & L. Austin Engineering Limited was executed by The Charterhouse Group Limited and the consideration was satisfied by an issue of their ordinary shares and debenture stock; on completion the company was transferred to Alenco Limited and for this purpose a loan of £750,000 was obtained from Charterhouse Industrial Holdings Limited. The results of the Alenco group include those of H. & L. Austin Engineering Limited and its subsidiary companies for the full year ended 30th September, 1969. The charge for interest on the loan from Charterhouse Industrial Holdings Limited amounted to £23,000 for the four months ended on that date and would have amounted to £68,000 for a full year.

Devaluation

The devaluation of the French franc took place on 11th August, 1969. This resulted in a decrease of £204,000 in the sterling value of the group's net assets which has been subtracted from the capital and revenue reserves. It will be recalled that when sterling was devalued on 18th November, 1967 there was an increase in the sterling value of the group's net assets amounting to £272,000.

The results of the Alenco group include those of the French subsidiary company for approximately 10½ months converted into sterling at the rate of exchange ruling at 10th August, 1969, and for approximately 1½ months converted into sterling at the rate of exchange ruling at 30th September, 1969. This devaluation has not had a material effect on the group's sales and net profit for the year.

Directors' Report continued

Copper

During the year the cost of copper based metals continued to fluctuate and selling prices of the group's gunmetal and brass products were adjusted to keep pace with these and other raw material cost changes. As a result the group benefited in the year ended 30th September, 1969 by approximately £50,000 – the same extent as in the previous year – but this additional profit cannot be regarded as exceptional.

New group headquarters

For many years Alenco Limited had occupied premises adjoining those of their major U.K. subsidiary company, British Ermeto Corporation Limited, at Maidenhead. The continued expansion of that company, however, created a need for additional accommodation and during the year the opportunity was taken to establish a new group headquarters at Slough.

Principal activities

The principal activities of the group comprise the manufacture and sale of pipe fittings, valves, hose, tube, thread sealing tape and other industrial components.

Further details of the particular activities of each company in the group are shown on Page 24.

Dividends

An interim dividend of 8¼% was paid on 29th August, 1969. The directors now recommend the payment of a final dividend of 19¼% making a total for the year of 27¾% (1968 – 25%).

Directors

The directors at the date of this Report are shown on Page 2

**Changes since
30th September, 1968**

On 1st October, 1969 Mr. J. M. Blake was appointed Managing Director and Chief Executive in place of Mr. E. Fawcett who resigned on 30th September, 1969.

Re-election

In accordance with the company's Articles of Association Mr. P. N. M. Rudder retires and being eligible, offers himself for re-election.

Directors' interests

The interests of the directors and their families in shares in the company's ultimate holding company as required to be disclosed by the Companies Act, 1967, were:

The Charterhouse Group Limited

Directors at the end of the financial year	30th September, 1969		30th September, 19	
	5/– Ordinary shares	6% Cum. 2nd Pref. shares of £1 each	£1 Ordinary shares	6% Cum. 2nd Pr shares of £1 ea
P. N. M. Rudder	3,672	100	823	
J. M. Blake	–	–	–	
R. E. Burrows	–	–	–	
R. Couraud	–	–	–	
S. A. Gardner	5,400	–	1,350	
R. B. Halford	–	–	–	
K. M. S. Maconick	–	–	–	

During the year each of the existing £1 ordinary shares of The Charterhouse Group Limited was sub-divided into four ordinary shares of 5/– each.

The directors had no interest in any other shares or debentures of the company, ultimate holding company or any fellow subsidiary company.

The Charterhouse Group

Charterhouse Industrial Holdings Limited, a wholly owned subsidiary company of The Charterhouse Group Limited, continues to hold the whole of the company's issued ordinary and preference share capital.

Other information

Exports

During the year the group exported from the United Kingdom goods to the value of £1,059,000 (1968 – £410,000). This figure includes sales to overseas subsidiary companies but excludes substantial indirect export sales.

This increase largely reflects the export performance of H. & L. Austin Engineering Ltd.

Employees

The number of persons employed in the group at 30th September, 1969 was:

	1969	1968
United Kingdom	1,398	1,296
France and Holland	715	675
	2,113	1,971

The average number of persons employed in the United Kingdom during the year ended 30th September, 1969 was 1,331 and their aggregate remuneration for the year amounted to £1,455,000.

Charitable and political contributions

Donations made by the group during the year for charitable purposes in the United Kingdom amounted to £418.

The group made no political contributions

Auditors

During the year Messrs. Thomson McLintock & Co. resigned as joint auditors. Messrs. Touche Ross & Co. (formerly Messrs. Radford Edwards & Co.) continue in office in accordance with Section 159 (2) of the Companies Act, 1948.

By order of the Board

S. A. Gardner, Secretary, 22nd January, 1970

Alenco Limited   **Consolidated Profit and Loss Account**

and subsidiary companies

For the year ended 30th September		Note	1969	1968
Sales	Excluding inter-company sales	5	9,669,000	8,085,000
Cost of sales	Raw materials		3,835,000	2,873,000
	Wages and salaries	6	3,183,000	2,847,000
	Depreciation	7	324,000	305,000
	All other expenses	3	1,348,000	1,082,000
			8,690,000	7,107,000
Trading profit			979,000	978,000
Interest	Payable less receivable	4	29,000	15,000
Profit attributable to proprietors before taxation			950,000	963,000
Proprietors' charges	Management charge		5,000	5,000
	Loan interest	4	23,000	—
			28,000	5,000
Profit chargeable to taxation			922,000	958,000
Taxation		8	407,000	401,000
			515,000	557,000
Proprietors' appropriations	Preference dividends		10,000	10,000
	Ordinary dividends			
	Interim paid – 8½% (1968 – 3%)		149,000	53,000
	Final proposed – 19¼% (1968 – 22%)		339,000	387,000
			498,000	450,000
Balance of profit	Added to revenue reserves		**£17,000**	**£107,000**

Changes in the composition of the group and the treatment of foreign currencies consequent upon the devaluation of the French franc are explained in Notes 1 and 2.

The Notes are on pages 12–19

Explanations

The Consolidated Profit and Loss Account is a statement showing the combined results of Alenco Limited and its eight subsidiary companies for the year ended 30th September, 1969; it shows the sales executed, profits earned, taxation charged, dividends appropriated and the balance of profit retained in the group.

The value of goods sold to customers outside the Alenco group

Raw materials, bought out parts and sub-contractors' charges

Including directors' emoluments, agents' commission, contributions to state welfare schemes and the cost of company pension schemes

The amount by which the fixed assets and patents have been written down during the year

The cost of all other factory, selling and administrative expenses (including auditors' remuneration)

Interest payable on bank and other short and medium term borrowings less interest receivable on bank and other deposits

The profit of the group for the year before taxation which has been earned for the proprietors

A charge which the proprietors have made for management services rendered to the group (including the chairman's fee)

Interest payable to the proprietors on their unsecured loan

The total of the proprietors' charges which are met out of the profit of the group for the year before taxation

Taxation chargeable on the profit for the year

Payable half yearly on 31st March and 30th September

Paid on 29th August, 1969

Payable on 6th March, 1970 (subject to the approval of the proprietors at the annual general meeting)

The total of the proprietors' appropriations which are met out of the profit of the group for the year after taxation

The balance of profit for the year retained and added to the funds of the group

Alenco Limited   **Consolidated Balance Sheet**

and subsidiary companies

As at 30th September	Note	1969	1968
Source of Funds			
Ordinary share capital and reserves			
Ordinary share capital of Alenco Limited	9	1,760,000	1,760,000
Share premium account		207,000	207,000
Other capital reserves	10	502,000	620,000
Revenue reserves	12	2,277,000	2,353,000
		4,746,000	4,940,000
Preference share capital Preference share capital of Alenco Limited	9	165,000	165,000
Unsecured loan Loan from Charterhouse Industrial Holdings Ltd	11	750,000	—
		£5,661,000	£5,105,000
Employment of Funds			
Fixed assets Land, buildings, plant, equipment and vehicles	15	2,550,000	2,625,000
Patents	16	42,000	46,000
Current assets Stocks	13	2,685,000	2,432,000
Debtors	14	2,786,000	2,032,000
Cash and bank balances and deposits	14	67,000	477,000
		5,538,000	4,941,000
		8,130,000	7,612,000
Less			
Current liabilities Creditors	14	1,816,000	1,308,000
Current taxation		468,000	324,000
Bank loans and overdrafts	19	169,000	95,000
Proposed dividend		339,000	387,000
		2,792,000	2,114,000
And less			
Deferred taxation	17	636,000	681,000
		4,702,000	4,817,000
Add			
Goodwill	18	959,000	288,000
		£5,661,000	£5,105,000

Changes in the composition of the group and the treatment of foreign currencies consequent upon the devaluation of the French franc are explained in Notes 1 and 2.

The Notes are on pages 12–19

Explanations

The Consolidated Balance Sheet is a statement showing the combined financial position of Alenco Limited and its eight subsidiary companies at 30th September, 1969 as if they were one company; it shows the source of the group's funds and how they were employed at that date.

The par value of the issued ordinary shares of Alenco Limited all of which are now owned by Charterhouse Industrial Holdings Limited

Some of the ordinary shares were originally issued above their par value i.e. at a premium; these premiums cannot be distributed as dividends

Comprising capital profits which are regarded as not normally being available for distribution by way of dividend

Representing the balance, after charging taxation and deducting dividends, of all other profits retained in the group

The par value of the issued preference shares of Alenco Limited all of which are now owned by Charterhouse Industrial Holdings Limited

Representing monies advanced by the proprietors by way of additional investment in the group

The proprietors' interest in the group

Those assets of a more or less permanent nature which enable the group to manufacture and sell its products

Representing rights which the group has acquired to manufacture certain specialised products

Consisting of raw materials, work in progress and finished parts

Amounts due to the group – largely from customers for sales made in the normal course of business

The group's favourable cash and bank balances and short term deposits

The gross tangible assets

Amounts owed by the group – largely for materials supplied and expenses incurred in the normal course of business

Taxation which has been charged against profits and which is currently payable

Short and medium term bank borrowings

The cost of the final dividend which it is recommended be paid on the ordinary shares

Taxation which has been charged against profits but which is not currently payable

The net tangible assets

Representing the excess of the cost of shares in subsidiary companies over the book value of their net tangible assets at the dates of acquisition

The total net assets

Alenco Limited **Balance Sheet**

As at 30th September	Note	1969	1968

Source of Funds

Ordinary share capital and reserves

	Note	1969	1968
Ordinary share capital	9	1,760,000	1,760,000
Share premium account		207,000	207,000
Other capital reserves	10	39,000	27,000
Revenue reserves	12	1,466,000	1,510,000
		3,472,000	3,504,000

Preference share capital

	9	165,000	165,000

Unsecured loan

	Note	1969	1968
Loan from Charterhouse Industrial Holdings Ltd	11	750,000	—
		£4,387,000	**£3,669,000**

Employment of Funds

Subsidiary companies

	Note	1969	1968
Shares at cost		2,520,000	1,746,000
Amounts owed by subsidiary companies		2,404,000	1,931,000
		4,924,000	3,677,000
Less: Amounts owed to subsidiary companies		38,000	6,000
		4,886,000	3,671,000

Other fixed assets

	Note	1969	1968
Leasehold building, equipment and vehicles	15	81,000	—

Current assets

	Note	1969	1968
Debtors	14	10,000	9,000
Bank balances and deposits	14	—	393,000
		10,000	402,000
		4,977,000	4,073,000

Less

Current liabilities

	Note	1969	1968
Creditors	14	41,000	14,000
Current taxation		1,000	1,000
Bank overdrafts		205,000	—
Proposed dividend		339,000	387,000
		586,000	402,000

And less

Deferred taxation

	Note	1969	1968
	17	4,000	2,000
		£4,387,000	**£3,669,000**

Signed on behalf of the Board P. N. M. Rudder, J. M. Blake, Directors

Changes in the composition of the group and the treatment of foreign currencies consequent upon the devaluation of the French franc are explained in Notes 1 and 2.

The Notes are on pages 12–19

Explanations

It is a requirement of the Companies Acts 1948 and 1967 that a holding company shall present to its shareholders not only a Consolidated Balance Sheet showing the group position (see pages 8 and 9) but also a Balance Sheet showing its own financial position; it shows the source of Alenco Limited's funds at 30th September, 1969 and that at that date they were mainly employed by investment in its subsidiary companies.

The par value of the issued ordinary shares of Alenco Limited all of which are now owned by Charterhouse Industrial Holdings Limited

Some of the ordinary shares were originally issued above their par value i.e. at a premium; these premiums cannot be distributed as dividends

Comprising capital profits which are regarded as not normally being available for distribution by way of dividend

Representing the balance, after charging taxation and deducting dividends, of all other profits retained in the company

The par value of the issued preference shares of Alenco Limited all of which are now owned by Charterhouse Industrial Holdings Limited

Representing monies advanced by the proprietors by way of additional investment in the company

The proprietors' interest in Alenco Limited

This is the cost to Alenco Limited of the 100% interests which it has in its eight subsidiary companies

Representing monies advanced by Alenco Limited to its subsidiary companies by way of additional investment

This is money lent to Alenco Limited by subsidiary companies which have funds surplus to their immediate requirements

Mainly building improvement and equipment costs associated with the new group headquarters at Alenco House, Slough

Sundry amounts due to the company

Last year there were favourable bank balances and short term deposits; this year there are bank borrowings

Sundry amounts owed by the company

Taxation which has been charged against profits and which is currently payable

Short term bank borrowings; last year there were favourable bank balances and short term deposits

The cost of the final dividend which it is recommended be paid on the ordinary shares

Taxation which has been charged against profits but which is not currently payable

Alenco Limited   **Notes**

and subsidiary companies

All figures (except those in Note 6) have been rounded off to the nearest £1,000

1   The Alenco Group

During the year the following changes have taken place in the composition of the group:

Acquisition

On 30th May, 1969 the whole of the issued share capital of H. & L. Austin Engineering Ltd and its subsidiary companies was acquired with effect from 1st October, 1968. For this purpose a loan of £750,000 was obtained from Charterhouse Industrial Holdings Ltd.

Disposal

On 12th August, 1969 the whole of the issued share capital of S. S. Stott Ltd was sold.

Accounting treatment

The cost of the shares in subsidiary companies shown in the Balance Sheet of Alenco Limited reflects the above transactions.

The Consolidated Profit and Loss Account includes the results of H. & L. Austin Engineering Limited and its subsidiary companies for the full year ended 30th September, 1969. The charge for interest on the loan from Charterhouse Industrial Holdings Limited amounted to £23,000 for four months ended on that date and would have amounted to £68,000 for a full year. The net assets of this sub-group are included in the Consolidated Balance Sheet.

The results and net assets of S. S. Stott Limited have been excluded from the accounts for the whole year.

2   Foreign currencies

For the purpose of preparing the Consolidated Balance Sheet foreign currencies have been converted into sterling at the rates of exchange ruling at 30th September, 1969. These rates reflect the devaluation of the French franc which took place on 11th August, 1969. This resulted in a decrease of £204,000 in the sterling value of the group's net assets which has been subtracted from the capital and revenue reserves (Notes 10 and 12).

For the purpose of preparing the Consolidated Profit and Loss Account, French francs have been converted into sterling at the rates of exchange ruling at 10th August, 1969, and 30th September, 1969, for periods of approximately $10\frac{1}{2}$ months and $1\frac{1}{2}$ months ended on those dates respectively. Other foreign currencies have been converted at the rates of exchange ruling at 30th September, 1969. The devaluation of the French franc has not had a material effect on the sales and net profit for the year.

3   Auditors' remuneration

		1969	1968
Alenco Limited		1,000	1,000
Subsidiary companies		15,000	11,000
		£16,000	£12,000

4   Interest

		1969	1968
Payable	On bank loans and overdrafts	41,000	28,000
Less: Receivable	On bank and other deposits	12,000	13,000
		£29,000	£15,000
Loan interest	Payable to Charterhouse Industrial Holdings Limited	£23,000	—

5   Turnover

Turnover comprises the invoiced value (after deduction of trade discounts and sales rebates) of goods despatched to and accepted by customers outside the group during the year.

6   Directors' emoluments

		1969	1968
Total emoluments	The emoluments of the directors of Alenco Limited were:		
	Fees as directors	750	750
	Remuneration as executives, including pension contributions	85,321	63,410
		£86,071	£64,160

Particulars of emoluments

Particulars of the emoluments (excluding all pension contributions) are stated below for those directors whose duties were mainly performed in the United Kingdom

	1969	1968
Chairman	£750	£750
Highest paid director	£10,834	£10,834
Number of other directors		
Not more than £2,500	—	3
£2,501– £5,000	—	—
£5,001– £7,500	1	—
£7,501–£10,000	4	2

Former director's pension	Pension paid to a former director of Alenco Limited	£5,000	£5,000

7   Depreciation

	1969	1968
The charge for depreciation for the year was:		
Fixed assets	313,000	296,000
Less: Adjustments on disposals	4,000	3,000
	309,000	293,000
Patents	15,000	12,000
	£324,000	£305,000

Depreciation is calculated on a straight line basis by reference to the original cost (reduced by investment grants) or subsequent revaluation of the assets. Substantially the assets are written off over the following periods:

Freehold land and buildings	Over 50 years or their estimated economic lives, whichever is the shorter
Leasehold land and buildings	Over the periods of the leases
Plant and equipment	Over 10 years
Motor vehicles	Over 5 years
Patents	Over their legal lives or their estimated economic lives if shorter

8 Taxation

	1969	1968
United Kingdom taxation based on the profit for the year		
Corporation Tax	387,000	382,000
Taxation equalisation account	5,000	—
	392,000	382,000
Less: Relief for foreign taxation	51,000	—
	£341,000	£382,000
Foreign taxation based on the profit for the year		
Company taxation	69,000	24,000
Taxation equalisation account	(3,000)	(5,000)
	£66,000	£19,000
Total	£407,000	£401,000

United Kingdom corporation tax has been provided at a rate of 45% (1968 – 42½%).

The charge for foreign company taxation was reduced by £30,000 (1968 – £10,000) by reason of differences between the bases used for calculating profits for taxation purposes and those adopted for accounts purposes. In 1969 this figure was mainly the result of change in the taxation treatment of certain accrued expenses.

9 Share capital

	Authorised	Issued and fully paid
The share capital at 30th September, 1969 was:		
Ordinary shares of 5/– each	£2,000,000	£1,760,000
6% cumulative preference shares of £1 each	£500,000	£165,000

10 Other capital reserves

	Alenco Ltd	Group
As at 30th September, 1968	27,000	620,000
Adjustments arising on disposal of former subsidiary company		
Profit on sale of shares	12,000	12,000
Reserve no longer available to the group	—	(15,000)
Decrease resulting from devaluation of the French franc (Note 2)	—	(115,000)
As at 30th September, 1969	£39,000	£502,000

11 Unsecured loan

	1969	1968
Unsecured loan from Charterhouse Industrial Holdings Limited – repayable at call	£750,000	

12 Revenue reserves

	Alenco Ltd	Group
As at 30th September, 1968	1,510,000	2,353,000
Adjustment arising on disposal of former subsidiary company		
Reserves relieved of accumulated losses	—	21,000
Adjustments relating to earlier years		
Taxation	—	(8,000)
Taxation equalisation account	(1,000)	(9,000)
Amount provided for proposed change in stockholding policy of a subsidiary company	—	(8,000)
Decrease resulting from devaluation of the French franc (Note 2)	—	(89,000)
Excess of dividends over profit dealt with in Alenco Limited	(43,000)	—
Balance of profit for the year	—	17,000
As at 30th September, 1969	£1,466,000	£2,277,000

Consolidation adjustments amounting to £59,000 (1968 – £77,000) have been made in connection with the overseas subsidiary companies and to this extent group revenue reserves are not available for distribution.

No provision has been made for additional taxation which would only be payable in the event of retained profits of foreign subsidiaries being distributed to the parent company. It is estimated that at 30th September, 1969 the liability attributable to retained post acquisition profits of foreign subsidiaries would not have exceeded £41,000 (1968 – £40,000).

13 Stocks

Stocks were in the main valued on the following bases:

Raw materials at the lower of cost and net realisable value

Finished parts and work in progress at the lower of cost and net realisable value. Cost in this context is confined to the cost of direct materials, variable wages and variable expenses; no addition has been made for fixed overhead expenses or depreciation.

14 Other Charterhouse Group indebtedness

Other amounts of indebtedness between Alenco group companies and their fellow subsidiaries of The Charterhouse Group Limited have been included in the accounts as follows:

	Alenco Limited		Group	
	1969	1968	1969	1968
In current assets				
Debtors	—	2,000	3,000	3,000
Bank balances and deposits	—	220,000	—	226,000
In current liabilities				
Creditors	3,000	4,000	12,000	10,000

Alenco Limited   Notes continued

and subsidiary companies

15 Fixed assets

Group

	1968	Disposals on sale of S. S. Stott Ltd	Additions on acquisition of H & L Austin Engineering Limited	Other movements during the year		
				Additions	Investment Grants	Disposals and other adjustments
Land and buildings						
Cost or valuation	1,521,000	87,000	14,000	63,000	—	—
Accumulated depreciation	96,000	7,000	2,000			—
	£1,425,000	£80,000	£12,000	£63,000	—	—
Plant, equipment and vehicles						
Cost or valuation	3,094,000	129,000	149,000	369,000	67,000	78,000
Accumulated depreciation	1,894,000	78,000	63,000			71,000
	£1,200,000	£51,000	£86,000	£369,000	£67,000	£7,000
Total						
Cost or valuation	4,615,000	216,000	163,000	432,000	67,000	78,000
Accumulated depreciation	1,990,000	85,000	65,000			71,000
	£2,625,000	£131,000	£98,000	£432,000	£67,000	£7,000

Fixed assets at 30th September, 1969 were made up as follows:

	Land Cost or valuation
As valued at 30th September, 1966	1,290,000
As valued at 31st December, 1959	—
At cost (after deducting investment grants)	149,000
	£1,439,000

Land and buildings largely comprise freehold factories. Other premises stated at cost i
and buildings held on short leases the book value of which was £103,000 (1968 – £

The additions on acquisition of H. & L. Austin Engineering Limited are shown after p
for depreciation of £9,000 for the period from 1st October, 1968 to 30th May, 1969.

Capital expenditure

Capital expenditure and investment grants receivable not dealt with in the consolidat
accounts were as follows:

	196 Estimated cost
Contracts placed	137,000
Authorised only	67,000
	£204,000

Alenco Limited

crease on French franc uation	1969	1968	Additions	Inter-group transfers	Disposals	Depreciation	1969
,000	1,439,000	—	52,000	—	—		52,000
,000	121,000	—	—	—	—	—	—
000	£1,318,000	—	£52,000	—	—	—	£52,000
000	3,223,000	—	25,000	14,000	3,000		36,000
000	1,991,000	—		5,000	1,000	3,000	7,000
000	£1,232,000	—	£25,000	£9,000	£2,000	£3,000	£29,000
000	4,662,000	—	77,000	14,000	3,000		88,000
000	2,112,000	—		5,000	1,000	3,000	7,000
000	£2,550,000	—	£77,000	£9,000	£2,000	£3,000	£81,000

Fixed assets at 30th September, 1969 were made up as follows:

quipment and vehicles st or ation	Book value		Land and buildings Cost or valuation	Book value	Plant, equipment and vehicles Cost or valuation	Book value
—	—		—	—	—	—
000	1,000		—	—	—	—
000	1,231,000		52,000	52,000	36,000	29,000
000	£1,232,000		£52,000	£52,000	£36,000	£29,000

Land and buildings represents the costs associated with the company's recent acquisition of a short term lease of Alenco House.

Capital expenditure and investment grants receivable not dealt with in the accounts were as follows:

1968 ed ost	Investment grants		1969 Estimated cost	Investment grants	1968 Estimated cost	Investment grants
000	41,000		5,000	—	—	—
00	1,000		—	—	—	—
00	£42,000		£5,000	—	—	—

16 Patents

As at 30th September, 1968	46,000
Acquired during the year	13,000
Decrease resulting from devaluation of the French franc (Note 2)	(2,000
Depreciation for the year	(15,000
As at 30th September, 1969	£ 42,000

17 Deferred taxation

	Alenco Limited		Group	
	1969	1968	1969	1968
Corporation tax				
Payable on 1st January, 1971	—	2,000	326,000	382,000
Payable on 1st June, 1971	—	—	24,000	—
	—	2,000	350,000	382,000
Taxation equalisation account				
As at 30th September, 1968	—	—	299,000	304,000
Adjustments arising from changes in the composition of the group	—	—	(5,000)	—
Adjustments relating to earlier years	1,000	—	9,000	—
Decrease resulting from devaluation of the French franc (Note 2)	—	—	(19,000)	—
Charged against profit for the year	3,000	—	2,000	(5,00
As at 30th September, 1969	4,000	—	286,000	299,00
Total	£ 4,000	£ 2,000	£ 636,000	£ 681,00

The taxation equalisation account represents taxation the payment of which is deferre
by reason of the fact that depreciation written off fixed assets for taxation purposes is t
date greater than the depreciation provided on those assets for accounts purposes.

18 Goodwill

As at 30th September, 1968	288,00
Adjustment in respect of the disposal of S. S. Stott Limited	102,0
Addition in respect of the acquisition of H. & L. Austin Engineering Limited	569,00
As at 30th September, 1969	£ 959,00

Goodwill represents the excess of the cost of shares in subsidiary companies over th
book value of their net tangible assets at the dates of acquisition. In the case of S. S. Sto
Limited the above adjustment arises because its net tangible assets at the date
acquisition exceeded the cost of shares.

19	**Bank loans and overdrafts**	A bank loan of £46,000 (1968 – £52,000) to a foreign subsidiary company was secured. Its bank overdraft of £39,000 (1968 – £43,000) was guaranteed by Alenco Limited.
		A bank overdraft of £6,000 (1968 – Nil) was secured
20	**Contingent liabilities**	There were contingent liabilities at 30th September, 1969 in respect of bills discounted by a foreign subsidiary company amounting to £214,000 (1968 – £271,000) and of guarantees of loans to employees amounting to £14,000 (1968 – £13,000)
21	**Unquoted trade investments**	The group has a 15% interest in the equity share capital of P. Arnold Sales and Engineering Limited, which is a company incorporated in Great Britain, and less than a 10% interest in the equity share capitals of two other companies. The Directors estimate that the value of these unquoted trade investments does not exceed their original cost of £2,000 which figure is included in the accounts under debtors.

22 Related companies

Subsidiary companies	Details of the company's subsidiary companies are shown on Page 24
Immediate holding company	The company's immediate holding company is Charterhouse Industrial Holdings Limited
Ultimate holding company	The company's ultimate holding company is The Charterhouse Group Limited, a company incorporated in Great Britain.

Report of the Auditors

Alenco Limited   **Source and Disposition Statement**

and subsidiary companies

For the year ended 30th September, 1969

Source

Profit before taxation	Profit attributable to proprietors before taxation	950,000
Depreciation		324,000
Disposal	Amount realised on disposal of S. S. Stott Limited	218,000
Unsecured loan	Received from Charterhouse Industrial Holdings Limited	750,000
		£ 2,242,000

Disposition

Acquisition	Acquisition of H. & L. Austin Engineering Limited		
	Increase in net tangible assets	276,000	
	Addition to goodwill	569,000	
			845,000
Expenditure on fixed assets	Land and buildings	63,000	
	Plant, equipment and vehicles	369,000	
		432,000	
	Less		
	Investment grants	67,000	
	Proceeds of sales	11,000	
			354,000
Expenditure on patents			13,000
Taxation paid			391,000
Proprietors' charges and appropriations	Management charge and loan interest	28,000	
	Dividends paid	546,000	
			574,000
Increase in working capital	Increase in stocks	343,000	
	Increase in debtors	566,000	
		909,000	
	Less: Increase in creditors	470,000	
			439,000
Foreign currency	Disposition resulting from the devaluaton of the French franc (Note 2 on Page 12)		33,000
			£ 2,649,000

Reduction in net cash and bank resources	**£ 407,000**

Explanation	The above statement shows the source of the group's cash funds during the year, their disposition and the resulting effect on the overall cash position.

The Alenco Group **Statistics and Ratios**

30th September	**1969**

Sales and Profits

Sales	£ 9,669,000
Profit attributable to proprietors before tax	£ 950,000
Profit attributable to proprietors after tax (adjusted)	£ 530,000

Consolidated Balance Sheet

Source of funds

Proprietors' funds	Share capital, reserves and unsecured loan	£ 5,661,000

Employment of funds

Fixed assets and patents	At cost or valuation less accumulated depreciation	2,592,000
Current assets	Stocks	2,685,000
	Debtors	2,786,000
	Cash and bank balances and deposits	67,000
		5,538,000
	Gross tangible assets	8,130,000
Less:		
Current liabilities	Creditors	1,816,000
	Current taxation	468,000
	Bank loans and overdrafts	169,000
	Proposed dividend	339,000
		2,792,000
And less:		
Deferred taxation		636,000
	Net tangible assets	4,702,000
Goodwill		959,000
Total net assets		£ 5,661,000

Ratios

Profit attributable to proprietors before tax as a percentage of:		
	Sales	9·8%
	Gross tangible assets	11·7%
	Net tangible assets	20·2%
	Proprietors' funds	16·8%
Profit attributable to proprietors after tax as a percentage of:		
	Proprietors' funds	9·4%

Expenditure on fixed assets	Net of investment grants	£ 354,000

1968	1967	1966	1965	1964	1963	1962	1961	1960
£8,085,000	£7,544,000	£7,708,000	£7,415,000	£6,924,000	£5,682,000	£5,410,000	£4,502,000	£2,467,000
£963,000	£951,000	£1,135,000	£1,281,000	£1,212,000	£831,000	£779,000	£679,000	£508,000
£560,000	£548,000	£679,000	£726,000	£555,000	£398,000	£393,000	£337,000	£256,000
£5,105,000	£4,981,000	£4,599,000	£3,830,000	£3,334,000	£3,007,000	£2,816,000	£2,582,000	£1,093,000
2,671,000	2,737,000	2,663,000	2,146,000	2,037,000	1,793,000	1,661,000	1,367,000	668,000
2,432,000	2,287,000	2,294,000	2,317,000	2,057,000	1,752,000	1,833,000	1,595,000	866,000
2,032,000	1,974,000	1,879,000	1,686,000	1,713,000	1,241,000	1,126,000	1,197,000	489,000
477,000	186,000	46,000	55,000	41,000	131,000	42,000	17,000	1,000
4,941,000	4,447,000	4,219,000	4,058,000	3,811,000	3,124,000	3,001,000	2,809,000	1,356,000
7,612,000	7,184,000	6,882,000	6,204,000	5,848,000	4,917,000	4,662,000	4,176,000	2,024,000
1,308,000	1,118,000	1,069,000	1,116,000	1,196,000	1,000,000	940,000	981,000	274,000
324,000	358,000	394,000	445,000	395,000	300,000	380,000	320,000	273,000
95,000	109,000	282,000	383,000	547,000	456,000	449,000	181,000	82,000
387,000	255,000	202,000	181,000	178,000	135,000	121,000	108,000	66,000
2,114,000	1,840,000	1,947,000	2,125,000	2,316,000	1,891,000	1,890,000	1,590,000	695,000
681,000	651,000	618,000	531,000	480,000	301,000	227,000	250,000	236,000
4,817,000	4,693,000	4,317,000	3,548,000	3,052,000	2,725,000	2,545,000	2,336,000	1,093,000
288,000	288,000	282,000	282,000	282,000	282,000	271,000	246,000	—
£5,105,000	£4,981,000	£4,599,000	£3,830,000	£3,334,000	£3,007,000	£2,816,000	£2,582,000	£1,093,000
11·9%	12·6%	14·7%	17·3%	17·5%	14·6%	14·4%	15·1%	20·6%
12·7%	13·2%	16·5%	20·6%	20·7%	16·9%	16·7%	16·3%	25·1%
20·0%	20·3%	26·3%	36·1%	39·7%	30·5%	30·6%	29·1%	46·5%
18·9%	19·1%	24·7%	33·5%	36·4%	27·6%	27·7%	26·3%	46·5%
11·0%	11·0%	14·7%	19·0%	16·6%	13·2%	14·0%	13·1%	23 4%
£239,000	£151,000	£256,000	£336,000	£412,000	£305,000	£453,000	£287,000	£113,000

The Alenco Group

As at 30th September, 1969

Name of company	Locations	Principal activities	Country of incorporation
Alenco Limited	Slough	Management and holding company owning directly (or indirectly where indicated) the whole of the issued share capitals, comprising preference and ordinary shares, of the following subsidiary companies.	Great Britain

United Kingdom

British Ermeto Corporation Limited	Maidenhead Barnstaple Slough	Manufacturers of 'Ermeto' pipe fittings and valves for the highest industrial pressures. Suppliers of flexible rubber hose and ranges of hose-end fittings.	Great Britain
Kay & Company (Engineers) Limited	Bolton	Manufacturers of 'Kontite' and other high quality gunmetal pipe fittings, valves and cocks for the building trade and for the lowest range of industrial pressures.	Great Britain
Simplifix Couplings Limited *Incorporating* *S. & C. (Plastics) Limited* *a fellow subsidiary company*	Slough	Manufacturers of 'Simplifix' pipe fittings and valves for the medium industrial pressure range. Extruders of nylon and thermoplastic tube and formers of nylon air and electrical coils.	Great Britain
H. & L. Austin Engineering Limited *Incorporating* *William Rose Limited and* *Hilyn Industrial Equipment Limited* *its wholly owned subsidiaries*	Enfield	Manufacturers of industrial hoses, thread sealing tape, tubes and mouldings – mainly in polytetrafluorethylene (PTFE).	Great Britain
Kent Nail Works Limited	Barnstaple Slough	Manufacturers of upholstery nails, plated and plastic-capped drawing pins.	Great Britain

Overseas

Ermeto S.A. *Incorporating* *Hydexco S.A.R.L.* *its wholly owned subsidiary*	Paris Blois	Manufacturers of 'Ermeto' products and high pressure valves for industry and certain accessories for the motor trade. Suppliers of flexible rubber hose and ranges of hose-end fittings.	France
De Ridder N.V. *Incorporating* *Ermeto Productie Maatschappij N.V.* *its wholly owned subsidiary*	Naarden	Manufacturers of 'Ermeto' products and selling company for certain other engineering products.	Holland
Patex S.A.	Glarus	A company holding 7% of the shares of Ermeto S.A. and certain patents.	Switzerland

H. & L. Austin Engineering Limited owns all the issued share capital in a non-trading company Hilyn N.V. incorporated in Holland

The Alenco Group **Graphs**

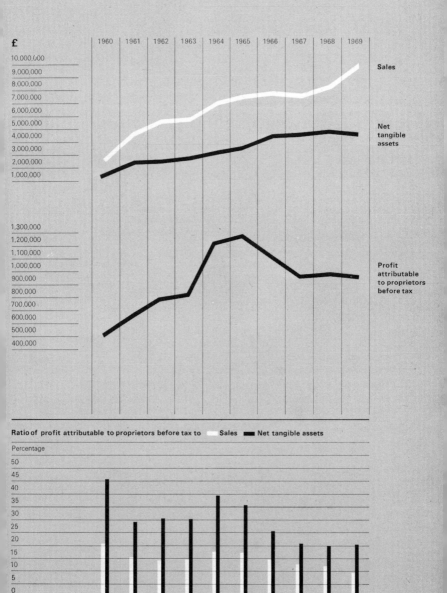

Sales

Net tangible assets

Profit attributable to proprietors before tax

Ratio of profit attributable to proprietors before tax to ☐ Sales ■ Net tangible assets

Appendix D

REPORT & ACCOUNTS 1970

1970 IN BRIEF	1
NOTICE OF MEETING	2
FINANCIAL CALENDAR	3
CHAIRMAN'S STATEMENT	4
DIRECTORS	8
REPORT OF THE DIRECTORS	8
GKN—1970	17
MEMBER COMPANIES	30
ASSOCIATED COMPANIES	32
CONSOLIDATED PROFIT AND LOSS ACCOUNT	33
CONSOLIDATED BALANCE SHEET	34
BALANCE SHEET	35
NOTES ON PROFIT AND LOSS ACCOUNT	36
NOTES ON BALANCE SHEETS	38
REPORT OF THE AUDITORS	42
FINANCIAL INFORMATION 1961-1970	44
STOCKHOLDERS	48

Registered Office
GROUP HEAD OFFICE,
SMETHWICK, WARLEY,
WORCESTERSHIRE

London Office
GKN HOUSE,
22 KINGSWAY,
LONDON WC2

1970 IN BRIEF
(IN STERLING AND VARIOUS OTHER CURRENCIES)

THE 1969 FIGURES HAVE BEEN ADJUSTED TO DEAL
WITH JOHN LYSAGHT (AUSTRALIA) LIMITED
AS IF IT HAD BEEN AN ASSOCIATED COMPANY
IN THAT YEAR (see Report of Directors)

TURNOVER
CHIFFRE D'AFFAIRES
UMSATZ
CIFRA DE NEGOCIOS

SURPLUS ON TRADING
BÉNÉFICE BRUT D'EXPLOITATION
UEBERSCHUSS
EXCEDENTE COMERCIAL

PROFIT BEFORE TAX
BÉNÉFICE AVANT DÉDUCTION DES IMPÔTS
GEWINN VOR STEUERN
BENEFICIO SIN DEDUCCIÓN DE IMPUESTOS

TAXATION
IMPÔTS
STEUERN
IMPUESTOS

PROFIT AFTER TAX
BÉNÉFICE IMPÔTS DÉDUITS
GEWINN NACH STEUERN
BENEFICIO DESPUÉS DE IMPUESTOS

NET PROFIT ATTRIBUTABLE
TO ORDINARY STOCKHOLDERS
BÉNÉFICE NET IMPUTABLE AUX PORTEURS D'ACTIONS ORDINAIRES
DEN STAMMAKTIONÄREN VERTEILBARER NETTO GEWINN
BENEFICIO NETO IMPUTABLE A ACCIONISTAS ORDINARIOS

COST OF ORDINARY DIVIDENDS
VALEUR DES DIVIDENDES ORDINAIRES
GEWINNAUSSCHUETTUNG AUF DIE STAMMAKTIEN
COSTO DE DIVIDENDOS ORDINARIOS

PROFIT RETAINED
BÉNÉFICE REPORTÉ
GEWINNVORTRAG
BENEFICIO RETENIDO

EQUITY INTEREST
INTÉRÊT DES PORTEURS D'ACTIONS ORDINAIRES
EIGENMITTEL
INTERÉS DE LOS ACCIONISTAS ORDINARIOS

NET PROFIT TO EQUITY INTEREST
BÉNÉFICE NET RELATIF À L'INTÉRÊT DES PORTEURS D'ACTIONS ORDINAIRES
NETTO GEWINN IM VERGLEICH MIT EIGENMITTEL
RELACIÓN DE BENEFICIO NETO AL INTERÉS SOBRE ACCIONES ORDINARIAS

TOTAL NET ASSETS EMPLOYED
TOTAL DE L'ACTIF UTILISÉ
GESAMTAKTIVEN
TOTAL DE ACTIVO NETO UTILIZADO

PROFIT TO TOTAL NET ASSETS EMPLOYED
BÉNÉFICE RELATIF À L'ACTIF NET TOTAL UTILISÉ
GEWINN IN BEZUG AUF GESAMTAKTIVEN
RELACIÓN DE BENEFICIO AL TOTAL DE ACTIVO NETO UTILIZADO

EARNINGS PER ORDINARY SHARE
PRODUIT NET PAR ACTION ORDINAIRE
GEWINN JE STAMMAKTIE
BENEFICIO POR ACCIÓN ORDINARIA

DIVIDENDS PER ORDINARY SHARE (GROSS)
DIVIDENDES PAR ACTION ORDINAIRE (BRUT)
DIVIDENDE JE STAMMAKTIE (BRUTTO)
DIVIDENDO POR ACCIÓN ORDINARIA (BRUTO)

EXPENDITURE ON FIXED ASSETS
DÉPENSES SUR ACTIF IMMOBILISÉ
INVESTITIONEN IM SACHANLAGEVERMÖGEN
GASTOS EN ACTIVOS FIJOS

DEPRECIATION
AMORTISSEMENT
ABSCHREIBUNGEN
AMORTIZACIÓN

"CASH FLOW" *(DEPRECIATION AND RETAINED PROFITS)*
AMORTISSEMENT ET BÉNÉFICE REPORTÉ
ABSCHREIBUNGEN UND UEBERTRAGENDER GEWINN
AMORTIZACIÓN Y BENEFICIO RETENIDO

£	AUSTRALIAN $ 2·145 = £	DEUTSCHE MARK 8·78 = £	USA $ 2·40 = £	FRS SUISSES 10·30 = £	RAND 1·70 = £	GUILDER 8·70 = £	SVENSKA KRONOR 12·50 = £
485·2	1,040·8	4,260·1	1,164·5	4,997·6	824·8	4,221·2	6,065·0
421·3	903·7	3,699·0	1,011·1	4,339·4	716·2	3,665·3	5,266·3
37·5	80·4	329·3	90·0	386·3	63·8	326·3	468·8
30·8	66·1	270·4	73·9	317·2	52·4	268·0	385·0
43·1	92·4	378·4	103·4	443·9	73·3	375·0	538·8
35·4	75·9	310·8	85·0	364·6	60·2	308·0	442·5
21·0	45·0	184·4	50·4	216·3	35·7	182·7	262·5
17·5	37·5	153·7	42·0	180·3	29·8	152·3	218·8
22·1	47·4	194·0	53·0	227·6	37·6	192·3	276·3
17·9	38·4	157·2	43·0	184·4	30·4	155·7	223·8
21·2	45·5	186·1	50·9	218·4	36·0	184·4	265·0
17·7	38·0	155·4	42·5	182·3	30·1	154·0	221·3
13·2	28·3	115·9	31·7	136·0	22·4	114·8	165·0
11·6	24·9	101·8	27·8	119·5	19·7	100·9	145·0
8·0	17·2	70·2	19·2	82·4	13·6	69·6	100·0
6·1	13·1	53·6	14·6	62·8	10·4	53·1	76·3
256·4	550·0	2,251·2	615·4	2,640·9	435·9	2,230·7	3,205·0
234·3	502·6	2,057·2	562·3	2,413·3	398·3	2,038·4	2,928·8
8·3%	8·3%	8·3%	8·3%	8·3%	8·3%	8·3%	8·3%
7·6%	7·6%	7·6%	7·6%	7·6%	7·6%	7·6%	7·6%
299·6	642·6	2,630·5	719·0	3,085·9	509·3	2,606·5	3,745·0
280·9	602·5	2,466·3	674·2	2,893·3	477·5	2,443·8	3,511·3
14·9%	14·9%	14·9%	14·9%	14·9%	14·9%	14·9%	14·9%
13·3%	13·3%	13·3%	13·3%	13·3%	13·3%	13·3%	13·3%
20·5p	$0·44cts	DM1·80pf	$0·49cts	FR2·11cts	Rand0·35cts	DF1·78cts	KR2·56ore
18·1p	$0·39cts	DM1·59pf	$0·43cts	FR1·86cts	Rand0·31cts	DF1·57cts	KR2·26ore
12·8p	$0·27cts	DM1·12pf	$0·31cts	FR1·32cts	Rand0·22cts	DF1·11cts	KR1·60ore
11·9p	$0·26cts	DM1·04pf	$0·29cts	FR1·23cts	Rand0·20cts	DF1·04cts	KR1·49ore
22·5	48·3	197·6	54·0	231·8	38·3	195·8	281·3
17·3	37·1	151·9	41·5	178·2	29·4	150·5	216·3
14·7	31·5	129·1	35·3	151·4	25·0	127·9	183·8
13·8	29·6	121·2	33·1	142·1	23·5	120·1	172·5
21·0	45·0	184·4	50·4	216·3	35·7	182·7	262·5
18·9	40·5	165·9	45·4	194·7	32·1	164·4	236·3

NOTICE OF MEETING

Notice is hereby given that the seventy-first annual general meeting of Guest, Keen and Nettlefolds, Limited will be held at Group Head Office, Smethwick, Warley, Worcestershire, on Tuesday the 11th day of May 1971 at 12.15 p.m.

The business of the meeting will be:

1 To consider and, if thought fit, pass the following resolutions as ordinary resolutions:

(a) That the report of the Directors and the audited statement of accounts for the 52 weeks ended 2nd January 1971 be approved and adopted.

(b) That a final dividend on the ordinary stock of 9p per £1 unit for the 52 weeks ended 2nd January 1971 be declared payable to ordinary stockholders on the register at the close of business on 26th April 1971.

2 To elect Directors.

3 To fix the remuneration of the Auditors.

4 To transact any other business which may be transacted at an annual general meeting.

Any member of the Company entitled to attend and vote may appoint another person (whether a member or not) as his proxy to attend and vote instead of him. A form of proxy is included with this annual report for the use of members who are unable to attend the meeting. To be effective this must be deposited at the registered office of the Company not less than forty-eight hours before the meeting.

By order of the Board
J. F. HOWARD,
Secretary

Group Head Office,
Smethwick,
Warley,
Worcestershire

15th April 1971

ALTHOUGH THIS ANNUAL REPORT IS SENT TO BOTH ORDINARY AND LOAN STOCKHOLDERS, ONLY HOLDERS OF ORDINARY STOCK ARE ENTITLED TO ATTEND OR VOTE AT THIS MEETING. THERE WILL BE AVAILABLE FOR INSPECTION BY MEMBERS AT THE REGISTERED OFFICE OF THE COMPANY DURING USUAL BUSINESS HOURS FROM THE DATE OF THIS NOTICE UNTIL THE CONCLUSION OF THE ANNUAL GENERAL MEETING:

(a) PARTICULARS OF TRANSACTIONS OF DIRECTORS AND OF THEIR FAMILY INTERESTS IN SHARES OR DEBENTURES OF THE COMPANY AND ITS SUBSIDIARIES AND

(b) COPIES OR PARTICULARS OF CONTRACTS OF SERVICE (UNLESS EXPIRING OR DETERMINABLE BY THE EMPLOYING COMPANY WITHOUT PAYMENT OF COMPENSATION WITHIN ONE YEAR) OF DIRECTORS WITH THE COMPANY OR WITH ANY OF ITS SUBSIDIARIES.

DIVIDENDS ON ORDINARY STOCK

INTERIM

announced 18th August 1970
paid 6th October 1970

FINAL

announced 24th March 1971
to be paid 13th May 1971

INTEREST ON LOAN CAPITAL

payable on 28th June and
28th December 1971 on

$6\frac{1}{2}$% convertible unsecured loan stock
and
6% convertible unsecured loan stock

For conversion terms see page 41; in
May 1971 the conversion rights for
the 6% loan stock become exercisable and
remain exercisable for the $6\frac{1}{2}$% loan stock.

RESULTS

HALF YEAR ENDED 4th JULY 1970

announced 18th August 1970

FULL YEAR ENDED 2nd JANUARY 1971

announced 24th March 1971

FINANCE ACT 1965

CAPITAL GAINS TAX

In certain circumstances the liability of a
stockholder to long term capital gains tax
is computed by reference to the market
value of shares on 6th April 1965.

The market value of £1 GKN ordinary stock
on 6th April 1965 (adjusted for the
1 for 3 scrip issue in 1970) was 183p.

NOTE: THIS ANNUAL REPORT WAS RELEASED
TO THE PRINTERS ON 24th MARCH 1971.

STATEMENT BY THE CHAIRMAN

SIR RAYMOND BROOKES

Necessarily this Annual Report is released to the printers on March 24th and cannot therefore take cognisance of the Government's Budget proposals due for announcement on March 30th 1971.

TRADING RESULTS
For 1970 we are pleased to report another record year, well ahead of the sound performance in 1969. On a comparable basis we increased :

Profit before tax from
£35·4 million in 1969 to
£43·1 million in 1970

Earnings per £1 ordinary share
from 18·1p to 20·5p

Earnings on net assets employed
from 13·3% to 14·9%

We had good reason to expect and perhaps deserved more but the cumulative misfortunes of strikes, both internal and external, and the Rolls-Royce debacle have taken their toll. The Sankey strike alone is calculated to have cost the Group £1·8 million in loss of profits. In relation to the Rolls-Royce situation we have deemed it necessary to provide £1·5 million against possible losses. These exceptional burdens totalling £3·3 million had the effect of seriously distorting results in the second half of the year.

PRESENTATION OF
REPORT AND ACCOUNTS
Influenced by the increasing significance of our investments in associated companies and mindful of the progressive effect which our arrangements with The Broken Hill Proprietary Company Limited will have on the measure of our participation in John Lysaght (Australia) Limited, we have introduced changes in the presentation of the profit and loss account, balance sheet and report appropriate to the reflection of these circumstances.

The salient feature is that we have brought into the profit and loss account, at 'profit before tax', profits or losses attributable to the GKN investments in associated companies. Such inclusion is subject to two prior conditions, which are :

1. That the GKN investment is 20% or more of the total equity capital of the associate

2. That GKN is participant to management or the determination of policy.

This method of presentation conforms with modern accounting practice and with the views of the Institutes of Chartered Accountants.

Stockholders are asked to give special attention to pages 8 and 9 of the report which explains more fully the nature and effect of this departure from our more traditional form of reporting.

THE YEAR IN RETROSPECT
Operating conditions have been a mixture of the significantly favourable and unfavourable. On the credit side we have on balance benefited in the first half year from a world steel shortage. On the other hand, three major internal strikes—at Guest, Keen, Williams, India, Scottish Stampings and GKN Sankey—caused exceptional reductions in profitability. In the United Kingdom we have traded against an economic background of inflation at an unprecedented rate ; overseas, we have had a variety of economic conditions —inflation, recession, monetary restriction or external trade imbalance leading in some cases to governmental control. High interest rates continued world-wide.

Group sales were at a record rate : the total of £485 million was, on a comparable basis £64 million more than in 1969. Sales per working day (excluding John Lysaght (Australia) Limited) rose from £1·75 million at the beginning of the year to a peak of £2·10 million in November, ending the year at a very slightly lower level. The reduced level of sales in December may be indicative of the trend for the early months of 1971.

UNITED KINGDOM OPERATIONS
Compared with 1969 :

Turnover increased from £359 million to £408 million

Surplus on trading increased from £26·1 million to £29·0 million

% Surplus decreased from 7·3% to 7·1%

All in all not bad particularly when related to the back-cloth of industrial irresponsibility and economic palsy against which management has had to perform. In these circumstances it has not always been possible for prices to keep pace with costs.

For the car, truck and tractor industries 1970 was a lean year, inevitably affecting the results of GKN companies orientated toward them. Disregarding special and exceptional provisions, Forgings achieved an improved and fair performance and Transmissions did well to maintain their position. Sankey inevitably reflecting the adversities of the prolonged strike fell back but the undertone was encouraging. Vandervell although improving toward the end of the year was nevertheless disappointing.

Improving or recovering areas, some of which are not yet secure or satisfactory, include Bolts & Nuts, Engineering, Building Supplies & Services. BKL Alloys was adversely affected by the development of their new factory at Redditch. Screws & Fasteners turned in an improved and typically steady performance.

The really 'high fliers', materially assisted by exceptionally heavy demands, were Rolled & Bright Steel and Distribution which includes steel, fasteners, engineers' tools and hardware, etc.

Viewing the United Kingdom performance as a whole, the conclusion is that our alleged vulnerability to the vicissitudes of the vehicle industries may have been over-emphasised and that the results once again demonstrate strengths inherent in the selective 'spread' of our activities, allied to the philosophy of management which achieves a sensible balance between effective delegation and federated cohesion. There is, however, no sense of complacency; on the contrary, we constantly question and seek to improve our competences.

OVERSEAS OPERATIONS
Compared with 1969 adjusted to exclude John Lysaght (Australia) Limited):

Turnover increased from £63 million to £77 million

Surplus on trading from £4·7 million to £8·5 million

Surplus from 7·5% to 11·0%

In themselves these figures are most encouraging and even more so when associated with those of Lysaght Australia. Viewed as a whole our foreign operations and investments have the potential to

contribute an increasing proportion of Group activity and earnings.

In Australia GKN (Aust.) improved but more is needed : Lysaghts (whose figures are not included above) although losing momentum at the year end, did exceptionally well.

In India, Guest, Keen, Williams achieved significant and most necessary improvement and would have done better if raw material supplies had been adequate.

New Zealand maintained the previous year's recovery.

In Scandinavia and Holland, Stenman declined and immediate prospects are discouraging.

In Southern Africa, through GKN (S.A.) there was a pronounced improvement.

In relation to overseas affairs, it is necessary to refer to our interests in Uni-Cardan. This is a 'holding' company with sixteen subsidiaries and associates operating factories in West Germany, France and Italy. The major products are transmission drives for automotive, agricultural and general engineering applications, universal and constant velocity joints, forgings and sintered products.

Uni-Cardan is a virile and successful organisation, whose turnover in 1970 approximated £62 million. In the European Common Market countries it has in its specialised field deservedly established a situation of commercial and technical leadership. Forecasts for the ensuing five years indicate an exceptionally high rate of growth. At the end of 1970 GKN held 39·5% of the equity and negotiations directed toward increasing this proportion to not less than 50% are in an advanced state.

In this connection Stockholders will appreciate the significance of the inter-national strategic values attaching to the closer co-ordination of technical and commercial policies between Uni-Cardan and our important United Kingdom subsidiary, GKN Birfield Transmissions.

EXPORTS
With justification we are proud of our export performance. Since 1967, when we adopted a new approach to the international marketing of our products, Group exports have increased by more than 150% and our

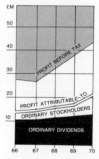

PROFITS AND DIVIDENDS

PROFIT BEFORE TAX

PROFIT ATTRIBUTABLE TO ORDINARY STOCKHOLDERS

ORDINARY DIVIDENDS

£M
50
40
30
20
10

66   67   68   69   70

export proportion (of total sales) has advanced from 7% to 12% in 1970. Yet, as essentially a component manufacturer and supplier of other industrial 'intermediates', GKN is not a 'natural' exporter. At £51·6 million in 1970 (1969—£40·2 million) —an increase of 28%—our physical exports from the United Kingdom are themselves of national significance ; indirect exports (of GKN components incorporated in our customers' products sold overseas) contributed an estimated further £110 million (1969—£95 million) to Britain's export effort. The increase in 1970 over the previous year was especially heartening when world trading conditions worsened because of the American recession and the adverse movement of cost trends, particularly in the United Kingdom.

As labour and other costs continue to move against us, it will become increasingly difficult to maintain this high rate of export expansion. With demand stagnant in the United Kingdom and in some of the overseas areas in which we operate, the maintenance, however, of an effective export expansion policy continues to be given high priority.

CAPITAL EXPENDITURE

United Kingdom	£19·3 million
Overseas (excluding Lysaghts)	£3·2 million
	£22·5 million

At the end of 1970 outstanding approvals totalled £20 million, of which £18 million related to the United Kingdom and £2 million to overseas operations.

Although as influenced by earlier commitments expenditure in 1970 was a record, restraint was exercised on new approvals, particularly for the United Kingdom. For the present these selective attitudes will be maintained.

Expenditure by John Lysaght (Australia) Limited, which is excluded from the above table, was £7·4 million ; this high figure reflects the commencement of expenditure on the development of the plant at Western-port to which reference was made last year. Outstanding approvals at the end of 1970 for John Lysaght (Australia) Limited totalled £44·2 million.

FINANCE

The effect on profits of inflation, and the demands for industry to absorb more and

more of the cost increases imposed on it, are now given general prominence in company statements, but it must also be recognised that these pressures, which have persisted over the last ten years and accelerated since 1968, have probably had a more severe effect on corporate liquidity in most countrie of the world than the tight money policies imposed by governments. In conditions prevailing in 1970, it was virtually impossibl for industry in the United Kingdom to finance the maintenance—let alone the expansion—of operations from its own cash flow.

The deficiency has had to be met by capital markets, the demands on which, coupled with an insistence by investors that long ter interest rates must also have some regard to continuance of inflation, have forced long term interest rates up to a level which would have astounded our predecessors. Suggestions that these rates might go even higher are frightening and must cause company policies on investment and pricinc of products to be examined critically. Even under present conditions investment overall will have to be directed only into projects where the pay-off is much higher than it has been formerly and weak corporate liquidity (resulting in some cases in liquidations) increases the risk element which has to be taken into account.

The Group source and disposition of funds statement included in the report of the Directors (page 15) shows that the mo notable factor affecting liquidity during 197 was the substantial increase in stocks. This feature applied both in the United Kingdom and overseas and was in the main a direct reflection of higher volume, inflation and the disruptive effect of strikes.

To safeguard the Group's liquid position we felt it necessary in the middle of 1970 to issue £20 million of 10½% guaranteed debenture stock at a price of 98¾, the net proceeds of which, after paying commissions and expenses, amounted to £19·45 million ; of this £5·5 million was received in 1970 and the balance in January 1971. This is specifically intended to provide funds for financing United Kingdom operations. Overseas, £950,000 was raised by companies in Scandinavia to meet their requirements. Additional funds needed by other overseas companies have been provided by Bank loans. Whilst the rates of interest on these loans are currently relatively attractive, we have to bear the exchange risk. In this respect, some relaxation of Exchange Control regulations on outflows of funds from the United Kingdom would be welcome.

The financing of the John Lysaght (Australia) Limited expansion is being carried out as a separate operation ; during 1970 that company issued a debenture for $40 million on the Australian market at interest rates varying between $8\frac{1}{2}$% to 9%. The aim is for John Lysaght (Australia) Limited to finance the whole of phase I of the Westernport development by issues of loan capital and internal cash flow.

As at the end of 1970 Group borrowing, including guarantees, etc., amounted to £45 million which represents only 30% of the limit imposed under the Articles of Association. GKN is still comparatively lowly geared and, therefore, has the ability to raise further substantial debt finance. Whether this ability will be used in future will depend entirely on conditions at the time, but our aim is to use our financial strength to the maximum for the benefit of the ordinary Stockholders.

THE PROSPECT FOR 1971

An assessment which accepted the figures projected by our thoroughly prepared business plans, budgets and forecasts, and discounted them by the historic margin of short-fall, would justify forecasting another major advance in 1971. I am disinclined to do this largely because of the immediate unpredictability of the United Kingdom economic/industrial environment.

The chronic and persisting lack of effective growth in United Kingdom productivity has at its roots years of unrewarding obsession with outdated political prejudices and discredited economic theories, enforced adherence to restrictive practices, confusion of liberty with licence, excessive tax disincentives, diminishing cash flows and depleted investment confidence. This situation is alien to the real preferences of our people, is not truly reflective of their capabilities and frustrates legitimate aspirations for enhanced living standards.

In these circumstances confrontation between Government and extremists who, without regard to the real wishes and best interests of the majority, seek to maintain

disruptive power and privilege outside the law was and is inevitable. Necessarily these problems must be resolved before safely embarking upon fiscal/economic policies directed towards significant economic expansion. Having so quickly dissipated the questionable and transient values of the enforced 1967 devaluation we must, as a first priority, avoid another.

Accordingly, for the United Kingdom economy as a whole it is prudent to assume modest growth, continuing but diminishing inflation, and in the short term a high level of intentionally inspired industrial unrest.

Despite these discouraging portents and the expectation that for the first half of 1971 results may fall short of the exceptionally good figures for 1970, my belief is that in Britain the nation is at long last realistically facing and resolving fundamental problems and that the outcome will be successful. In this situation, and viewing the year as a whole, I expect GKN to continue to move ahead of national trends. Overseas the prospect is that we should at least maintain last year's good figures.

ACKNOWLEDGEMENTS

To my Board colleagues, and Directors, management and personnel throughout the world, my gratitude for the coalescence of commitment and capability which protects our heritage, vitalises our present and will assuredly sustain our future.

Raymond Brookes

RAYMOND BROOKES

24th March 1971

REPORT OF
THE DIRECTORS

DIRECTORS

SIR RAYMOND BROOKES
CHAIRMAN AND CHIEF EXECUTIVE

SIR HENRY WILSON SMITH, KCB, KBE
DEPUTY CHAIRMAN
(NON-EXECUTIVE)

JAMES F. INSCH
DEPUTY CHAIRMAN AND MANAGING DIRECTOR

WILLIAM W. FEA
DEPUTY CHAIRMAN
ADMINISTRATION AND SPECIAL OPERATIONS

CLAUDE C. BIRCH
CHAIRMAN
GKN CASTINGS LTD.
GKN FORGINGS LTD.
GKN POWDER MET. LTD.
VANDERVELL PRODUCTS LTD.

SIR ANTHONY BOWLBY, Bt.
CORPORATE DIRECTOR
CHAIRMAN
GKN BOLTS & NUTS LTD.
GKN SCREWS & FASTENERS LTD.

SIR DOUGLAS BRUCE-GARDNER, Bt.
CHAIRMAN
GKN ROLLED & BRIGHT STEEL LTD.

G. TREVOR HOLDSWORTH
GROUP CONTROLLER

H. SPENCER KILLICK, MC, TD
CHAIRMAN
GKN SANKEY LTD.

RICHARD G. LEWIS, TD
CHAIRMAN
GKN ENGINEERING LTD.

STEPHEN LLOYD
CHAIRMAN
GKN DISTRIBUTORS LTD.

LESLIE MAXWELL-HOLROYD
CHAIRMAN
GKN BIRFIELD TRANSMISSIONS LTD.

WILLIAM A. NICOL
(NON-EXECUTIVE)

MARK S. PEARCE
CHAIRMAN
GKN BUILDING SUPPLIES & SERVICES LTD.

FREDERICK C. ROWBOTTOM
GROUP FINANCIAL DIRECTOR

SIR CHARLES WHEELER, KBE
(NON-EXECUTIVE)

GROUP SECRETARY:
JOHN F. HOWARD

The Directors present their annual report together with the audited accounts of the Company for the 52 weeks ended 2nd January 1971.

GROUP RESULTS

Two significant changes affect the accounts for 1970, the first concerning John Lysaght (Australia) Limited :

(i) As reported in the interim statement, the arrangements necessary to implement the proposals under which Guest, Keen and Nettlefolds, Limited and The Broken Hill Proprietary Company Limited ('BHP') now jointly own and control John Lysaght Australia were concluded in July 1970. In order to equalise the GKN and BHP shareholdings, John Lysaght Australia then issued to BHP an additional 16,992,361 shares, but BHP subscribed only 1 cent for each share of A$1 nominal value issued at A$4·20. Although John Lysaght Australia is no longer a legal subsidiary of GKN, the Group continues for the time being, and until BHP are required to subscribe further capital, to participate in profits and dividends in approximately the same proportion as hitherto, i.e., 75·65%. Accordingly the Group turnover and trading surplus, which up to 1969 included John Lysaght Australia as a subsidiary, exclude John Lysaght Australia in 1970. The Group's proportion of John Lysaght Australia's pre-tax earnings is, however, now included in the profit before tax earnings of the Group under the heading 'share of profits less losses of associated companies'. In order to facilitate comparison with the previous year, the consolidated profit and loss account includes 1969 figures adjusted to deal with John Lysaght Australia as if it had been an associated company.

(ii) The other significant change is that for the first time the Group share of the pre-tax earnings of other associated companies has been included.

Realising that views may have been formed of Group results for the year based on the interim report for the six months ended

4th July 1970 which included John Lysaght Australia as a subsidiary, the following comparison may be helpful ; this includes the 1970 results of John Lysaght Australia as though it had remained a subsidiary for that year and, in respect of associated companies, includes only dividends received instead of underlying earnings :

TURNOVER (excluding inter-group sales)	1970 52 WEEKS £M	1969 53 WEEKS £M
	584·03	511·71
SURPLUS ON TRADING	46·11	38·33
Investment income and interest receivable	1·56	2·13
Interest payable	3·76	3·33
PROFIT BEFORE TAXATION	43·91	37·13
Taxation	21·20	18·31
NET PROFIT FOR THE YEAR	22·71	18·82
Exceptional items	0·14	0·25
	22·57	19·07
Profit attributable to outside shareholders' interests	1·85	1·34
NET PROFIT ATTRIBUTABLE TO ORDINARY STOCKHOLDERS	20·72	17·73
Earnings per share (1969 adjusted for 1 for 3 scrip issue in 1970)	20·0p	18·1p

The inclusion of John Lysaght Australia as an associated company in the consolidated profit and loss account on page 33 has had no effect on the earnings attributable to ordinary Stockholders of Guest, Keen and Nettlefolds, Limited, nor therefore on the earnings per ordinary share ; the difference between such earnings shown above and those shown in the consolidated profit and loss account, amounting to £0·49 million (0·5p per share) is wholly attributable to the inclusion of underlying earnings of associated companies other than John Lysaght Australia instead of dividends received as hitherto.

The results of John Lysaght Australia are shown separately under the heading 'associated companies' on page 12 and hereafter in this report ; the comparison of Group trading and results between 1970 and 1969 is on the basis of the exclusion of John Lysaght Australia as a subsidiary in each year.

GROUP TURNOVER
Group turnover of subsidiaries (excluding sales within the Group) for 1970 totalled £485 million compared with £422 million in 1969 (excluding John Lysaght Australia). Companies acquired during the year had no material effect on turnover.

UNITED KINGDOM OPERATIONS
Sales of United Kingdom subsidiaries (including exports) rose from £359 million in 1969 to £408 million in 1970. In general a high rate of activity was achieved throughout a year in which rapid inflation and a low rate of real growth were the main features of the domestic economy.

By mid-year the boom in world steel demand had passed its peak. This condition was reflected in some slackening of demand for steel in the United Kingdom towards the end of the year when domestic conditions became more competitive, particularly in sheet and reinforcing bar. Against this background sales for the year of Group re-rolled steel products and sales of steel products generally by the distribution companies were at very high levels, although in the second half of the year sales of bright steel were affected by the unsettled condition of the United Kingdom motor industry and the recession in the U.S.A. economy. Exports of re-rolled products increased by 17% over 1969, despite intensifying price competition.

In unit terms, United Kingdom vehicle production (passenger, commercial and tractor) was lower than in 1969 and remained below the peak of 1964 for the sixth successive year. This was largely attributable to the unprecedented level of industrial unrest and plant stoppages, causing disruption of production schedules. Commercial vehicle production was badly affected, while car production suffered so much that United Kingdom manufacturers of cars lost world and domestic market shares.

However, the demand in world markets for United Kingdom commercial vehicles remained strong, particularly for the heavier types requiring larger components of higher value. This benefited Group companies, and, with direct exports of many products increasing significantly as a result of sustained efforts, enabled sales of automotive components to be generally maintained, and in some cases improved.

Sales of transmission products—in particular commercial vehicle crankshafts and clutches for tractors and passenger cars—were higher ; sales of pressed steel wheels for commercial vehicles and tractors and other pressings and fabrications, although suffering from the serious strike at GKN Sankey in August/September 1970, showed improvement with direct exports maintaining a rapidly rising trend. Direct exports of forged components, bearings and bushes compensated to some extent for the considerable dislocation of home sales caused by strikes and stoppages. Demand for castings (cylinder blocks and heads) fluctuated widely during the year and tonnage output was less than in 1969.

Fastener demand, which is dependent on the level of industrial activity, changed little in the United Kingdom between 1969 and 1970, although exports continued to expand. In these conditions Group distributors of fasteners and hardware did well to achieve increased industrial sales ; demand from the retail and house building sectors continued low.

For plant and machinery producers, the home market in 1970 was rather better than in 1969. Export deliveries in 1970 also rose strongly. Taking home and export markets together, higher levels of activity were spread widely over all types of machinery. Group contracting and heavy engineering activities experienced a recovery of demand from the steel and process industries. Several contracts were completed during the year and substantial orders were obtained (more than half for overseas) for completion in 1971 and 1972. In medium and light engineering, sales of injection moulding machines in the United Kingdom were somewhat reduced in the second half of the year ; similar conditions in demand for welding equipment were offset by a large export contract.

In 1970, construction output in the United Kingdom was below that of 1969—itself a poor year. Private housing suffered most, and conditions were little better in other sectors. There were some signs of a revival in demand in the second half of the year, but inflation was responsible for much of the apparent increase. This background provided little encouragement for Group companies serving the construction industry ; and demand for foundation work was weak, although sales of steel

reinforcements for concrete, in conditions of national shortage, were high and scaffolding business was satisfactory. Demand for domestic central heating installations suffered a severe decline, but conversion of appliances to use natural gas increased in volume.

Sales of BKL aluminium ingots, tubular welding fittings and other products were maintained. The Group's major stake in the vending machine industry was strengthened. Sales of brewery equipment also made further progress.

OVERSEAS OPERATIONS
Sales of overseas subsidiaries rose from £63 million in 1969 (excluding John Lysaght Australia) to £77 million in 1970.

In Australia, strong growth continued throughout most of the year, though demand from agricultural and rural markets was weak. Measures taken to control inflation in mid-year affected building markets, but industrial and consumer demand generally remained firm. Group activities experienced strong demand from the commercial building sector but sales of wheels to the automotive and tractor industries showed only a marginal increase, the major customer having lost ground. The setback in domestic building in the second half of the year affected fastener sales.

In New Zealand economic developments closely resembled those in Australia—high growth of domestic demand coupled with spiralling wage, cost and price increases. Sales showed a marked increase, attributable both to an increase in capacity of the wire mill and to diversification, including entry into the automotive spare parts field.

Economic conditions in India remained relatively favourable, continuing the trend of 1969 and demand was generally satisfactory. Group companies achieved a substantial increase in turnover, despite a lock-out which closed down a major part of the operation during the first two months of 1970, and an acute shortage of raw material.

Sales also increased significantly in South Africa where buoyant economic conditions prevailed despite credit restrictions. Construction demand was strong and units serving the automotive and general engineering industries operated on

TURNOVER

(excluding inter-Group sales)	1966 £M	1967 £M	1968 £M	1969 £M	1970 £M
UNITED KINGDOM					
GKN Steel Company Limited	27	—	—	—	—
Other United Kingdom companies	236	249	301	359	408
Total United Kingdom sales and exports from the United Kingdom	263	249	301	359	408
OVERSEAS					
Asia	16	14	17	19	25
Australasia	14	13	16	17	20
Europe	8	8	11	13	15
North America	1	2	4	4	4
Southern Africa	6	7	8	10	13
	308	293	357	422	485
John Lysaght (Australia) Limited	49	62	77	90	—
Group total	357	355	434	512	485

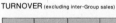
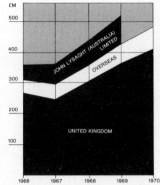

TURNOVER (excluding inter-Group sales)

improved levels. In Sweden, Holland and Denmark, price restrictions of varying degrees (most severe in Denmark) coupled with reduced building activity in Sweden and Holland, affected sales adversely, but in West Germany sales of plastics injection moulding machines were increased.

EXPORTS
The value of exports from the United Kingdom in 1970 (defined as direct exports of manufactured goods only) was £41·8 million compared with £33·2 million in 1969. In addition the value of goods sold specifically by the Group in the United Kingdom through known agencies and designated for export in their original state amounted to £9·8 million (1969 £7·0 million). Income from contracts undertaken abroad and sales of know-how, technical aid, etc., totalled £1·8 million (1969 £1·5 million) whilst indirect exports—parts and components sold to manufacturers and included in products exported by them— are estimated at a further £110 million (1969 £95 million). The achievement in the export market (in the first two categories) represents an improvement of approximately 28% on the previous year—more than three times the increase in the national rate of exports of manufactured goods. All sections of the Group recorded significant increases, the main markets being E.F.T.A., E.E.C. and North America—despite difficult conditions in the U.S.A.

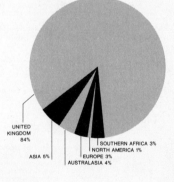

ANALYSIS OF 1970 TURNOVER

UNITED KINGDOM 84%
ASIA 5%
AUSTRALASIA 4%
EUROPE 3%
NORTH AMERICA 1%
SOUTHERN AFRICA 3%

GROUP TRADING RESULTS

The Group trading surplus was £37·5 million compared with £30·8 million (excluding John Lysaght Australia) for 1969. The contribution of companies acquired during the year was not material.

United Kingdom companies achieved a surplus to sales of 7·1% compared with 7·3% in 1969, and overseas companies 11·0% as against 7·5% in 1969.

In the second half of 1970, the effect of industrial disputes, both in our own and customers' plants, was far more severe than in the first part of the year. The Sankey strike alone is calculated to have cost the Group £1·8 million in loss of profits. In addition it was deemed necessary to provide £1·5 million in respect of possible losses arising from the collapse of Rolls-Royce Ltd.

In the United Kingdom the effect of inflation on costs was particularly severe and although selling prices were increased, in some cases the increases were not fully effective until towards the end of the year. The exceptional demand for steel, and the increases in steel prices in January and October, contributed to profitability in the re-rolled products (including steel reinforcements) and distributive sectors ; the profits of the automotive components companies as a whole were adversely affected not only by escalation in costs of raw material and labour, but also by industrial unrest which caused fluctuations in customers' scheduled requirements on a scale never previously experienced, as well as disrupting production at Group works—particularly GKN Sankey and The Scottish Stamping & Engineering Company. The poorer performance in the automotive area largely counterbalanced the improvements achieved in other areas— particularly bolts and nuts and machinery and capital equipment.

Overseas, shortage of labour in Australia, and strikes and stoppages at Group and customer works, restricted profits in that territory to little more than the previous year's level. In New Zealand, although shortage of locally produced steel made it necessary to import steel at inflated prices, and costs were also affected by inflation, profits were maintained with the benefit of additional installed capacity.

In Southern Africa, which also experienced acute shortage of labour, increased turnover yielded substantially higher profits than in the previous year.

In India there were significantly better results from Guest, Keen, Williams despite the difficulty in obtaining adequate supplies of most varieties of steel ; margins were improved, management deployed more effectively, and labour relations, after the serious strike early in the year, improved.

In Sweden, after a promising start, results were adversely affected by lower demand and inflation, particularly in the latter part of the year. In Denmark, profits were affected by severe and unrealistic price control.

ASSOCIATED COMPANIES

The principal associated company, John Lysaght (Australia) Limited, experienced strong demand for its products throughout the year. Turnover increased and sales of sheet and coil exceeded 1 million tons for the first time, reflecting the continued growth in the main sectors of the economy, notably the automotive industry and the building industry (particularly non-domestic). Export sales were also a record although interruptions in the supply of steel caused by industrial unrest prevented full advantage being taken of profitable export opportunities. Shortage of steel also restricted the ability to compete in the Australian market (contributing to the continued high level of imports of sheet and coil into Australia) and affected productivity.

Stage 1 of the development at Westernport was commenced during the year, involving the construction and commissioning of a second cold strip plant by 1972-73. This will initially be fed by hot strip from Australia Iron & Steel Limited, Port Kembla (a subsidiary of The Broken Hill Proprietary Company Limited) and a new agreement for the supply of hot strip to John Lysaght Australia was concluded during the year. Work on Stage 1 has since progressed as planned. The physical characteristics, timing and investment required for Stage 2—the installation of a hot strip mill at Westernport—are now being studied.

The results of John Lysaght Australia for 1970, with comparative figures for 1969, are shown below :

	1970 £M	1969 £M
Turnover	98·78	90·88
Surplus on trading	8·58	7·51

TRADING SURPLUS	1966 £M	1967 £M	1968 £M	1969 £M	1970 £M
UNITED KINGDOM					
GKN Steel Company	2·5	—	—	—	—
Other United Kingdom companies	18·1	19·0	22·3	26·1	29·0
Total United Kingdom	20·6	19·0	22·3	26·1	29·0
OVERSEAS					
Asia	2·0	0·9	0·8	1·4	4·6
Australasia	0·8	0·8	1·2	1·3	1·4
Europe	0·9	0·2	0·4	0·9	1·0
North America	0·2	0·4	0·4	0·4	0·3
Southern Africa	0·4	0·3	0·6	0·7	1·2
	24·9	21·6	25·7	30·8	37·5
John Lysaght (Australia) Limited	3·9	4·6	5·4	7·5	—
Group total	28·8	26·2	31·1	38·3	37·5

The West German associated company, Uni-Cardan AG, in which the Group has a substantial interest and with which there are close commercial and technological relations, broadly maintained its position in the supply of automotive transmission equipment through its subsidiaries and associated companies in West Germany, Italy, France and Holland, achieving a turnover of approximately £62 million in 1970. The Group's associated companies in other parts of the world achieved improved results in most cases.

PRINCIPAL ACTIVITIES AND CLASSIFICATION OF BUSINESS
The principal products of the Group are listed on page 19 and Group activities are described on pages 20 to 29 of this report.

The proportions in which the 1970 turnover and profit of the Group were divided between classes of business which, in the opinion of the Directors, were substantially different, are as follows:

	PROPORTION OF TURNOVER %	PROPORTION OF SURPLUS ON TRADING %
MATERIAL MANIPULATION (ferrous, non-ferrous and synthetic) including rolling, drawing, forging, extruding, moulding, casting, pressing and fabrication	48	48
ENGINEERING including machining, metal finishing and assembly	33	27
SERVICES, STOCKHOLDING AND DISTRIBUTION	19	25
	100	100

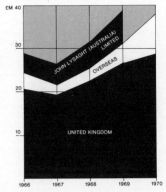

TRADING SURPLUS

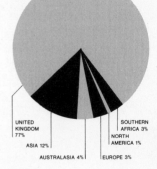

ANALYSIS OF 1970 TRADING SURPLUS

UNITED KINGDOM 77%
ASIA 12%
AUSTRALASIA 4%
EUROPE 3%
NORTH AMERICA 1%
SOUTHERN AFRICA 3%

PROFITS

Profits before tax for the year amounted to £43·1 million as compared with £35·4 million in 1969 (including John Lysaght Australia on the same basis as in 1970).

The inclusion of the attributable earnings of associated companies (other than John Lysaght Australia) in place of dividends received increased pre-tax earnings of 1970 by £1·2 million.

The effect on working capital of the higher level of sales and continued cost inflation, particularly in the United Kingdom, was the main factor contributing to the decrease in investment income and increase in interest payable in 1970.

Taxation in relation to profits was lower in 1970 than in the previous year due mainly to United Kingdom corporation tax being provided at $42\frac{1}{2}$% as compared with 45% for 1969. On the other hand the rate of tax on profits in Australia was increased from 45% in 1969 to $47\frac{1}{2}$%.

Allowing for exceptional items and after deducting the profit attributable to outside shareholders, the net profit attributable to ordinary Stockholders amounted to £21·2 million (including £2·0 million in the accounts of associated companies) compared with £17·7 million in 1969.

The return on net assets employed for the year was 14·9% compared with 13·3% in 1969 (see table below). Earnings per ordinary share again increased—to 20.5p (including 0.5p attributable to the inclusion of other associated companies on an earnings basis) compared with 18.1p in 1969 (after adjusting for the 1 for 3 scrip issue in 1970).

DIVIDEND

The Directors recommend that a final dividend on the ordinary stock of 9·00p per £1 unit be declared for the 52 weeks ended 2nd January 1971. The interim and final dividends for 1970 are payable on the ordinary stock as increased during that year both by the 1 for 3 scrip issue of £24,431,040 ordinary stock made in May 1970, and the £5,911,333 ordinary stock issued by way of conversion for £11,083,751 $6\frac{1}{2}$% convertible unsecured loan stock 1986/91 in June 1970. The total dividend for 1970 of 12·75p per £1 unit compares with 11·875p per £1 unit (adjusted for the 1 for 3 scrip issue in 1970) paid in respect of 1969.

ORGANISATION

As reported in the interim statement, it was decided in 1970, for organisational, financial and management reasons, to separate the bulk of the United Kingdom and overseas activities into two groups, each with its own holding company. Following establishment of Guest Keen and Nettlefolds (U.K.) Limited in July 1970, as holding company for substantially all United Kingdom activities, Guest Keen and Nettlefolds (Overseas) Limited has now been set up and will own the share capital of the majority of Group companies overseas. Guest, Keen and Nettlefolds, Limited owns the whole of the share capitals of the two new holding companies and will continue to maintain overall responsibility for all the companies which it controls.

FINANCE

In May 1970, the right to convert the £11,713,685 $6\frac{1}{2}$% unsecured loan stock 1986/91 into ordinary stock became exercisable : in the event holders of £11,083,751 of the $6\frac{1}{2}$% loan stock (94·6% in value) exercised their right, and were allotted £5,911,333 ordinary stock of the Company. Under the terms of conversion, holders who converted were not entitled to any interest on the loan stock in 1970, but became entitled to the interim and final dividends payable on the ordinary stock for that year.

In August 1970, arrangements were made for the placing by Guest Keen and Nettlefold (U.K.) Limited of £20 million $10\frac{1}{2}$% guaranteed debenture stock 1990/95 at £98·75, providing funds to finance the

	TOTAL NET ASSETS EMPLOYED AT END OF YEAR (BOOK VALUES)		PROFIT BEFORE LOAN CAPITAL INTEREST AND TAXATION		RATIO	
	1970	1969	1970	1969	1970	1969
	£M	£M	£M	£M	%	%
United Kingdom	206·6	195·9	28·1	27·2	13·6	13·9
Overseas	93·0	85·0	16·5	10·1	17·7	11·9
Total	299·6	280·9	44·6	37·3	14·9	13·3

THE 1969 FIGURES HAVE BEEN ADJUSTED
(a) TO DEAL WITH JOHN LYSAGHT AUSTRALIA AS IF IT HAD BEEN AN ASSOCIATED COMPANY.
(b) TO PRESENT THE OTHER ASSOCIATED COMPANIES ON A COMPARABLE BASIS WITH 1970.

maintenance and expansion of United Kingdom operations. At 2nd January 1971, £5·47 million had been received and the balance was received by 18th January 1971.

In accordance with the principle that Guest Keen and Nettlefolds (U.K.) Limited should wherever possible provide finance for the companies it controls, further series of guaranteed debenture stock of Guest Keen and Nettlefolds (U.K.) Limited were issued on 28th December 1970 in exchange for the outstanding debenture and loan stocks of subsidiaries of that company : the new series, which are identical as to rate of interest and redemption to the subsidiary stocks they replaced, and in other respects are identical to the original £20 million 10½% debenture of Guest Keen and Nettlefolds (U.K.) Limited, are as follows :

£1,369,760 4½% guaranteed debenture stock 1970/84
£3,500,000 6½% guaranteed debenture stock 1976/81
£2,055,000 6½% guaranteed debenture stock 1980/85
£4,000,000 7½% guaranteed debenture stock 1986/91
£119,220 8% guaranteed debenture stock 1986/91

Overseas, in order to finance increased requirements in Scandinavia, secured loans of £950,000 were raised by Group companies in Sweden and Denmark.

In 1970 the capital expenditure of the Group, after taking credit for United Kingdom investment grants, was £22·5 million.

At the end of the year the total outstanding on schemes approved by the Directors amounted to £20·0 million (United Kingdom £18·0 million, overseas £2·0 million).

The movements in fixed assets in the Group during the year are set out on page 38.

There has been no recent independent valuation of all the Group's properties. The properties are employed in the business of the Group and are predominantly of an industrial nature. Many of them were acquired at dates when market values were considerably lower than at present. The Directors are of the opinion, however, that any difference between market value and book value at 2nd January 1971 would not be of such significance as to require the attention of the members and loan stockholders to be drawn thereto.

CAPITAL EXPENDITURE	1966 £M	1967 £M	1968 £M	1969 £M	1970 £M
UNITED KINGDOM					
GKN Steel Company Limited	1·8	—	—	—	—
Other United Kingdom companies	8·8	11·7	10·7	14·5	19·3
Total United Kingdom	10·6	11·7	10·7	14·5	19·3
OVERSEAS					
Asia	2·0	1·3	0·7	0·4	0·4
Australasia	0·5	0·7	0·7	0·7	0·7
Europe	0·8	0·9	0·6	0·6	1·2
North America	0·1	0·2	0·2	0·3	0·2
Southern Africa	0·5	0·2	0·3	0·8	0·7
	14·5	15·0	13·2	17·3	22·5
John Lysaght (Australia) Limited	3·8	3·3	5·0	3·4	—
Group total	18·3	18·3	18·2	20·7	22·5

SOURCE AND DISPOSITION OF FUNDS IN 1970

	U.K. £M	OVERSEAS £M	TOTAL £M
SOURCE			
Profit retained :			
By GKN Ltd. and subsidiaries	4·0	2·0	6·0
Attributable to outside shareholders	—	0·4	0·4
Depreciation charged against profits	12·2	2·5	14·7
Subscription to share capital of subsidiaries by outside shareholders	0·3	—	0·3
Issue/redemption of loan capital	5·3	0·9	6·2
Sundry	0·6	0·2	0·4
	22·4	5·6	28·0
DISPOSITION			
Net additions to fixed assets	17·6	2·8	20·4
Investment in associated companies	0·5	0·2	0·7
Movements in :			
Stocks	17·0	5·0	22·0
Debtors, less creditors, taxation and dividends	6·1	2·4	8·5
Inter-group items :			
Share capital and loan subscriptions to overseas companies	0·7	0·7	—
Current account movements	1·4	1·4	—
	31·1	3·5	34·6
INCREASE/DECREASE DURING THE YEAR	8·7	2·1	6·6
Net liquid resources at beginning of year	9·9	2·2	7·7
Net liquid resources at end of year	1·2	0·1	1·1

Stocks and work in progress in the United Kingdom showed a significant increase during 1970, reflecting the higher level of sales and cost inflation.

The Group investments in associated companies (listed on page 32) are now included in the consolidated balance sheet at book value of the investments plus the Group share of their post acquisition reserves. In the 1969 published figures they were included at book value with a note of the Directors' valuation based on net assets or book value if lower, or in the case of quoted investments, market value. In order to facilitate comparison with the previous year, the consolidated balance sheet includes the 1969 figures adjusted to deal with John Lysaght Australia as if it had been an associated company.

Investments other than associated companies, i.e., trade investments, have been included in both years at book value with a note of the Directors' valuation based on net asset value or book value if lower, or in the case of quoted investments, market value.

During 1970 capital expenditure of John Lysaght Australia was A$15·8 million (£7·4 million) of which A$8·8 million (£4·1 million) related to the first stage of development at Westernport (No. 2 cold strip plant). The total outstanding on the Westernport cold strip project and other schemes approved by the Directors of John Lysaght Australia at 2nd January 1971 was A$94·7 million (£44·2 million) and in order to provide part of the finance required for these expenditures John Lysaght Australia issued a public debenture of A$40 million (£18·65 million) on the Australian capital market towards the end of 1970, at interest rates varying from between 8½% and 9% and maturities ranging from 8 to 25 years. Further loan finance (in addition to financing arrangements made with suppliers of major units of equipment) will be raised outside Australia during 1971, in accordance with the Australian Treasury borrowing guide lines.

BOARD OF DIRECTORS

The Directors record their great pleasure at the honour of Knighthood conferred on the Group Chairman, Sir Raymond Brookes, in the 1971 New Year's Honours List.

The composition of the Board of Directors of the Company is given on page 8. Mr. G.F. Brown and Mr. G. B. Sankey retired from the Board on 31st March 1970, and acknowledgement of their services was recorded in last year's report.

Mr. C. C. Birch, Sir Douglas Bruce-Gardner, Bt., Mr. W. A. Nicol, Mr. M. S. Pearce and Mr. F. C. Rowbottom retire at the annual general meeting by rotation and, being eligible, offer themselves for re-election.

(Certain statutory information relating to Directors and employees is given on page 37.)

CHARITABLE AND POLITICAL DONATIONS

Donations made during the year by the Group for charitable purposes amounted to £97,000, a large part of which was given to educational bodies, principally to universities, with which the Group has close relationships in the field of engineering, research and technology.

The following donations were made in the United Kingdom by the Group during the year for political purposes as defined by the Companies Act 1967:

	£
Conservative and Unionist Party	33,000
Aims of Industry	2,500
Aldnor Trust	1,500

In addition a contribution of £1,500 was made to the Economic League. This payment was not made for political purposes but might be held to come within the definition set out in Section 19 of the Companies Act 1967.

AUDITORS

The Auditors, Cooper Brothers & Co., will continue in office in accordance with Section 159 (2) of the Companies Act, 1948.

By order of the Board
J. F. HOWARD,
Secretary

23rd March 1971

FOUNDRY SERVICES TO
INDUSTRY; TRACTOR
COMPONENTS

BEARINGS
PLAIN BEARINGS, BUSHES AND
THRUST WASHERS; SINTERED
OIL-RETAINING BEARINGS,
COMPONENTS AND FRICTION
MATERIALS; PRESSED STEEL
ROCKER ARMS

FASTENERS
BOLTS, NUTS, SCREWS AND
FORMED PARTS; KEYS AND PINS;
HINGES; WIRE NAILS

STEEL
HOT RE-ROLLED PRODUCTS;
BRIGHT DRAWN, TURNED AND
GROUND AND HEAT TREATED BARS;
COLD ROLLED STRIP;
SPRING WIRE, SEATING WIRE,
WIRE FOR EXTRUDED COMPONENTS,
WELDING WIRE

ALUMINIUM
ALLOY INGOTS AND
ALUMINIUM EXTRUSIONS

FILTRATION EQUIPMENT
AND STRAINERS

PLATING
ELECTRO-PLATING AND METAL
FINISHING

GARAGE EQUIPMENT
WHEEL BALANCERS, DYNAMOMETERS,
ENGINE DIAGNOSTIC TEST
EQUIPMENT, BATTERY CHARGERS,
BRAKE TESTERS

AEROSPACE
COMPRESSOR AND TURBINE DISCS
AND BLADES, AIR INTAKE
HOUSINGS, GEAR CASINGS AND
CONTROL BOX CASTINGS,
INSTRUMENT CASES AND CHASSIS;
JET AIRCRAFT ENGINE
FABRICATIONS; FASTENERS

INDUSTRIAL EQUIPMENT AND SUPPLIES

CONTRACTORS FOR THE SUPPLY OF
COMPLETE PROJECTS, INDUSTRIAL
PLANTS AND PROCESS LINES,
INCLUDING THOSE USING GKN
KNOW-HOW; STEELWORKS PLANT;
INGOT MOULDS; FURNACES FOR
OIL REFINERIES AND CHEMICAL
PLANTS; INDUCTION HEATING AND
MELTING FURNACES; HEAT
EXCHANGERS; EXTRUSION AND
POWER PRESSES; PLASTICS
EXTRUSION AND PLASTICS
INJECTION MOULDING MACHINES;
INDUSTRIAL GAS CONVERSION;
INSTALLATION OF LPG-FIRED
SYSTEMS

TRANSMISSIONS AND POWER
TAKE-OFF SHAFTS; INDUSTRIAL
COUPLINGS; BRONZE BEARING AND
BUSH MATERIALS; SINTERED
OIL-RETAINING BEARINGS,
COMPONENTS, FRICTION MATERIALS
AND FILTER ELEMENTS; WHITE
METAL BEARINGS; ELECTRICAL
LAMINATIONS FOR MOTORS,
TRANSFORMERS AND GENERATORS;
STEAM TURBINE BLADES

HOT ROLLED STEEL BARS, FLATS,
STANDARD AND SPECIAL SECTIONS;
BRIGHT DRAWN, TURNED AND
GROUND AND HEAT TREATED BARS;
WIRE RODS AND COILED BARS;
HOT AND COLD ROLLED STRIP;
MILD STEEL, ALLOY AND HIGH
TENSILE PATENTED STEEL WIRE AND
WIRE PRODUCTS; ANODISING;
ALUMINIUM ALLOY INGOTS,
ALUMINIUM EXTRUSIONS, ANODES
AND SERVICES FOR CATHODIC
PROTECTION; TUBULAR WELDING
FITTINGS; BREWERY EQUIPMENT
AND CONTAINERS;
FILTRATION EQUIPMENT AND
FILTER MEDIA; CASTINGS FOR
MACHINE TOOL AND GENERAL
INDUSTRIAL USE;
CONTINUOUS-CAST PHOSPHOR
BRONZE ROD AND TUBE;
PRECISION FERROUS, NON-FERROUS
AND PLASTIC COMPONENTS FOR
ENGINEERING AND ELECTRONIC
APPLICATIONS; BOLTS, NUTS,
SCREWS, OTHER FASTENERS AND
FORMED PARTS; PLATING; WELDED
FABRICATIONS; PRESSWORK FOR
ELECTRICAL AND DOMESTIC
APPLIANCE INDUSTRIES; WELDING
MACHINES AND EQUIPMENT;
STRAPPING AND BALING SYSTEMS

DISTRIBUTION OF FASTENERS,
TOOLS, HARDWARE AND GENERAL
ENGINEERS' SUPPLIES;
STOCKHOLDERS OF STEEL AND
OTHER MATERIALS—BLACK BARS,
STRUCTURAL SECTIONS, PLATES,
FLAT PRODUCTS, BRIGHT STEEL,
TUBES, ALUMINIUM, BRASS,
PHOSPHOR BRONZE AND
INDUSTRIAL NYLON

TRADE SALES AND SERVICES

BOLTS, NUTS, SCREWS, OTHER
FASTENERS AND FORMED PARTS;
WIRE NAILS; HINGES; LOCKS;
BUILDERS' AND GENERAL
HARDWARE; BRIGHT DRAWN,
TURNED AND GROUND AND HEAT
TREATED BARS; HOT ROLLED STEEL
BARS, FLATS, STANDARD AND
SPECIAL SECTIONS; WIRE RODS AND
COILED BARS; HOT AND COLD
ROLLED STRIP; MILD STEEL, ALLOY
AND HIGH TENSILE PATENTED STEEL
WIRE AND WIRE PRODUCTS;
TUNGSTEN CARBIDE DIES AND
TIPPED TOOLS; ALUMINIUM ALLOY
INGOTS, ALUMINIUM EXTRUSIONS,
ANODES AND SERVICES FOR
CATHODIC PROTECTION;
TUBULAR WELDING FITTINGS;
TRANSMISSION AND GARAGE
EQUIPMENT; FILTRATION
EQUIPMENT AND FILTER MEDIA

BUILDING AND CONSTRUCTION

SCAFFOLDING
INCLUDING SPECTATOR STANDS;
FORMWORK, BUILDERS' AND CIVIL
ENGINEERING EQUIPMENT

STEEL
FOR REINFORCED CONCRETE;
MILD STEEL AND HIGH TENSILE
BARS; WELDED MESH;
"STABILIZED" WIRE AND STRAND
FOR PRE-STRESSED CONCRETE

ALUMINIUM
EXTRUSIONS, STAINLESS STEEL CLAD
ALUMINIUM SECTIONS AND
ARCHITECTURAL ANODISING

PILING
AND SOIL ENGINEERING

PLASTIC COMPONENTS
INCLUDING CEILING PANS,
"STENNI" WALL PANELS;
SPECIALISED FLOORING

HINGES,
LOCKS, BUILDERS' HARDWARE

FASTENERS
BOLTS, NUTS, SCREWS AND
FORMED PARTS; WIRE NAILS

PARTITIONING
SHELVING, "UNISTRUT"
FRAMING SYSTEM AND RACKING

CENTRAL HEATING
SYSTEMS AND EQUIPMENT,
PRESSED STEEL RADIATORS,
STAINLESS STEEL FLEXIBLE
FLUE LINING; FILTRATION
EQUIPMENT AND FILTER MEDIA;
DOUBLE GLAZING SYSTEMS

GOVERNMENT AND PUBLIC UTILITIES

ARMAMENT CASTINGS; X-RAY AND
GAMMA-RAY TESTING OF CASTINGS;
ARMOURED FIGHTING VEHICLES AND
DEFENCE EQUIPMENT; TRAILERS;
DEFENCE COMPONENTS IN PLASTICS;
STEEL FOR REINFORCED CONCRETE;
"STABILIZED" WIRE AND STRAND
FOR PRE-STRESSED CONCRETE;
BOLTS, NUTS, SCREWS, OTHER
FASTENERS AND FORMED PARTS;
WIRE NAILS; SPECIAL FORGINGS,
PERMANENT WAY AND TRACK
EQUIPMENT, PERMANENT WAY
FASTENINGS; CONVERSION OF
APPLIANCES TO USE NATURAL GAS;
PIPE FITTINGS FOR GAS
TRANSMISSION LINES; FILTRATION
EQUIPMENT AND FILTER MEDIA

CONSUMER PRODUCTS

AUTOMATIC VENDING MACHINES;
BOLTS, NUTS, SCREWS, OTHER
FASTENERS AND FORMED PARTS;
WIRE NAILS; HINGES AND
HARDWARE; DOMESTIC CENTRAL
HEATING AND DOUBLE GLAZING
SYSTEMS; MOULDINGS, PRESSINGS,
CASTINGS AND EXTRUSIONS IN
STEEL, ALUMINIUM AND PLASTICS
FOR HOUSEHOLD APPLIANCES;
PLASTIC DUSTBINS; OFFICE
FURNITURE; SAFETY FOOTWEAR AND
PROTECTIVE CLOTHING

AUSTRALIA

SCAFFOLDING, FORMWORK AND
BUILDERS' AND CIVIL ENGINEERING
EQUIPMENT AND SERVICES;
"UNISTRUT" FRAMING SYSTEM;
"DURAFRAME" STEEL HOUSE
FRAMES; BUILDING BOARDS;
BOLTS, NUTS, SCREWS AND OTHER
FASTENERS; WHEELS, RIMS AND
OTHER PRESSINGS
*ALSO MANUFACTURED BY
ASSOCIATED COMPANY, JOHN
LYSAGHT (AUSTRALIA) LTD:*
COATED AND UNCOATED STEEL
SHEET AND COIL; ELECTRICAL
LAMINATIONS FOR MOTORS,
TRANSFORMERS AND GENERATORS;
EXPANDED METAL; RURAL
PRODUCTS INCLUDING FARM
BUILDINGS AND SILOS; STEEL
FURNITURE AND OFFICE EQUIPMENT;
STRUCTURAL DECKING, ROOFING,
WALLING AND FLOORING MEMBRANES;
TRANSPORTABLE BUILDINGS

NEW ZEALAND

BRIGHT AND GALVANISED WIRE;
ROLL FORMING, ROOFING AND
WALLING SHAPES; SCAFFOLDING
AND FORMWORK FOR CONSTRUCTION
INDUSTRY; "UNISTRUT" FRAMING
SYSTEM; EXPANDED METAL AND
CABLE LADDERS; BOLTS, NUTS,
SCREWS AND OTHER FASTENERS;
DISTRIBUTION OF COATED AND
UNCOATED SHEET AND COIL AND
OF AUTOMOTIVE PARTS AND
ACCESSORIES

INDIA

DROP, UPSET AND PRESS
FORGINGS FOR AUTOMOTIVE,
RAILWAY AND OTHER INDUSTRIES;
PRECISION PRESSWORK FOR
ELECTRICAL, AUTOMOTIVE AND
TEXTILE INDUSTRIES; STAMPINGS
AND STRIP WOUND CORES FOR
ELECTRICAL INDUSTRY; ELECTRICALLY
MELTED ALLOY STEELS, ROLLED
AND BRIGHT STEEL BARS; PLASTICS
INJECTION MOULDING MACHINES;
TRACK FASTENERS FOR THE
RAILWAYS; BOLTS, NUTS, SCREWS
AND OTHER FASTENERS

PAKISTAN

WOODSCREWS AND ROOFING
SCREWS; AGENCY FOR GROUP AND
OTHER PRODUCTS

SOUTHERN AFRICA

DESIGN, MANUFACTURE, SALE
AND HIRE OF STEEL SCAFFOLDING, .
FORMWORK AND BUILDERS'
EQUIPMENT; STRUCTURAL DESIGN,
STEEL REINFORCEMENT
AND WIREWELD FABRIC FOR
CONCRETE; STEEL FLOORING;
"UNISTRUT" FRAMING SYSTEM,
PARTITIONING AND SHELVING;
ELECTRICAL STAMPINGS, SMALL
ELECTRICAL TRANSFORMERS AND
RELAYS; GENERAL PRESSWORK
FOR THE DOMESTIC APPLIANCE
AND ALLIED INDUSTRIES; STEEL
FURNITURE AND OFFICE EQUIPMENT;
COMMERCIAL VEHICLE CAB
ASSEMBLIES AND GENERAL
PRESSWORK; PERMANENT WAY
FASTENERS; BOLTS, NUTS, SCREWS,
STUDS AND OTHER FASTENERS;
WIRE NAILS

SWEDEN, HOLLAND AND DENMARK

HINGES AND BUILDERS' HARDWARE;
CYLINDER AND LEVER LOCKS;
IGNITION AND DOOR LOCKS AND
OTHER CAR COMPONENTS; BICYCLE
LOCKS; DOOR, WINDOW AND
CURTAIN FITTINGS; COATED STEEL
TUBES; SCREWS; NEEDLE ROLLER
UNIVERSAL JOINTS, PROPELLER
SHAFTS AND POWER TAKE-OFF
SHAFTS

ITALY

WELDING MACHINES AND EQUIPMENT

WESTERN GERMANY

PLASTICS INJECTION MOULDING
MACHINES; FURNACES AND HEAT
EXCHANGERS FOR OIL REFINERIES
AND CHEMICAL PLANTS

NORTH AMERICA

OIL-RETAINING AND IRON
BEARINGS AND BUSHES;
SINTERED PARTS AND COMPONENTS
BY POWDER METALLURGY

MEMBER COMPANIES OF THE GKN GROUP

The following is a list of companies at 2nd January 1971 of which Guest, Keen & Nettlefolds, Ltd., either itself or through subsidiaries, is the beneficial owner of 100% of the issued share capital (of all classes) unless otherwise indicated. A number of smaller companies have been omitted.

	Country of registration or incorporation
GKN BIRFIELD TRANSMISSIONS LTD.	**ENGLAND**
BRD COMPANY LTD.	ENGLAND
HARDY SPICER LTD.	ENGLAND
HARDY SPICER WALTERSCHEID LTD. (85% Ordinary)	ENGLAND
LAYCOCK ENGINEERING LTD.	ENGLAND
NORDISKA KARDAN A.-B.	SWEDEN
SALISBURY TRANSMISSION LTD.	ENGLAND
AMBROSE SHARDLOW & CO. LTD.	ENGLAND
GKN BOLTS & NUTS LTD.	**ENGLAND**
SPECIALIST SECTOR	
AUTOMOTIVE DIVISION	
SPECIAL PRODUCTS DIVISION	
STANDARD BOLT & NUT SECTOR	
STANDARD BOLT & NUT DIVISION	
GKN ESLOK DIVISION	
ENGINEERING SERVICES SECTOR	
ENGINEERING MANUFACTURING DIVISION	
P.A.C.E. DIVISION	
GKN BUILDING SUPPLIES & SERVICES LTD.	**ENGLAND**
CROMPTON NETTLEFOLD STENMAN LTD.	ENGLAND
GKN FOUNDATIONS LTD.	ENGLAND
GKN REINFORCEMENTS LTD.	ENGLAND
MILLS SCAFFOLD COMPANY LTD.	ENGLAND
SERVOTOMIC LTD.	ENGLAND
GKN CASTINGS LTD.	**ENGLAND**
GKN (CWMBRAN) LTD.	ENGLAND
KENT ALLOYS LTD.	ENGLAND
SHOTTON BROS. LTD.	ENGLAND
C. & B. SMITH LTD.	ENGLAND
GKN DISTRIBUTORS LTD.	**ENGLAND**
BRINTON, ADAMS & RICHARDS LTD.	ENGLAND
C. C. DUNKERLEY & COMPANY LTD. (Ordinary, Preference and Employees)	ENGLAND
H. LEES (BRIDGE END) LTD.	ENGLAND
HARWIN TRANSPORT LTD.	ENGLAND
THOS. H. HOWELL LTD. (Ordinary and Preference)	ENGLAND
PIKE BROS. (IRON & STEEL) LTD.	ENGLAND
ROBERTS, SPARROW & CO. LTD.	ENGLAND
LYSAGHT STEEL SERVICE CENTRE	
B.A.R. FASTENERS LTD.	ENGLAND
DAVIS & TIMMINS LTD.	ENGLAND
DAVIS & TIMMINS (AIRCRAFT) LTD.	ENGLAND
GKN (NORTHERN IRELAND) LTD.	N. IRELAND
W. GALLOWAY & COMPANY LTD.	ENGLAND
JOHN & CHARLES MURRAY LTD.	SCOTLAND
MACNAYS LTD.	ENGLAND
MERRY & COMPANY (MANCHESTER) LTD.	ENGLAND
NETTLEFOLD & MOSER LTD.	ENGLAND

	Country of registration or incorporation
GKN ENGINEERING LTD.	**ENGLAND**
GKN BIRWELCO LTD.	ENGLAND
BIRWELCO G.m.b.H.	W. GERMAN
GKN BIRWELCO (USKSIDE) LTD.	ENGLAN
GKN CONTRACTORS LTD.	ENGLAN
GKN DOWLAIS LTD.	ENGLAN
GKN LINCOLN ELECTRIC LTD.	ENGLAN
LINCOLN ELECTRIC (ARCMAKER) S.p.A.	ITAL
GKN MACHINERY LTD. (Ordinary and Preference)	ENGLAN
GKN WINDSOR LTD. (Ordinary and Deferred Ordinary)	ENGLAN
GKN WINDSOR G.m.b.H.	W. GERMAN
R. H. WINDSOR (INDIA) LTD. (51% Ordinary)	INDI
GKN FORGINGS LTD.	**ENGLAN**
BIRFIELD EXTRUSIONS LTD.	ENGLAN
FORGINGS & PRESSWORK LTD.	ENGLAN
GARRINGTONS LTD.	ENGLAN
OSWALD TRANSPORT LTD.	SCOTLAN
PRECISION FORGINGS LTD.	ENGLAN
THE SCOTTISH STAMPING & ENGINEERING COMPANY LTD.	SCOTLAN
SMETHWICK DROP FORGINGS LTD.	ENGLAN
SMITH-CLAYTON FORGE LTD.	ENGLAN
GKN INTERNATIONAL TRADING (HOLDINGS) LTD.	**ENGLAN**
GKN INTERNATIONAL TRADING (LONDON) LTD.	ENGLAN
GKN INTERNATIONAL INC.	U.S.
GKN INTERNATIONAL (CANADA) LTD.	CANAD
GKN INTERNATIONAL (IRELAND) LTD.	EI
GKN BIRFIELD OVERSEAS VERTRIEB G.m.b.H.	AUSTR
GKN INTERNATIONAL TRADING (GERMANY) G.m.b.H.	W. GERMAN
GKN INTERNATIONAL (AUSTRALIA) PTY. LTD.	AUSTRAL
GKN INTERNATIONAL (S.E. ASIA) LTD.	HONG KON
GKN ROLLED & BRIGHT STEEL LTD.	**ENGLAN**
SOUTH WALES DIVISION	
GKN (SOUTH WALES) LTD.	ENGLAN
GKN SOMERSET WIRE LTD.	ENGLA
NORTHERN & MIDLAND DIVISION	
EXORS. OF JAMES MILLS LTD.	ENGLA
CABLE STREET MILLS DIVISION	
LEDLOY LTD.	ENGLA
F. A. POWER LTD.	ENGLA
PARSON LTD.	ENGLA
GKN SANKEY LTD.	**ENGLA**
AUTOMOTIVE OPERATION	
WHEEL DIVISION	
PLASTICS DIVISION	
GENERAL PRODUCTS OPERATION	
AUTOMATIC VENDING DIVISION	
BANKFIELD DIVISION	
BREWERY DIVISION	
SANKEY-SHELDON AND UNISTRUT DIVISION	
GKN SANKEY FINANCE LTD. (Ordinary and Deferred Ordinary)	ENGLA
GKN SANKEY (EUROPE) G.m.b.H.	W. GERMA

KN SCREWS & FASTENERS LTD.	ENGLAND
ARGE VOLUME SECTOR	
EATH STREET DIVISION	
OCKETEX DIVISION	
LEXANDER SOCKET SCREWS LTD.	ENGLAND
HE BRITISH SCREW COMPANY LTD.	ENGLAND
HOMAS HADDON & STOKES LTD.	ENGLAND
REDK. MOUNTFORD (BIRMINGHAM) LTD.	ENGLAND
METAL FINISHING SECTOR	
NIC PLATING COMPANY LTD.	ENGLAND
ILTON & TUCK LTD.	
Ordinary and Deferred Ordinary)	ENGLAND
PECIALIST SECTOR	
INGS NORTON DIVISION	
J. BROOKS (LEICESTER) LTD.	ENGLAND
KN FLOFORM LTD.	ENGLAND
KN SHARDLOW METROLOGY LTD.	ENGLAND
HE PREMIER SCREW & REPETITION	
OMPANY LTD.	ENGLAND
NGINEERING SERVICES SECTOR	
NGINEERING MANUFACTURING DIVISION	
KN TOOLS (MALTA) LTD.	MALTA G.C.

KN POWDER MET. LTD.	ENGLAND
OUND BROOK LTD.	ENGLAND
OUND BROOK BEARING CORPORATION	
F AMERICA	U.S.A.

ANDERVELL PRODUCTS LTD.	ENGLAND
ANDERVELL CANADA (1968) LTD.	CANADA

KL ALLOYS LTD.	
rdinary and Unclassified)	ENGLAND
UNDRY DIVISION	
ATHODIC PROTECTION DIVISION	
TTINGS DIVISION	
RAWN & ROLLED SECTIONS LTD.	
rdinary and Preference)	
DLAND EXTRUSIONS LTD.	ENGLAND
LIABLE ANODISING LTD.	ENGLAND
N FARR FILTRATION LTD.	
0% Ordinary)	ENGLAND
RLSON-FORD LTD.	
rdinary and Preference)	ENGLAND
DENTON & SON LTD.	
3.1% Ordinary, 100% Preference)	ENGLAND
TERNATIONAL SAFETY PRODUCTS LTD.	
4.5% Ordinary)	ENGLAND

OLDING AND SERVICE COMPANIES	
EST KEEN AND NETTLEFOLDS (U.K.) LTD.	ENGLAND
EST KEEN AND NETTLEFOLDS	
VERSEAS) LTD.	ENGLAND
N INDUSTRIES LTD.	ENGLAND
FIELD LTD.	ENGLAND
N GROUP SERVICES LTD.	ENGLAND

GKN IN AUSTRALIA (HOLDINGS) LTD.	AUSTRALIA
GUEST KEEN & NETTLEFOLDS (AUST.) LTD.	AUSTRALIA
GKN BUILDING AND ENGINEERING DIVISION	
GKN SANKEY-BENSON DIVISION	
NETTLEFOLDS DIVISION	

GKN (NEW ZEALAND) HOLDINGS LTD.	NEW ZEALAND
GKN (NEW ZEALAND) LTD.	
(75% Ordinary)	NEW ZEALAND
KELLY AUTOMOTIVE PRODUCTS LTD.	
(75% Ordinary)	NEW ZEALAND
JOHN LYSAGHT (NEW ZEALAND) LTD.	NEW ZEALAND
NORSTEEL ROLL FORMED PRODUCTS	
LTD. (60% Ordinary)	NEW ZEALAND
TRANSPORT SERVICES LTD.	
(66.6% Ordinary)	NEW ZEALAND

GUEST KEEN & NETTLEFOLDS SOUTH AFRICA (PTY.) LTD.	SOUTH AFRICA
GKN MILLS (PTY.) LTD.	SOUTH AFRICA
GKN SANKEY (PTY.) LTD.	SOUTH AFRICA
GKN WALTER & DEANE (PTY.) LTD.	SOUTH AFRICA
GKN TWISTEEL (PTY.) LTD.	SOUTH AFRICA
COMBINED REINFORCING SERVICES (PTY.) LTD. (73% Ordinary)	SOUTH AFRICA

BOLT MANUFACTURERS AFRICA LTD.	
(51% Ordinary)	ZAMBIA

GKN-STENMAN A.-B.	
(86.1% Ordinary)	SWEDEN
ASSA-STENMAN A.-B.	SWEDEN
GKN :S NORDISKA FÖRSÄLJNINGS A.-B.	SWEDEN
A/S RUKO	DENMARK
STENMAN HOLLAND N.V.	HOLLAND

GUEST KEEN WILLIAMS LTD.	
(60.3% Ordinary)	INDIA
GKW (OVERSEAS TRADING) LTD.	INDIA

GUEST KEEN & NETTLEFOLDS IN PAKISTAN LTD.	
(60% Ordinary)	PAKISTAN

ASSOCIATED COMPANIES
AT 2ND JANUARY 1971

	Country of registration or incorporation	Description of shares held	Percentage GKN Group holding of total equity
UNITED KINGDOM			
NTN BEARINGS-GKN LTD.	ENGLAND	'B' SHARES	50·0
TELCON MAGNETIC CORES LTD.	ENGLAND	ORDINARY	33·3
OVERSEAS			
ASIA			
SANKEY WHEELS LTD.	INDIA	EQUITY SHARES	43·2
SHARDLOW INDIA LTD.	INDIA	EQUITY SHARES	33·3
MAHINDRA SINTERED PRODUCTS LTD.	INDIA	ORDINARY	49·0
AUSTRALASIA			
BHP-GKN HOLDINGS LTD. (OWNS THE WHOLE OF THE VOTING SHARES IN JOHN LYSAGHT (AUSTRALIA) LTD. IN WHOSE PAID-UP SHARE CAPITAL GKN HAS A 75·65% INTEREST)	AUSTRALIA	'Y' SHARES	50·0
AJAX GKN HOLDINGS LTD. (HOLDS 74% OF EQUITY OF AJAX GKN LTD. NEW ZEALAND)	NEW ZEALAND	ORDINARY	50·0
BROWNBUILT METAL SECTIONS (NEW ZEALAND) LTD.	NEW ZEALAND	'B' ORDINARY	50·0
EUROPE			
UNI-CARDAN A.G. (INCLUDING GELENKWELLENBAU G.m.b.H., LÖHR & BROMKAMP G.m.b.H. AND JEAN WALTERSCHEID K.G.)	W. GERMANY	GRUNDKAPITAL	39·5
BIRFIELD TRASMISSIONI S.p.A.	ITALY	REGISTERED AND BEARER	50·0
BIRFIELD (NEDERLAND) TRANSMISSIE N.V.	HOLLAND	UNCLASSIFIED	50·0
GLAENZER SPICER S.A.	FRANCE	UNCLASSIFIED	33·0
RHEINMETALL SCHMIEDE- UND PRESSWERK TRIER G.m.b.H.	W. GERMANY	UNCLASSIFIED	15·0
BOUND BROOK ITALIA S.p.A.	ITALY	UNCLASSIFIED	50·0
S.A. TAGA	SPAIN	UNCLASSIFIED	30·0
NORTH AMERICA			
PRESMET CORPORATION	U.S.A.	COMMON STOCK	33·6
SOUTH AFRICA			
GUEST KEEN ANGLOVAAL AUTOMOTIVE COMPONENTS LTD.	SOUTH AFRICA	UNCLASSIFIED	50·0
BIRFIELD-RUBEROWEN (PTY.) LTD.	SOUTH AFRICA	ORDINARY	25·0
BORG-WARNER S.A. (PTY.) LTD.	SOUTH AFRICA	ORDINARY	20·0

PRINCIPAL TRADE INVESTMENTS
AT 2ND JANUARY 1971

NEW ZEALAND STEEL LTD.	NEW ZEALAND	ORDINARY	9·2
PACIFIC STEEL LTD.	NEW ZEALAND	UNCLASSIFIED	8·0
NATIONAL BOLTS & RIVETS LTD.	SOUTH AFRICA	ORDINARY	12·5
SWAZILAND IRON ORE DEVELOPMENT CO. LTD.	SWAZILAND	UNCLASSIFIED	8·0

STATEMENT OF ACCOUNTS

CONSOLIDATED PROFIT AND LOSS ACCOUNT

	NOTES SEE PAGES 36 AND 37	1970 52 WEEKS		1969 53 WEEKS AS ADJUSTED (SEE NOTE 1)	AS PUBLISHED (SEE NOTE 2)
		£M	£M	£M	£M
TURNOVER (excluding inter-group sales)			485·25	421·34	511·71
SURPLUS ON TRADING (after depreciation)	1		37·53	30·82	38·33
INVESTMENT INCOME AND INTEREST RECEIVABLE	2		1·02	1·80	1·80
INTEREST PAYABLE	3		*3·41*	*2·92*	*3·33*
			35·14	29·70	36·80
SHARE OF PROFITS *LESS* LOSSES OF ASSOCIATED COMPANIES	4				
John Lysaght (Australia) Limited		6·28		5·34	—
Others		1·73	8·01	0·33	0·33
PROFIT FOR THE YEAR BEFORE TAXATION			43·15	35·37	37·13
TAXATION	5		*21·04*	*17·48*	*18·31*
NET PROFIT FOR THE YEAR			22·11	17·89	18·82
EXCEPTIONAL ITEMS	6		*0·12*	0·25	0·25
			21·99	18·14	19·07
PROFIT ATTRIBUTABLE TO OUTSIDE SHAREHOLDERS INTERESTS			*0·78*	*0·41*	*1·34*
NET PROFIT ATTRIBUTABLE TO ORDINARY STOCKHOLDERS			21·21	17·73	17·73
DIVIDENDS Paid 6th October, 1970 : Interim at 3·75p per £1 unit on £103,635,000 (1969—5·00p per £1 unit on £73,293,000)		3·88		3·67	
Proposed : Final at 9·00p per £1 unit on £103,635,000 payable 13th May, 1971 (1969—10·83p per £1 unit on £73,293,000)		9·33	13·21	7·94	11·61
PROFIT RETAINED In accounts of parent company		2·47		4·41	
In accounts of subsidiaries		3·57		1·71	
In accounts of associated companies	4	1·96		—	
			8·00		6·12
			21·21		17·73

NOTES
(1) GROUP ADJUSTED TO DEAL WITH JOHN LYSAGHT (AUSTRALIA) LIMITED AS IF IT HAD BEEN AN ASSOCIATED COMPANY.
(2) GROUP INCLUDING JOHN LYSAGHT (AUSTRALIA) LIMITED AS SUBSIDIARY.

FIGURES IN ITALICS REPRESENT DEDUCTIONS
THE NOTES ON PAGES 36 AND 37 FORM PART OF THIS ACCOUNT

CONSOLIDATED BALANCE SHEET

	NOTES SEE PAGES 38 TO 42	1970 2ND JANUARY 1971		1969 3RD JANUARY 1970	
				AS ADJUSTED (SEE NOTE 1)	AS PUBLISHED (SEE NOTE 2)
		£M	£M	£M	£M
NET ASSETS EMPLOYED					
FIXED ASSETS	1		129·83	121·34	164·97
ASSOCIATED COMPANY AND TRADE INVESTMENTS	2		47·77	44·96	8·45
CURRENT ASSETS					
Stocks	3	121·06		99·06	116·61
Debtors		119·42		108·01	118·89
Quoted investments		0·01		0·01	0·01
(market value £12,000—1969 £13,000)					
Short term loans and deposits		1·74		8·19	8·19
Bank balances and cash		11·54		8·98	9·01
			253·77	224·25	252·71
CURRENT LIABILITIES					
Bank advances		*11·10*		*9·23*	*12·43*
(secured £1,537,000—1969 £1,844,000)					
Short term loans		*1·07*		*0·25*	*3·02*
(secured £567,000—1969 £120,000)					
Creditors		*82·69*		*66·10*	*75·15*
Taxation	4	*27·61*		*26·17*	*31·95*
Proposed final dividend		*9·33*		*7·94*	*7·94*
			131·80	*109·69*	*130·49*
			299·57	280·86	295·64
FINANCED BY					
SHARE CAPITAL AND RESERVES					
Ordinary stock	5	103·64		73·29	73·29
Reserves	6(i)	152·79		160·97	162·31
EQUITY INTEREST			256·43	234·26	235·60
OUTSIDE SHAREHOLDERS INTERESTS IN SUBSIDIARIES			5·81	5·00	17·31
LOAN CAPITAL	7		25·01	29·88	30·48
DEFERRED LIABILITIES	8		12·32	11·72	12·25

Signed on behalf of the Board

RAYMOND BROOKES
H. WILSON SMITH

Directors

| | | | 299·57 | 280·86 | 295·64 |

NOTES
(1) GROUP ADJUSTED TO DEAL WITH JOHN LYSAGHT (AUSTRALIA) LIMITED AS IF IT HAD BEEN AN ASSOCIATED COMPANY.
(2) GROUP INCLUDING JOHN LYSAGHT (AUSTRALIA) LIMITED AS SUBSIDIARY.

FIGURES IN ITALICS REPRESENT DEDUCTIONS
THE NOTES ON PAGES 38 TO 42 FORM PART OF THIS BALANCE SHEET

BALANCE SHEET
OF GUEST, KEEN AND NETTLEFOLDS, LIMITED

	NOTES SEE PAGES 39 TO 42	1970 2ND JANUARY 1971		1969 3RD JANUARY 1970	
		£M	£M	£M	£M
NET ASSETS EMPLOYED					
INTERESTS IN SUBSIDIARIES	11		207·68		195·20
CURRENT ASSETS					
Debtors		0·98		0·92	
Short term loans and deposits		—		7·15	
Bank balances		6·00		8·79	
			6·98		16·86
CURRENT LIABILITIES					
Bank advances		*2·81*		*1·93*	
(secured £294,000—1969 £335,000)					
Creditors		*0·40*		*2·61*	
Taxation	4	*2·12*		*1·91*	
Proposed final dividend		*9·33*		*7·94*	
			14·66		*14·39*
			200·00		197·67
FINANCED BY					
SHARE CAPITAL AND RESERVES		*Authorised*	*Issued*	*Authorised*	*Issued*
Ordinary stock and shares of £1 each	5	120·00	103·64	100·00	73·29
Reserves	6(ii)		92·77		109·70
			196·41		182·99
LOAN CAPITAL	7		3·59		14·68

Signed on behalf of the Board

RAYMOND BROOKES
H. WILSON SMITH

Directors

	200·00	197·67

FIGURES IN ITALICS REPRESENT DEDUCTIONS
THE NOTES ON PAGES 39 TO 42 FORM PART OF THIS BALANCE SHEET

NOTES ON PROFIT AND LOSS ACCOUNT

(THE 1969 FIGURES HAVE BEEN ADJUSTED TO DEAL WITH JOHN LYSAGHT (AUSTRALIA) LIMITED
AS IF IT HAD BEEN AN ASSOCIATED COMPANY IN THAT YEAR)

1 DEPRECIATION

Depreciation is calculated;

(a) in the case of all buildings throughout the Group and of plant of certain rolling mill companies in the United Kingdom and a number of companies outside the United Kingdom—on the original cost of the fixed assets

(b) for all other categories of assets and for all other companies both in the United Kingdom and overseas—on the written down value of the fixed assets at the beginning of the financial year.

Except in special cases no depreciation is charged on fixed assets capitalised during the year and available for use, but a full year's depreciation is charged on fixed assets sold or scrapped during the year. No depreciation is provided on general equipment but replacements are charged against trading profits.

The total depreciation charged against profits takes into account the reduced purchasing power of money. The amount provided in excess of that required to write off the original cost of fixed assets over their estimated life is transferred to the depreciation reserve (see note 6, page 40).

	1970 £M	1969 £M
Written off fixed assets	12·00	11·67
Transferred to depreciation reserve	2·67	2·10
	14·67	13·77

Rental for hire of equipment and motor vehicles amounted to £1,730,000 (1969—£1,545,000).

2 INVESTMENT INCOME AND INTEREST RECEIVABLE

Investments:		
Trade:		
quoted	0·04	0·03
unquoted	0·16	0·13
Loans	0·23	0·16
Quoted securities	—	0·25
Short term loans and deposits	0·59	1·23
	1·02	1·80

3 INTEREST PAYABLE

Loan capital:		
short term	0·08	0·08
long term	1·37	1·88
Bank advances	1·45	0·91
Short term and other loans	0·51	0·05
	3·41	2·92

FIGURES IN ITALICS REPRESENT DEDUCTIONS

4 SHARE OF PROFITS *LESS* LOSSES OF ASSOCIATED COMPANIES

ASSOCIATED COMPANIES
Associated Companies are those companies listed on page 32 which, although not subsidiaries, satisfy the following requirements:—

(a) the Group has a beneficial interest of at least 20% in the equity capital and

(b) the Group is represented on the Board of Directors.

PROFITS BEFORE TAXATION
The proportion of the profits and losses of such companies attributable to the Group shareholding is included under this heading.

The figures are derived from the latest audited or reliable management accounts.

Except for John Lysaght (Australia) Limited, only dividends received were brought in as 'Investment Income' in previous years. The effect of this change in presentation on profits before taxation is dealt with in the Report of the Directors on pages 8 and 9.

PROFIT RETAINED	1970 £M
The profit retained attributable to the Group is as follows:—	
Share of profits less losses	8·01
Taxation thereon (note 5)	*4·21*
	3·80
Exceptional items (note 6)	0·02
	3·82
Dividends (unquoted companies)	*1·86*
Profit retained in accounts of associated companies	1·96

5 TAXATION

	1970 £M	1969 £M
United Kingdom:		
Corporation tax	13.31	13·84
Less:		
Double taxation relief	*1·85*	*1·72*
	11·46	12·12
Overseas	4·32	2·10
	15·78	14·22
Transfer to taxation equalisation account	1·05	0·66
	16·83	14·88
Taxation charge on associated companies earnings	4·21	2·60
	21·04	17·48

United Kingdom corporation tax has been charged at 42½% (1969—45%).
The charge for taxation is after deducting surplus taxation of previous years amounting to £920,000 (1969—£824,000).

TAXATION (Continued)

The transfer to taxation equalisation account represents deferred taxation on the difference between taxation allowances for the year on fixed assets and the amount of depreciation written off book values, together with expenditure charged in the accounts not immediately allowable for tax purposes.

6 EXCEPTIONAL ITEMS

	1970· £M	1969 £M
Surplus on realisation of properties	0·11	0·32
Miscellaneous charges less income	*0·25*	*0·07*
Associated companies	0·02	—
	0·12	*0·25*

7 DIRECTORS' AND EMPLOYEE EMOLUMENTS

Emoluments of Directors of Guest, Keen and Nettlefolds, Limited paid by the company and its subsidiaries, including **£15,000** (1969—£9,000) for services as directors, amounted to **£408,000** (1969—£362,000).

Pensions to and in respect of former Directors amounted to **£28,000** (1969—£25,000).

The emoluments of the Chairman of the company amounted to **£47,000** (1969—£36,000).

The emoluments of the other Directors (excluding pension scheme contributions) fall within the following scales:

Scale of Emoluments £	Number of Directors 1970	1969
0— 2,500	4	2
5,001— 7,500	1	1
10,001—12,500	1	—
12,501—15,000	—	3
15,001—17,500	3	8
17,501—20,000	5	1
20,001—22,500	1	—
22,501—25,000	1	—
25,001—27,500	—	1
35,001—37,500	1	—

One employee of the parent company, who was not a director, received emoluments in 1969 and 1970 (excluding pension scheme contributions) within the scale £10,001—£12,500.

8 DIRECTORS' INTERESTS IN SHARES AND DEBENTURES

Interests in shares or debentures of the Company and its subsidiaries of persons who were Directors of Guest, Keen and Nettlefolds, Limited on 2nd January 1971:

Holding of GKN ordinary stock (including family interests) at

Name	1970 (or date of appointment) 4th January £	1971 2nd January £
C. C. Birch	1,185	1,930
Sir Anthony Bowlby, Bt.	2,431	3,241
Sir Raymond Brookes	6,611	8,814
Sir Douglas Bruce-Gardner, Bt.	4,749	6,332
W. W. Fea	1,000	1,333
G. T. Holdsworth	Nil	1,332
J. F. Insch	10,550	4,166
H. S. Killick, MC, TD	2,300	5,798
R. G. Lewis, TD	1,439	1,918
S. Lloyd	3,040	4,053
L. Maxwell-Holroyd	1,000	1,500
W. A. Nicol	7,000	9,366
M. S. Pearce	1,000	1,333
F. C. Rowbottom	1,050	1,700
Sir Henry Wilson Smith, KCB, KBE	2,500	3,333
Sir Charles Wheeler, KBE	2,349	3,132

The above holdings reflect the 1 for 3 scrip issue made in 1970.

The reduction in Mr. J. F. Insch's holding of ordinary stock is wholly attributable to the transfer of stock to his children (who are of full age) during 1970.

9 EMPLOYEES

The number of persons employed in the GKN Group at 2nd January 1971 was as follows:

UNITED KINGDOM		77,662
OVERSEAS		
Asia	12,109	
Australasia	2,399	
Europe	2,884	
North America	260	
Southern Africa	3,529	21,181
World total		98,843

The average number of persons employed in the United Kingdom companies during the year was 77,662 and their aggregate remuneration was £109 million.

10 AUDITORS' REMUNERATION

Remuneration of auditors of the company was **£2,500** (1969—£2,000) and of the Group **£222,000** (1969—£189,000).

NOTES ON BALANCE SHEETS

(THE 1969 FIGURES HAVE BEEN ADJUSTED TO DEAL WITH JOHN LYSAGHT (AUSTRALIA) LIMITED AS IF IT HAD BEEN AN ASSOCIATED COMPANY IN THAT YEAR)

1 FIXED ASSETS

(i) SUMMARY	Land and Buildings Freehold £M	Leasehold £M	Plant, Machinery and Vehicles £M	General Equipment £M	Development Schemes £M	Total £M
COST OR VALUATION: (see (iii) below)						
Totals at 3rd January 1970	50·55	8·44	169·27	0·97	4·45	233·68
Additions:						
companies acquired	0·05	—	0·05	—	—	0·10
capital expenditure (see below)	1·96	0·20	13·21	0·11	7·03	22·51
Reclassifications	0·91	*0·95*	0·04	—	—	—
Development schemes completed during the year	1·12	0·15	4·82	—	*6·09*	—
Disposals	*0·63*	*0·11*	*5·87*	*0·12*	—	*6·73*
Revaluation by overseas subsidiary (see (iii) below)	*0·38*	—	—	—	—	*0·38*
Totals at 2nd January 1971	53·58	7·73	181·52	0·96	5·39	249·18
ACCUMULATED DEPRECIATION:						
Totals at 3rd January 1970	9·22	2·34	100·78	—	—	112·34
Companies acquired	—	—	0·02	—	—	0·02
Reclassifications	0·29	*0·29*	—	—	—	—
Disposals	*0·14*	*0·07*	*4·28*	—	—	*4·49*
Charge for the year	1·01	0·22	10·77	—	—	12·00
Revaluation by overseas subsidiary (see (iii) below)	*0·52*	—	—	—	—	*0·52*
Totals at 2nd January 1971	9·86	2·20	107·29	—	—	119·35
NET BOOK VALUES AT 2ND JANUARY 1971	43·72	5·53	74·23	0·96	5·39	**129·83**
NET BOOK VALUES AT 3RD JANUARY 1970	41·33	6·10	68·49	0·97	4·45	**121·34**

Capital expenditure is after deducting estimated investment grants receivable in the United Kingdom amounting to £3,379,000 (1969—£2,204,000).

(ii) ANALYSIS OF LEASEHOLD LAND AND BUILDINGS

	Cost £M	Accumulated Depreciation £M	Net Book Value At 2.1.71 £M	At 3.1.70 £M
Long leases	5·47	1·53	3·94	4·62
Leases with 50 years to run or less at date of balance sheet	2·26	0·67	1·59	1·48
	7·73	2·20	5·53	6·10

(iii) 'COST OR VALUATION' OF FIXED ASSETS INCLUDES:

(a) For acquisitions before 1937 the net book values at that date and for certain subsidiaries the net book values at 1st July 1948.

(b) The directors of an overseas company have revalued the freehold land and buildings at 2nd January 1971 having regard to the assessed values for taxation purposes.

(c) For 13 companies valuations by their directors or professional valuers. The amounts included are:

Year of Valuation	£M
1946	0·42
1950	0·67
1951	0·21
1952	0·31
1953	4·35
1960	2·59
1965	0·29
1966	0·35
1970	1·44
	10·63

FIGURES IN ITALICS REPRESENT DEDUCTIONS

2 ASSOCIATED COMPANY AND TRADE INVESTMENTS

		1970 £M	1969 £M
(i)	ASSOCIATED COMPANIES (see note below)		
	QUOTED		
	At cost less amounts written off	0·30	
	Share of post acquisition reserves	*0·07*	
	Market value £320,000	0·23	
	Book value 3rd January 1970 Market value £288,000		0·36
	UNQUOTED		
	At cost less amounts written off	14·63	
	Share of post acquisition reserves	29·15	
		43·78	
	Book value 3rd January 1970		40·73
		44·01	41·09
	LOANS	3·15	2·86
(ii)	TRADE		
	at cost less amounts written off		
	QUOTED Market value £1,441,000 1969 £1,739,000	0·54	0·84
	UNQUOTED Directors valuation £235,000 1969 £273,000	0·07	0·12
	LOANS	—	0·05
		0·61	1·01
(iii)	TOTAL	47·77	44·96

Notes:
(1) The Group share of post acquisition reserves of associated companies is included in RESERVES (see note 6).

		1970 £M	1969 £M
(2)	In respect of unquoted associated company investments: Group's share of aggregate profits less losses		
	before tax	7·99	6·17
	after tax	3·81	2·96
	Group's share of aggregate undistributed profits less losses accumulated since the investments were acquired	29·15	27·14

FIGURES IN ITALICS REPRESENT DEDUCTIONS

3 STOCKS

Stocks have been consistently valued at the beginning and end of the year at the lower of Group cost and net realisable value.

4 TAXATION

	Parent Company		Group	
	1970 £M	1969 £M	1970 £M	1969 £M
United Kingdom corporation tax:				
current year's profits	2·07	0·90	12·23	12·87
earlier years' profits	*0·06*	0·99	11·77	11·55
Overseas taxation	0·11	0·02	3·61	1·75
	2·12	1·91	27·61	26·17

In the event of any taxation liability arising from the nationalisation of GKN Steel Co. Ltd. the amount will be charged against Revenue Reserve.

5 SHARE CAPITAL

	Ordinary Stock £M
Total at 3rd January 1970	73·29
Scrip issue approved at Annual General Meeting held 12th May 1970	24·43
Issued to holders of 6½% convertible unsecured loan stock 1986/91 on 31st May 1970	5·92
Total at 2nd January 1971	103·64

6 RESERVES

(i) GROUP

	Share Premium £M	Depreciation £M	General Capital £M	Goodwill Arising on Consolidation £M	Revenue £M	Total £M
Totals at 3rd January 1970 (as published)	—	19·90	17·06	25·97	151·32	162·31
Movement due to:						
John Lysaght (Australia) Limited becoming an associated company	—	2·33	0·12	1·61	2·48	1·34
Totals at 3rd January 1970 (as adjusted)	—	17·57	17·18	27·58	153·80	160·97
Associated companies	—	—	0·17	—	0·77	0·94
Adjustment to taxation provisions and taxation equalisation account mainly arising from variations in taxation rates	—	—	—	—	1·00	1·00
Scrip issue on 12th May 1970	—	—	—	—	24·43	24·43
Share premium arising on shares issued to holders of 6½% unsecured loan stock 1986/91	5·17	—	—	—	—	5·17
Discount on and expenses of issue of debenture and stamp duty on increase in share capital	0·10	—	0·56	—	—	0·66
Amounts written off investments in subsidiaries	—	—	—	0·80	0·80	—
Amounts provided against investments less surplus on realisations	—	—	—	—	1·03	1·03
Other variations	—	—	—	0·47	0·19	0·28
Transfer for the year £2,670,000 less outside shareholders proportion £121,000	—	2·55	—	—	—	2·55
Profit retained	—	—	0·05	—	7·95	8·00
Totals at 2nd January 1971	5·07	20·12	16·84	26·31	137·07	152·79
Group companies excluding associated company reserves	5·07	20·12	2·57	26·31	122·26	123·71
Associated company reserves	—	—	14·27	—	14·81	29·08
	5·07	20·12	16·84	26·31	137·07	152·79

(ii) PARENT COMPANY

	Share Premium £M	Revenue £M	Total £M
Total at 3rd January 1970	—	109·70	109·70
Adjustment to taxation provision arising from reduction in taxation rate	—	0·07	0·07
Stamp duty on increase in share capital	0·10	—	0·10
Scrip issue on 12th May 1970	—	24·43	24·43
Share premium arising on shares issued to holders of 6½% unsecured loan stock 1986/91	5·17	—	5·17
Amount written off investment in subsidiary	—	0·40	0·40
Other variations	—	0·29	0·29
Profit retained	—	2·47	2·47
Totals at 2nd January 1971	5·07	87·70	92·77

FIGURES IN ITALICS REPRESENT DEDUCTIONS

	Loan Outstanding	
	1970	1969
7 **LOAN CAPITAL**	£M	£M

7 **LOAN CAPITAL**
(redeemable at par unless otherwise stated)

SHORT TERM
(repayable within five years from 2nd January 1971)

SUBSIDIARY COMPANIES OUTSIDE UNITED KINGDOM
**Guest, Keen and Nettlefolds South Africa
(Proprietary) Limited**

	1970 £M	1969 £M
7½% registered notes 1971 (unsecured)	0·44	0·44
Guest, Keen, Williams, Limited, India		
6½% debenture stock 1966/71	—	0·66
	0·44	1·10

LONG TERM
PARENT COMPANY

6½% convertible unsecured loan stock 1986/91	0·63	11·72

The stock may be converted on 31st May 1971 or
1972 into ordinary stock on the following basis:
For each £100 of loan stock
in 1971 £50⅔ ordinary stock
in 1972 £48 ordinary stock
and so in proportion for any greater or lesser
amount of loan stock.

6% convertible unsecured loan stock 1988/93	2·96	2·96

The stock may be converted at 31st May in any of
the years 1971 to 1975 inclusive into ordinary
stock at the rate of £1 ordinary stock for every
£3⅞ nominal of loan stock.

SUBSIDIARY COMPANIES IN UNITED KINGDOM
Guest Keen and Nettlefolds (UK) Limited
10½% guaranteed debenture stock 1990/95
£20,000,000 less par value of amounts due to be

subscribed 18th January 1971 £14,530,000	5·47	—
4½% guaranteed debenture stock 1970/84 redeemable at £103 per cent.	1·37	1·47
6½% guaranteed debenture stock 1976/81	3·50	3·50
6½% guaranteed debenture stock 1980/85	2·06	2·06
7½% guaranteed debenture stock 1986/91	4·00	4·00
8% guaranteed debenture stock 1986/91	0·12	0·12

Guest Keen and Nettlefolds (Overseas) Limited

5½% redeemable debenture stock redeemable at £103 per cent.	0·48	0·55

All the above stocks are guaranteed unconditionally
as to principal and interest by Guest, Keen and
Nettlefolds, Limited.

Others (secured £22,000—1969 £24,000) at a
maximum interest rate of 9½% repayable

in period 1971 to 1983	0·02	0·02

SUBSIDIARY COMPANIES OUTSIDE UNITED KINGDOM
Guest, Keen, Williams, Limited, India

7% debenture stock 1973/78	0·75	0·80
7¾% debenture stock 1976/81	1·07	1·08

GKN (New Zealand) Limited
6½% debenture stock 1973/78 (including accrued

interest of £3,000)	0·28	0·28

Others (secured £1,858,000—1969 £217,000)
at a maximum rate of 9·6% repayable

in period 1971 to 2000	1·86	0·22
	24·57	28·78

**GROUP TOTAL (secured £20,980,000
1969 £7,137,000)**

	25·01	29·88

8 DEFERRED LIABILITIES

	1970 £M	1969 £M
Overseas taxation	1·90	1·97
Taxation equalisation account	9·50	8·87
	11·40	10·84
Superannuation funds	0·92	0·88
	12·32	11·72

9 CAPITAL EXPENDITURE

	1970	1969
Capital expenditure sanctioned by the Board and outstanding at 2nd January 1971 amounts to	20·00	25·00
Contracts placed against these sanctions so far as not provided for in these accounts amount to	11·00	11·00

Note:
John Lysaght (Australia) Limited is now an Associated Company and its capital expenditure sanctions are therefore excluded (see Report of Directors)

10 CONTINGENT LIABILITIES OF SUBSIDIARIES

Bank and other guarantees and liability on negotiated bills	1·30	2·37

11 INTERESTS IN SUBSIDIARIES

	1970 £M	1970 £M	1969 £M	1969 £M
Shareholdings at or under cost		104·98		111·41
Amounts owing from subsidiaries	104·07		95·58	
Amounts owing to subsidiaries	1·37		11·79	
		102·70		83·79
		207·68		195·20

12 GENERAL
(i) Assets and liabilities in foreign currencies have been converted to sterling at the rates of exchange ruling at 2nd January 1971.
(ii) Exchange restrictions on remittances are in force in certain countries in which subsidiaries operate.
(iii) The information relating to investments in subsidiary and associated companies is included on pages 30 to 32.

FIGURES IN ITALICS REPRESENT DEDUCTIONS

REPORT OF THE AUDITORS
TO THE MEMBERS OF GUEST, KEEN AND NETTLEFOLDS, LIMITED
In our opinion, based on our examination, on the reports of the auditors of certain subsidiaries and associated companies not audited by us, and on the management accounts of certain associated companies which have not been audited, the accounts set out on pages 30 to 42 read in conjunction with pages 8 and 9 of the Report of the Directors together give a true and fair view of the state of affairs at 2nd January 1971 and of the profit for the year ended on that date and comply with the Companies Acts 1948 and 1967.

COOPER BROTHERS & CO.
CHARTERED ACCOUNTANTS
BIRMINGHAM, 23rd MARCH 1971

FINANCIAL INFORMATION 1961-1970

FINANCIAL INFORMATION 1961-1970

SUMMARISED ACCOUNTS

	1961 (see note 3 above)	1962 (see note above)
	£M	£M
CONSOLIDATED PROFIT		
SURPLUS ON TRADING	21·37	21·18
Investment income and interest receivable	1·47	1·23
Interest on loan capital	*0·50*	*0·4*
Other interest payable	*0·08*	*0·1*
Share of profits less losses of Associated Companies	—	—
PROFIT FOR THE YEAR BEFORE TAXATION	22·26	21·8
Taxation	*11·33*	*10·2*
Net proft for the year	10·93	11·6
Exceptional items	0·13	*0·1*
	11·06	11·4
Outside shareholders interests in subsidiaries	0·54	0·8
Preference dividends	0·36	0·3
NET PROFIT ATTRIBUTABLE TO ORDINARY STOCKHOLDERS	10·16	10·2
	11·06	11·4
Depreciation charged	*9·99*	*11·2*
Cash flow (depreciation and retained profits)	15·76	17·1
NET ASSETS EMPLOYED		
Fixed assets	111·24	125·7
Associated company and trade investments	0·77	1·0
Investment in GKN Steel Co. Ltd.	—	—
Stocks	60·68	64·7
Debtors less creditors, current taxation and final dividend	8·85	6·9
Amounts receivable in respect of nationalisation of GKN Steel Co. Ltd.	—	—
Liquid resources (net)	20·62	19·4
TOTAL NET ASSETS EMPLOYED	202·16	217·8
Financed by:		
U.K. income tax	6·00	4·8
Deferred liabilities (taxation and superannuation funds)	10·57	11·8
Loan capital	8·86	10·9
Outside shareholders in subsidiaries	7·72	8·9
Preference stockholders	7·85	7·8
ORDINARY STOCKHOLDERS—EQUITY INTEREST	161·16	173·4
	202·16	217·8
Capital expenditure	19·84	19·4

FIGURES IN ITALICS REPRESENT DEDUCTIONS

E FIGURES IN THESE TABLES ARE TAKEN FROM THE PUBLISHED ACCOUNTS FOR THE YEARS LISTED.
MAKING COMPARISONS THE FOLLOWING SHOULD BE NOTED —
N STEEL CO, LTD WAS NATIONALISED IN 1967 AND IS EXCLUDED FROM THAT YEAR AND THEREAFTER.
HN LYSAGHT (AUSTRALIA) LIMITED CEASED TO BE A SUBSIDIARY IN 1970 AND IS DEALT WITH AS AN ASSOCIATED COMPANY IN THAT YEAR
T PROFIT FIGURES AND EARNINGS PER ORDINARY SHARE FOR THE YEARS 1961 TO 1965 ARE NOT COMPARABLE WITH THOSE OF
BSEQUENT YEARS DUE TO CHANGES INTRODUCED IN THE FINANCE ACT, 1965.

1963 (see note 3 above)	1964 (see note 3 above)	1965 (see note 3 above)	1966	1967 (see note 1 above)	1968	1969	1970 (see note 2 above)
£M	£M	£M	£M	£M	£M	£M	£M
23·74	31·44	30·41	28·81	26·21	31·09	38·33	37·53
1·01	1·47	1·75	1·31	3·21	3·68	1·80	1·02
0·58	0·63	0·63	1·18	1·75	1·86	2·00	1·45
0·23	1·17	1·43	1·53	1·32	1·43	1·33	1·96
—	—	—	—	—	—	0·33	8·01
23·94	31·11	30·10	27·41	26·35	31·48	37·13	43·15
11·79	15·45	12·07	11·81	10·91	14·47	18·31	21·04
12·15	15·66	18·03	15·60	15·44	17·01	18·82	22·11
0·27	0·04	0·30	0·32	1·07	0·72	0·25	0·12
12·42	15·62	18·33	15·92	16·51	17·73	19·07	21·99
0·87	1·27	1·25	1·14	0·77	0·98	1·34	0·78
0·37	0·37	0·37	0·63	0·63	0·59	—	—
11·18	13·98	16·71	14·15	15·11	16·16	17·73	21·21
12·42	15·62	18·33	15·92	16·51	17·73	19·07	21·99
12·09	13·20	14·34	16·33	14·13	15·19	16·49	14·67
18·44	21·47	22·66	20·70	19·26	20·66	23·40	21·05
36·69	144·55	147·31	167·34	131·53	145·51	164·97	129·83
1·90	2·04	2·31	7·84	8·99	8·56	8·45	47·77
—	—	—	—	15·22	—	—	—
67·77	75·96	85·74	92·61	93·32	100·28	116·61	121·06
8·17	13·62	10·28	2·63	1·42	8·10	3·85	0·21
—	—	—	—	—	42·00	—	—
12·22	4·57	0·74	8·65	4·42	28·16	1·76	1·12
26·75	240·74	244·90	261·77	243·22	276·29	295·64	299·57
5·71	7·42	—	—	—	—	—	—
13·02	14·51	13·44	14·51	7·95	11·05	12·25	12·32
10·72	11·53	12·63	30·22	27·22	30·57	30·48	25·01
11·58	12·11	11·77	13·09	13·02	15·50	17·31	5·81
7·85	8·05	8·05	8·05	8·05	—	—	—
77·87	187·12	199·01	195·90	186·98	219·17	235·60	256·43
26·75	240·74	244·90	261·77	243·22	276·29	295·64	299·57
18·24	18·74	17·48	18·26	18·34	18·23	20·69	22·51

SALIENT
FIGURES

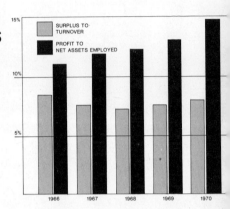

OPERATING STATISTICS

	Turnover (excluding inter-group sales)	Surplus on trading	Surplus to turnover	Total net assets employed	Profit before loan capital interest and taxation	Profit before interest and taxation to total net assets	
	£M	£M	%	£M	£M	%	tax
1961 (see note 3)	238·11	21·37	9·0	202·16	22·76	11·3	2
1962 (see note 3)	245·57	21·18	8·6	217·87	22·30	10·2	2
1963 (see note 3)	275·54	23·74	8·6	226·75	24·52	10·8	2
1964 (see note 3)	338·11	31·44	9·3	240·74	31·74	13·2	3
1965 (see note 3)	353·24	30·41	8·6	244·90	30·73	12·5	3
1966	356·58	28·81	8·1	261·77	28·59	10·9	2
1967 (see note 1)	354·74	26·21	7·4	243·22	28·10	11·6	2
1968	433·55	31·09	7·2	276·29	33·34	12·1	3
1969	511·71	38·33	7·5	295·64	39·13	13·2	3
1970 (see note 2)	485·25	37·53	7·7	299·57	44·60	14·9	4

THE FIGURES IN THESE TABLES ARE TAKEN FROM THE PUBLISHED ACCOUNTS FOR THE YEARS LISTED.
IN MAKING COMPARISONS THE FOLLOWING SHOULD BE NOTED:—
GKN STEEL CO. LTD WAS NATIONALISED IN 1967 AND IS EXCLUDED FROM THAT YEAR AND THEREAFTER.
JOHN LYSAGHT (AUSTRALIA) LIMITED CEASED TO BE A SUBSIDIARY IN 1970 AND IS DEALT WITH AS AN ASSOCIATED COMPANY IN THAT YEAR.
NET PROFIT FIGURES AND EARNINGS PER ORDINARY SHARE FOR THE YEARS 1961 TO 1965 ARE NOT COMPARABLE WITH THOSE OF
SUBSEQUENT YEARS DUE TO CHANGES INTRODUCED IN THE FINANCE ACT, 1965.

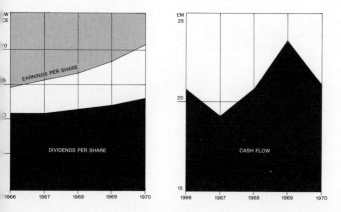

FINANCIAL STATISTICS

	Issued ordinary stock	Total equity interest	Net profit attributable to ordinary stockholders	Net profit to equity interest	Earnings per ordinary share (see note 3 above)	Ordinary dividends (see note 3 above) Amount per share	
						Net	Gross
	£M	£M	£M	%	p	p	p
1961	46·37	161·16	10·15	6·3	10·9	4·9	8·0
1962	48·38	173·40	10·30	5·9	10·6	4·9	8·0
1963	48·86	177·87	11·19	6·3	11·4	5·2	8·5
1964	73·29	187·12	13·98	7·5	14·3	6·3	10·5
1965	73·29	199·01	16·71	8·4	17·1		10·5
1966	73·29	195·90	14·15	7·2	14·5		10·5
1967	73·29	186·98	15·11	8·1	15·5		10·5
1968	73·29	219·17	16·16	7·4	16·5		11·2
1969	73·29	235·60	17·73	7·5	18·1		11·9
1970	103·64	256·43	21·21	8·3	20·5		12·8

STOCKHOLDERS
AT 2ND JANUARY 1971

Holdings	Ordinary Stockholders	Convertible Loan Stockholders	
£		6½%	6%
1 – 100	8,022	145	201
101 – 500	44,044	204	493
501 – 1,000	18,583	119	123
1,001 – 5,000	11,883	96	170
5,001 – 10,000	575	11	32
over 10,000	681	8	53
Total	83,788	583	1,072

ANALYSIS OF ORDINARY STOCKHOLDERS

	Number	%	Holding £000	%
INDIVIDUALS	78,293	93·4	48,670	47·0
INSTITUTIONS:				
Insurance companies	254	·3	21,188	20·4
Investment trusts	290	·3	3,016	2·9
Others	4,951	6·0	30,761	29·7
Total	83,788	100·0	103,635	100·0

So far as is known there is no person holding
or beneficially interested in more than 6% of
the share capital of the Company.

Index

(*Note* Appendixes B, C and D have not been indexed)

Accounting identity, 19–20, 101
Accounting policies, disclosure of, 87
Accounting principles, 84–91, 97
Accounting profession, influence on accounting principles, 84–8, 91, 97
Accounting standards, 85–7
Accounting Standards Steering Committee, 86, 90, 97
Accounts payable, 22
Accounts receivable, 21
Acid test ratio, 60–62
Aktiengesellschaften (A.G.), 14 n.
Alenco Ltd, 9–12, 14–15, 17–19, 21–38, 44–5, 48, 51–6, 60–73, 76–9, App. C
American Institute of Certified Public Accountants, 88
Analysis, tools of, 46–50, 95
Annual general meeting, 10–11
Arthur Bell & Sons Ltd, 72–3
Articles of association, 13, 15, 29, 92
Assets: as prepaid expenses, 100–101; classification of, 21, 93; revaluation of, 24, 79–80, 88, 90
Associated companies, 86
Audit and auditors, 23, 43–5, 95
Authorized share capital, 31
Average collection period, 62–3, 96

Balance sheet: consolidated, 21, 26–7; defined, 17–18, 93; diagram, 20; holding company's, 26–7; identity, 19–20, 101
Balancing allowance or charge, 39
Bell, P. W., 97

Bonus issue, 31–2, 77–80, 96
Briston, R. J., 97
Bull, R. J., 93, 94, 95

Calls on shares, 31
Capital allowances, 26, 39–41, 94
Capital gains tax, 42–3, 76, 94
Capitalization issue, *see* Bonus issue
Capital reserves, 32
Capital structure, 65–75, 96–7
Carsberg, B. V., 97
Cash budget, 57–60, 96
Cash flow, 35, 93
Centre for Interfirm Comparison, 48, 95
Chairman's statement, 15–16
Charterhouse Group Ltd, 11, 14, 27–8
Charterhouse Industries Ltd, 14, 27, 29
Clarkson, G. P. E., 97
Close companies, 43
Companies: associated, 86; characteristics of, 12; close, 43; corporate personality, 12; exempt private, 13, 15; guarantee, limitation of liability by, 14–15; holding, 13–14, 92; limitation of liability, 12, 14–15; objects, 15, 92; overseas, 14; private, 12–14, 92; proprietary, 12, 14 n.; public, 12–14, 92; registrar of, 13; subsidiary, 13–14, 92; unlimited, 15
Companies Act 1948, 12, 14, 15, 92, 94
Companies Act 1967, 12, 32, 92, 94; Second Schedule, 85
Company annual report, contents, 10–12

Company legislation, influence on accounting principles, 84–5, 87, 91, 97
Comparability, 47–8
Conservatism, 88–9, 97
Consistency, 48
Consolidated balance sheet, 17–18, 21, 26–7
Consolidated profit and loss account, 18, 32–3
Control, 67, 96
Convertible loan stock, 81–2
Corporate personality, 12
Corporation tax, 37–8, 94
Cost of capital, 67–71, 75–6, 96
Creditors, 22
Credits, 18, 99–101
Cummings, G., 98
Cumulative preference shares, 29–30
Current assets, 21–3
Current liabilities, 22
Current ratio, 46, 60–62, 96
Current taxation, 36–8, 94

Debenture discount, 28
Debentures, 27–8, 67–9, 71–5
Debits, 18, 99–101
Debtors, 21; average collection period, 62–3, 96
Deferred taxation, 36–8, 94
Depreciation, 19, 22, 44; defined, 23, 93; 'free', 39; inflation, 89–90; methods of, 23–6; on replacement cost, 89–90; 'source' of funds, 34–5
Dilution, 67
Directors' emoluments, 33
Directors' report, 11, 33
Disclosure, 85, 87
Distillers Company Ltd, 16, 68–70, 89–90
Dividend cover, 68, 76
Dividend policy, 75–9, 96
Dividends, 29–30, 33, 68–70, 75–9, 96
Dividend yield, 30, 68–70, 76, 96
Double entry, 18, 99–101

Earnings per share, 70, 76
Earnings yield, 70, 96
Edey, H. C., 97
Edwards, E. O., 97
Elliott, B. J., 97
Equity capital, 65–71, 93, 96
Exceptional items, 56
Exempt private companies, 13, 15
Exports, 33

Finance Act 1965, 42–3, 65, 72, 77
Financial ratios, 46–9
Financial statements, 17–35, 93–4
Financial Times, 16, 31, 68–70, 76
First-year allowance, 39, 94
Fixed assets, 22–6
Fixed charge, 28
Fixed overhead expenses, 22
Flat yield, 47
Floating charge, 27–8
Flow of funds statement, *see* Funds statement
Free depreciation, 39
Funds provided by operations, 35, 93
Funds statement, 11–12, 59; contents, 33–5; defined, 19–20, 93; diagram, 20

Gearing, 71–5, 96
Gesellschaften mit beschränkter Haftung (G.m.b.H.), 14 n.
Goethe, J. W. von, views on double entry book-keeping, 99
Goodwill, 26–7
Gower, L. C. B., 92, 94
Guarantee, companies limited by, 14–15
Guest, Keen and Nettlefolds Ltd, 9, 13, 16, 21, 42–3, 48, 79 n., 81–2, 86, 90, App. D
Gynther, R. S., 97

Harcourt, G. C., 97
Henry VIII, disclaims knowledge of taxation, 36

Historical cost, 23, 89, 91, 97
Holding companies, 13–14, 92

Imperial Chemical Industries Ltd, 26, 68
Imputation method of corporation tax, 38
Industry ratios, 48
Inflation: accounting for, 23, 84, 89–91, 97; cost of capital, 68; reverse yield gap, 69; taxable profits, 89–91
Initial allowance, 40
Institute of Chartered Accountants in England and Wales, 85, 88, 90, 94
Institute of Chartered Accountants of Scotland, 94
Interim dividend, 30
Interim reports, 16
Inventories, *see* Stock-in-trade
Investment grants, 25–6, 41
Investment incentives, 39–41
Issued share capital, 31

Jenkins Report on Company Law Amendment (1962), 12, 85, 87
Jones, F. H., 93, 94, 95

Leasing, 81–2
Leverage (gearing), 71–5, 96
Limited liability, 12, 14–15
Liquidity, 57–64, 96
Liquid ratio, 60–62
Loan capital (long-term debt), 27–9, 65–8, 71–5, 93, 96
Lynch, T. D., 94

Marley, C., 97
Memorandum of association, 15, 92
Minority interest, 21, 66
Moroney, M. J., 95

Naylor, G., 92
Naylor, M., 94, 98
Net current assets, 22

Net profit ratio, 51–3, 55, 95
Net worth, 17, 89
Newbould, G. D., 97
Non-cumulative preference shares, 29–30
No par value shares, 30 n.

Objectivity, 23, 26, 51, 88–9, 97
Objects (of company), 15, 92
Ordinary share capital, 29–32, 65–71, 93

Paid-up share capital, 31
Parker, R. H., 97
Par value, 30
Patents, 26–7
Personal investment, 98
Personal tax, 41–2, 94
Philips, accounting for inflation, 90
Preference share capital, 29–31, 65–6, 68, 71, 93
Price-earnings ratio, 68, 70, 76
Priority percentages, 73
Private companies, 12–14, 92
Profitability, 51–6, 95
Profit and loss account: analysis of, 53–6; consolidated, 32–3; contents, 32–3; defined, 18, 93; diagram, 20
Profit and loss appropriation account, 18 n.
Profits tax, 42
Proprietary companies, 12, 14 n.
Public companies, 12–14, 92

Quick ratio, 60–62, 96

Real capital, 89
Recommendations on accounting principles, 85, 88
Redeemable preference shares, 29
Redemption yield, 47
Reducing balance method of depreciation, 24–5, 39–40
Registered office, 11, 15
Registrar of Companies, 13

Reserves: capital reserves, 32; defined, 32; not same as cash, 32; revenue reserves, 18, 32–3 (*see also* Retained profits)
Retained profits, 19, 32–3, 35, 65–6, 73, 75–6, 96
Return on investment, 51–6, 95
Revaluation of assets, 24, 79–80, 88, 90
Revenue reserves, 18, 32–3
Reverse yield gap, 69
Rights issue, 31, 80–81, 96
Risk and capital structure, 67, 71–5, 96

Sales, 32–3, 51–5, 57–8, 62
Scrip issue, *see* Bonus issue
Securities and Exchange Commission, 87–8, 97
Share capital, types of, 29–30
Shareholders' funds, classification of, 29–32, 93
Share premium, 30–31, 80–81, 93
Share prices, 30–31, 68–70
Sizer, J., 95
Sociétés anonymes (S.A.), 14 n.
Sociétés à responsabilité limitée (S.A.R.L.), 14 n.
Source and disposition statement, *see* Funds statement
Sources of funds, 65–83, 96–7
Stamp, E., 97
Statements of standard accounting practice, 86–7
Stock dividend, *see* Bonus issue
Stock Exchange Daily Official List, 31

Stock-in-trade, 21–3, 28, 53–4, 60–61, 95
Stock turnover, 53–4, 95
Straight line depreciation, 24, 40–41
Subsidiary companies, 13–14, 92

Table A, 15
Taxation, 36–43, 94–5
Taxation equalization account, 38, 94
Tax legislation, 43; influence on accounting principles, 84, 87, 91, 97
Times interest earned, 71, 73, 96
Touche, A. G., 94
Touche Ross & Co., 44
Trading on the equity, 74
Transferability, 67, 96
True and fair view, 44, 85
Turnover, *see* Sales
Turnover of net tangible assets, 51–2, 95

Ultra vires doctrine, 15
Under-capitalization, 60
Uniformity of accounting principles and practice, 84–5, 91
Unlimited companies, 15
Unsecured loan, defined, 28

Van Horne, J. C., 97

Window-dressing, 63–4
Working capital, defined, 22
Work-in-progress, 23
Writing-down allowances, 39, 94

Yields, 47

More about Penguins and Pelicans

Penguinews, which appears every month, contains details of all the new books issued by Penguins as they are published. From time to time it is supplemented by *Penguins in Print*, which is a complete list of all available books published by Penguins. (There are well over four thousand of these).

A specimen copy of *Penguinews* will be sent to you free on request, and you can become a subscriber for the price of the postage. For a year's issues (including the complete lists) please send 3op if you live in the United Kingdom, or 6op if you live elsewhere. Just write to Dept EP, Penguin Books Ltd, Harmondsworth, Middlesex, enclosing a cheque or postal order, and your name will be added to the mailing list.

Note: *Penguinews* and *Penguins in Print* are not available in the U.S.A. or Canada

The Complete Guide to Investment

Gordon Cummings

FIFTH EDITION

During this century personal incomes – and with them savings
– have ballooned. People of all ages in every class now recognize
that idle money can be made to work and earn: they look
askance at the jar on the mantelpiece. Since the war the
number of share investors has roughly doubled.

This Penguin Handbook sets out to give help and advice on all
forms of personal investment and on house-purchase. It deals
with Savings Banks, Savings Certificates, Building Societies, and
Life Assurance, as well as the huge range of stocks and shares
handled through the Stock Exchange.

Personal investment can today be a perfectly sound and
predictable insurance against the future, and nobody is better
versed in it than Gordon Cummings, a chartered accountant
and financial expert who for years dealt with readers' financial
inquiries for one of the major publishing houses.

Pelican Library of Business and Management

The Genesis of Modern Management *Sidney Pollard*

Corporate Strategy† *H. Igor Ansoff*

An Insight into Management Accounting *John Sizer*

Computers, Managers and Society *Michael Rose*

Modern Management Methods* *Ernest Dale and L. C. Michelon*

Management Thinkers *Ed. A. Tillett, T. Kempner, G. Wills*

Operations Research† *Jagjit Singh*

Sales Forecasting* *Albert Battersby*

Management and Machiavelli* *Anthony Jay*

Progress of Management Research *Ed. Nigel Farrow*

Management Decisions and the Role of Forecasting *James Morrell*

*Not for sale in the U.S.A.
†Not for sale in the U.S.A. or Canada